Foundation Degree in Health and Social Care

Tina Tilmouth, Elizabeth Davies-Ward, Briony Williams

HODDER
EDUCATION
AN HACHETTE UK COMPANY

Orders: please contact Bookpoint Ltd, 130 Milton Park, Abingdon, Oxon OX14 4SB. Telephone: (44) 01235 827720. Fax: (44) 01235 400454. Lines are open from 9.00 to 5.00, Monday to Saturday, with a 24 hour message answering service. You can also order through our website www.hoddereducation.co.uk

If you have any comments to make about this, or any of our other titles, please send them to educationenquiries@hodder.co.uk

British Library Cataloguing in Publication Data

A catalogue record for this title is available from the British Library

ISBN: 978 1 444 135398

First Edition Published 2011

Impression number   10 9 8 7 6 5 4 3 2

Year   2015

Copyright © 2011 Tina Tilmouth, Elizabeth Davies-Ward, Briony Williams

Hachette UK's policy is to use papers that are natural, renewable and recyclable products and made from wood grown in sustainable forests. The logging and manufacturing processes are expected to conform to the environmental regulations of the country of origin.

Cover photo © nicolette wells / Flickr / Getty Images

Typeset by Pantek Media

Printed in Italy for Hodder Education, an Hachette UK Company, Carmelite House, 50 Victoria Embankment, London EC4Y 0DZ.

Contents

...rt has been made to trace and ...ledge ownership of copyright. The ...shers will be glad to make suitable ...ngements with any copyright holders ...hom it has not been possible to contact.

2.5 Swob Analysis, adapted with the permission of Nelson Thornes Ltd from *Foundations in Nursing and Healthcare: Beginning Reflective Practice*, Melanie Jasper, first published in 2003; **2.6** Based on Kolb, D.A (1984) Experiential Learning: Experience as the Source of Learning and Development, New Jersey: Prentice-Hall; **Table 2.5** SOLER (diagram from Egan 1990) taken from Egan G.E. (2002) 9th edition. The Skilled Helper, Brooks and Cole, California; **2.11** Lee Badham diagram. University of Worcester; **P.50** NMC Codes of Conduct www.nmc-uk.org; **Table 3.1** National Statistics Socio Economic Classifications, Crown copyright; **4.9** Caplan and Holland Model taken from Naidoo, Copyright Elsevier; **4.10** Beattie model taken from Naidoo and Wills, Copyright Elsevier; **4.11** Tannahill model taken from Naidoo and Wills, Copyright Elsevier; **pp.101–102** BBC News (July 2002); **Figure 8.2** Decisions in health care, Erickson, Owens and Kennedy; **9.1** Structure of the NHS Service, Office of Health Economics 2009 Copyright © OHE 2009; **9.2** Lee Badham University of Worcester; **9.4** Belbin The Management Network (2003); **9.5** Grow model, **9.6** Boost feedback, Alexander and Renshaw (2005) Supercoaching, Random House Business Books; **9.7** Lee Badham University of Worcester; **P.219** University of Worcester; **P.221** *Learning by Doing: A Guide to Teaching and Learning Methods,* Graham Gibbs, published by FEU (Further Education Unit, Oxford Polytechnic) 1988; **P.220** Text in box from Holm D and Stephenson S (1994) Reflection – A Student's Perspective. In Palmer A, Burns S and Bulman C (eds) *Reflective Practice in Nursing: the growth of the professional practitioner.* Blackwell Scientific Publications: Oxford 53–62; **10.2** Student British Medical Journal 2007 © BMJ Publishing Group Ltd 2011.

The authors and publishers would like to thank the following for the use of images in this volume:

Photo credits

1.1 © deanm1974 / Fotolia.com; **1.2** © Anatoly Tiplyashin / Fotolia.com; **1.4** © Yuri Arcurs / Fotolia.com; **1.5** © PA Archive/ Press Association Images; **1.7** © photogl / Fotolia.com; **2.1** © rgbspace / Fotolia. com; **3.2** © Monkey Business / Fotolia. com; **3.3** © MARK BOND / Fotolia.com; **3.5** ©TopFoto; **3.6** © dpa/Corbis; **4.1** © Kurhan / Fotolia.com; **4.4** © Yuri Arcurs / Fotolia. com; **4.5** © Dmitry Naumov / Fotolia.com; **4.6** © Crown Copyright; **5.1** © Andy Dean / Fotolia.com; **5.3** © Kablonk Micro / Fotolia. com; **5.4** © TheFinalMiracle / Fotolia. com; **5.5** © olly / Fotolia.com; **5.7** © Gary Salter/Corbis; **5.8** © Mary Evans Picture Library; **5.9** © The Granger Collection / TopFoto; **5.10** © Jon Le-Bon / Fotolia.com; **5.11** © Clive Goddard, CartoonStock; **5.12** © Crown Copyright; **5.13** © moodboard/ Corbis; **5.14** © dbvirago / Fotolia.com; **6.2** © Christian Noval / Fotolia.com; **6.3** © WALTER DAWN / SCIENCE PHOTO LIBRARY; **7.3** © KAKIMAGE / Alamy; **7.5** © David J. Green / Alamy; **7.7** © iofoto / Fotolia.com; **7.9** © Indigo Images / Alamy; **7.21** © Wellcome Photo Library, Wellcome Images; **7.23** © webking / iStockphoto; **7.24** © Phil Degginger / Alamy; **8.1** © carlosseller / Fotolia.com;

Author Biographies

Tina Tilmouth is currently working as a freelance writer, HE lecturer in Health and Social Care and has a private practice as a psychotherapist. Having worked for a number of years in all sectors of education and nursing, a career change led her to study as a psychotherapist. She is continuing this study at a higher level. She had worked on and been engaged in a host of publications including 'Contract Learning – A module for the Conversion course for SENS' (Open College 1990); 'NVQ Level 3 in Care' (Cable Education 2004); 'Safe Handling of Medications- A level 2 Certificate course' (Distance Learning – NCFE); 'Certificate in Contributing to the care setting' (Cable Education 2004) and 'NVQ Level 2 in Care' (Cable Education 2004).

Elizabeth Davies-Ward is currently Practice Development Manager and Senior lecturer on the Foundation Degree in Health and Social Care at the University of Worcester. She has been involved with Foundation Degree design and development since 2002. Her area of expertise is Work based Learning (WBL) and has supported students through their WBL modules for a number of years. She is a registered nurse and holds a BA (HONS) in Applied Community Studies and a Masters in Medical, Social Anthropology. She is currently registered on a Doctorate programme and the focus of her research is how Work Based learning can impact on policy and practice within the health and social care sector. She has previously worked in the Further Education Sector as Higher Education Coordinator.

Briony Williams is currently a Programme lead for Foundation degrees in Health and Social Care, Child and Adolescent Mental Health, Learning Disability and Mental Health at the University of Worcester. She is also a member of the Applied Social Science teaching team. Her main areas of teaching are mental health conditions, interventions in mental health, substance misuse and therapeutic group work. She has taught at Coventry University on the undergraduate BSc Hons in Occupational Therapy and the MSc in Occupational Therapy. Her recent clinical experience was working with young people with psychosis and in the past she has worked as an occupational therapist in community mental health services, substance misuse and acute mental health provision. She has contributed to and completed as joint author a textbook *Understanding and Dealing with Crisis*.

Introduction

Introduction to Health and Social Care for Foundation Degree Students

As an important and growing part of both national and local initiatives, Health and Social Care has increased opportunities for employment and emphasis has been placed on educating the workers in this field. One of the responses to this need has been the development of Foundation Degrees in vocational areas and, in particular, the focus has been on providing specific knowledge and skills within work based learning.

Foundation Degrees (FD) prepare students for a more effective role in the workplace and encourage them to pursue higher education beyond the FD itself.

The authors of this book were all part of the curriculum planning team at the University of Worcester who developed the new Foundation Degree in Health and Social Care validated in 2009. In developing the degree a collaborative approach to meet the need of key stake holders, including the student, the employer, the service user, the provider and the sector skills councils was employed and provided the expertise for the content to be included in the 13 Module Programme.

The content provided in the chapters to follow reflects the most common topics in Health and Social Care Advanced level courses, NVQs and Foundation Degrees and will therefore provide invaluable information for all students undertaking this vocational qualification.

Chapter 1: How to study effectively – provides a short introduction to the skills required for learning at higher levels. The writers unpick the major areas of concerns to students who may not have studied for some time. The mystique of academic styles of writing are addressed and the approaches to becoming an independent learner with the knowledge, skill and the confidence to find and use information in an evaluative way is developed throughout. Critical reflection and the introduction of approaches for successful academic study in higher education make this an essential opening chapter.

Chapter 2: Interpersonal skills and counselling relationships explores the theory and practice of effective communication and good listening skills and gives the student the opportunity to reflect on and explore self in relation to others. Models of reflection and basic counselling skills are explored.

Chapter 3: Diversity and inequality in health care work is a subject which underpins all Health and Social Care work. All the major areas of inequality in health care are addressed within a time line of events to show how social policy has been shaped by the public and political agenda. Together with a discussion about the need for non-judgemental attitudes the chapter helps the student to explore values and issues of prejudice, discrimination and inequality.

Chapter 4: Healthy living for individuals and communities deals with the complex area of defining health and the way in which it is promoted. The dynamic nature of the subject and the different perspectives that feed into the subject are debated and strategies for improving the health and well being of the nation and public health promotion is a core feature of this particular chapter

Chapter 5: Empowering people, politics and policy shows the legislative framework, policy making process and how these link to the empowerment of individuals who use the services. A historical overview of welfare is demonstrated within the chapter.

Chapter 6: The models of health and key theorists writing on social, biological and psychological models are explored. A comparison of the models shows how they can be used in practice.

Chapter 7: Managing health conditions and disease provides an overview of potential clinical problems and the common hazards encountered when in clinical practice. Common conditions and the first aid required to deal with these are also addressed and demonstrated. Health and safety and infection control and its prevention are major areas of concern for the Health and Social Care worker and are dealt with here.

Chapter 8: Research for practice enables the student to understand the wider organisational, ethical and service user-led considerations of evidence-based practice and research.

Chapter 9: Team working introduces the models of leadership across the care

sectors. Team working is essential to provide effective health and social care, and working in collaboration and partnership with others will ensure that happens. The chapter examines different models and strategies of leadership and team working offering practical strategies for success to enable the student to identify their own strengths, responsibilities and needs within the care context.

Chapter 10: Work-based learning. A feature of the FDSC is the link between theory and practice giving students the opportunity to integrate theory into practice in the reality of the workplace, in addition to reflecting on their role at work. This chapter will provide the student with generic and specific skills relevant to their workplace and they will be encouraged to use an online learning environment for the collation of their personal development documents.

1 How to study effectively – a short introduction

The aim of this chapter is to assist you in becoming an independent, reflective learner with the knowledge, skill and confidence to find and use information in an evaluative way. Students need to be able to use information technologies for data gathering and presentation and to be able to evaluate what they find. Critical reflection and the introduction of approaches for successful academic study in higher education are essential as a starting point for study.

Learning outcomes

By the end of the chapter you will be able to:

- understand what it means to be an independent, reflective learner and how this links with personal development planning

- plan and write an assignment with accurate written English

- organise written work and use correct conventions of referencing

- read in a critical manner and identify the key points, and construct defensible arguments.

Figure 1.1 Becoming a reflective learner requires thought

Intelligence, learning and reflection

You have made a decision to go to university and probably find yourself now faced with a huge change in your lifestyle and even in the way you are expected to learn.

Perhaps you have travelled a long way from home and are getting to grips with new accommodation and making new friends. As a mature student you may well be working and coming into university one day a week. The juggling you will need to do to ensure you are a success could be a major concern at this time. Some of your concerns will revolve around whether or not you will be able to complete the work required of you. You may worry about meeting deadlines since you are already so busy. Perhaps you haven't written anything for a

number of years and are concerned about your style of writing.

As you sat in the lecture room for the first time, I expect you took a look around you and sized the other people up. As a teacher, one of my first questions was always to ask how the students felt, and invariably the resounding answer was concern about not being 'intelligent' or clever enough to be successful at the course. When we discussed this further, students always had opinions of each other and more often than not felt that they themselves were probably the least intelligent person in the room. They also felt that they were not going to be quite good enough to do this course. Let's unpick these thoughts and also look in more depth at the term 'intelligence'.

You have come to university to learn about a subject in which you already have some

Figure 1.2 The first lecture at university can be daunting. Will I be clever enough?

Gardner's multiple intelligences are:

- Linguistic: reading writing, etc.
- Logical: maths ability with numbers and legal matters
- Spatial: navigating, driving or architecture
- Musical: singing, playing an instrument
- Body kinesthetics: sport, drama, dance
- Interpersonal: counselling and teaching skill
- Intrapersonal: self-understanding, self-awareness and self-management.

interest – and the first thing to establish is that learning is about a lot more than just being intelligent. We often have the mistaken belief that successful people are clever people, but this is not necessarily the case.

Early psychologists, such as Spearman (1927) and Terman (1916) (quoted in Cottrell, 2008), believed that each person has a fixed, general level of intelligence that they are born with, which they termed 'intelligence quotient' or IQ. You may have had the experience of being tested in this way and know your score. The general idea was that if a person did well on one IQ test they would do well on all others. However, later studies showed that the score gained on one form of IQ test may well change with a different test. The test provided, then, a mere snapshot of performance on a given day, using a specific type of test. Let's give an example here. How are you with maths? Or technology? If you undertook an IQ test, how do you think you would fare? I know I would probably do fairly badly since maths has never been a strong point for me. Maybe you will do brilliantly and gain a high score but then put in a poor performance on a test of verbal reasoning or spelling.

Thankfully, psychologists now believe that, rather than being a fixed entity, intelligence can be measured over a number of different disciplines and, more importantly, can be developed and learned through good study habits.

Gardner (1993, in Cottrell, 2008) identified seven 'main' intelligences and put forward the view that intelligence is indeed multifaceted and that individuals may show weakness in some areas but have highly developed skills in another.

Activity 1.1

Take a minute or two to think about things you are good at or have been successful with.

Where do you think this skill fits in with Gardner's seven intelligences?

As you look at the list of intelligences and your answer to Activity 1.1, you may have concluded that exposure in one way or another to one of those areas will undoubtedly develop knowledge and skills in that area and thus make the individual more 'intelligent'. For example, we can learn a sport or an instrument and if we practise hard we may be able to develop a high level of skill. This is good news for you as you embark upon your university career. If you expose yourself to intellectual pursuits such as reading around a subject and critically question what writers are saying, you can expect to develop your intellect and at the very least become more knowledgeable. We will look at this in more detail when we go on to look at how we can read in a more meaningful way and how we can take useful notes. The skills to enable you to critically analyse material will also be developed in this chapter. What we are saying here is that basically this premise means that intelligence is often the result of good study habits – and these can be learned.

But what exactly is learning? We will only briefly answer this here but you would be advised to look at Stella Cottrell's work in *The Study Skills Handbook* (2008) for a more in-depth discussion.

A common definition of learning is that it is a process that brings together influences and experiences in order to make changes in our knowledge, skills, values and attitudes. It is a process of change, and how we learn is a complex matter since we are all unique in our approach to it (Tilmouth, 2008).

One thing that will help you in your studies is to be aware of how you learn and what your preferences are. After the last few years of your education you will have realised the following:

- The time at which you study best
  - Are you a lark or an owl?
  - Do you prefer to stay up late or go to bed early?
  - When do you work best? In the morning or the evening?
- The space in which you need to work
  - Do you need a quiet environment or background music or chatter?
  - Does the room need a desk and computer or can you work lying on your bed?

- The time you need to spend to get the work done
  - Do you work for hours on end or for short snippets of time?
  - Do you plan from the deadline date and timetable backwards or do you spend a whole day and finish the work in that time?
- Your approach to assignment work
  - Do you like to get on with the assignment immediately in order to get it over with?
  - Or do you prefer to think about it and research it well before putting pen to paper?
- The type of teaching approach you prefer
  - Do you prefer to be spoon-fed the facts that go straight to the heart of the subject?
  - Do you need to understand everything before you can attempt an assignment?
  - Do you have to be interested in the subject in order to be motivated to go away and read?
  - Do you prefer to be active in class and like to discuss and take part in activities?

Figure 1.3 Preference for study

We all have our own approach to learning, but one thing you will find is that at university your styles of learning will undoubtedly be challenged and you will be asked to undertake new ways of gaining the information you need to complete assignments and to learn. There is an expectation that you will adopt independent strategies in your study and will be able to demonstrate that you can read and evaluate what you have read, making sense of it and constructing ideas and arguments.

Although you will attend lectures, you are expected to follow a lecture by seeking out more information to extend your knowledge. This can be quite a daunting task but can also be hugely liberating. It can free you to pursue areas of interest in the course you are studying and enable you to start to formulate your own thoughts on the subject.

One area of learning that is useful to develop at the outset of your studies is 'the art of reflection'. When we look in a mirror we may not always like what we see. Alternatively, we may be more than happy with the person we see and feel that change is not necessary.

I once knew a woman who continually upset people by her brusque manner. When this was pointed out to her she responded by saying 'That's just the way I am and if they don't like it, then I'm really not bothered. I just want them to do their jobs!'

That was one way of looking at it. But as a manager in a large team she failed to recognise that others were being affected by her approach. Her team was demotivated

and the 'job' she was so keen to get done was being done inefficiently at best and not at all in other instances. Her failure to reflect on her own approach would require a major change in her style of working and she was just not prepared to invest the time to do this. Had she done so, she might have found a better way of dealing with staff, with more positive results.

Reflective learning can be a little like this. We may read or hear something that does not quite fit with our previous understanding and this can be quite challenging. We may discuss our viewpoint on something with others in a seminar to find those views being challenged and this challenge being supported by eminent writers in the field. That can make us feel uncomfortable and we have a choice as to how we handle it. We can either reject the notion as unimportant or we can think about it and reformulate our own views.

Activity 1.2

Recall a time when you were challenged about an issue either at work or in your personal life. How did you react? Have you learned anything as a result? Reflect on this now!

As an undergraduate nearly 30 years ago I was challenged about my views on women. I had not come across the term 'feminism' at that time and held a somewhat stereotypical view about the place of women in our society. It may seem very strange to you now but I was firmly of the opinion that women with children should not go out to work and should not expect to earn the same as men in the workplace. My views, a result of a very traditional and somewhat unenlightened upbringing and education, were very real to me. But during a seminar they were challenged in a most erudite and forceful way and I was faced with a decision to make. Did I go away and allow them 'their opinions' and let the knowledge wash over me, firmly sticking to my own stance? Or should I reflect on what had been said and try to re-establish my own thoughts more in line with this idea? Of course, it was an uncomfortable time but a most interesting one in which I learned a huge

Figure 1.4 The art of reflection

amount and changed as a result. University was certainly a most liberating time in my life and one of great upheaval in terms of challenging views and values.

It will be the same for you. Reflection is certainly an agenda item for all universities, particularly since the Dearing report in 1997, and over the months ahead you will become aware of the importance of reflection and also of personal development planning (PDP).

As a result of the Dearing inquiry into higher education (1997), recommendations were made to universities to ensure that students not only became more aware of themselves and how they learn but also aware of how to improve their own personal performance, enabling them to develop the kinds of skills needed in the workplace.

You will have a progress file at university and one part of this file is the personal development planner, for which you are responsible. Through it you will be making continual adjustment to the ways in which you learn, develop new skills and plan for your future.

Most professions, particularly those in health care, expect you to undertake continuous professional development, so if you embrace this now through PDP while at university you will be making an important contribution to your future career.

Throughout most of the modules within a foundation degree, the link to the workplace is often made through assignments that make use of reflecting upon critical incidents. By embracing the PDP you will approach your own workplace with highly developed reflective and planning skills.

Your personal development planning file will therefore give you:

- a better understanding of how you learn

- a clearer indication of your goals

- better awareness of what you need and how you can meet these needs

- greater confidence in how to plan for your future career.

What do we actually do when we reflect on something?

Reflection often follows on from an incident that may have set us thinking (please see page 31–32 for more information on this). We sit back and review in our mind what happened, what we did and how we might have acted. Have you ever come away from a discussion and thought, 'I should have said this or done that'? Well, that's reflection in a way. You are reviewing what happened and thinking about what you might have said. If a similar situation presents itself at a later time you may well react differently due to this reflection.

Three things have happened here:

1. As a result of an incident we re-enact it and make sense of it.

2. We have gone over what we said and did and evaluated how we performed.

3. We weighed up our performance and drew conclusions as to how we might have handled it differently.

Let's apply these to learning:

1. We read something and make sense of it.

2. We go over it in our minds and evaluate it against our own knowledge or opinions.

3. We draw conclusions and consider how we might use this work in the future.

One thing that reflection is not, however, is description. Many students fall into the trap of describing an event or a piece of writing

Figure 1.5 Dearing report

rather than evaluating it, so you need to get into the habit of asking pertinent questions to focus your thinking.

The questions to ask revolve around *why* you did something or said something, *what you achieved* by doing or saying it, *what you learned* and *how* you might have improved. These are all the sorts of questions you must get into the habit of asking. You might also ask yourself *how* what you have read links in with other studies or *what* you thought about the materials you accessed and *why* you thought this. Look at Activity 1.3 to help you do this.

Activity 1.3

Example of descriptive writing

Read the following and then insert into the text some questions you might want answered in order to show reflective thinking.

I attended a study day on personal development planning. It was useful and I gained a lot of good ideas. I collected several handouts that will help me with my assignment for the education module. I thought the talk by Professor Higgins was good. She developed the theme of learning and disadvantage for young people. I did not enjoy Hazel Johnson's lecture. It was about how we can plan for our future careers.

These are the questions I would want the student to ask:

- Why was the study day useful?
- What 'good ideas' did I get and why were they 'good'?
- Why will the handouts be useful? How will they be used in my assignment?
- Why was Professor Higgins's talk 'good'?
- What did I learn?
- Why was her development of themes on disadvantage useful? What do I already know and how have I added to this knowledge as a result?

- Why was Hazel Johnson's lecture dismissed as unenjoyable?
- What would I have wanted from the lecture?
- What questions remain unanswered for me following the study day?

By answering these questions we gain a more in-depth knowledge of how useful this activity really was because we are being forced to think about what we are writing. When the student returns to look at the reflection, they will be faced with a journal entry that is more useful since it will be packed with examples of what they actually gained from the activity and how this has moved them forward in their learning. By contrast, descriptive accounts will merely remind us what we listened to and not what we learned or got out of that experience.

Reflection, then, is an important activity, and keeping your reflective accounts in a journal is part of your development and ongoing learning.

Using a computer to keep notes and jottings is fine; so too is the use of a notebook. The point is that you will be building a record of your own progress and development from the start of your course to its finish and then into your career.

By now you will have a better understanding of how to be more reflective in your studying and may also feel a little more reassured about your own ability to cope in higher education. As a summary, have a look at the following points. These are some of the things that might make life a little easier for you in the future.

Some dos and don'ts for effective independent learning

Do:

- become a reflective learner
- keep a learning journal
- prepare for lectures and formulate questions you need answered
- read!
- organise your time and your work in a logical and systematic manner
- discuss your learning with others.

Don't:

- waste time by rewriting notes to tidy them
- try to get down every word your lecturer speaks
- leave things until the last minute.

Some of these points will be developed in the following sections.

Plan and write an assignment with accurate written English

In this section we will tackle the process you need to go through in writing an assignment, in particular the essay.

While this type of writing generates feelings of terror for most students, it is a favoured device for university lecturers since it tests learning in a deep way. For example, the essay forces you to practise your research skills when you are gathering information to inform your writing, and to express your ideas and arguments in a clear manner. It helps you clarify your thoughts about a subject, and by having to write those thoughts down and argue for or against a given topic you are consolidating what you are learning.

We shall look at essay writing by addressing the following:

- what you are being asked to do
- the information you need
- organising your information
- reading efficiently
- taking meaningful notes
- structuring the piece of work
- the difference between a first class and a third class essay.

What you are being asked to do

Let's use an example essay title throughout this section to demonstrate how you might tackle it:

> Compare and contrast the consequences of social disadvantage on achievement in education for children aged 5 to 8.

So you are faced with your first assignment and are expected to construct an essay on the above subject. How do you start?

The first step is to fully understand what it is you are being asked to do. This requires your reflection on the actual title of the piece. I do as follows:

1. Read the question and highlight the main points.

2. Make sure I understand what I am being asked to do and rewrite the question in another way.

3. Check my understanding of it with somebody else.

4. Check the word limit and the marking criteria.

5. Refer to the learning objectives.

While all of the above is necessary I feel that the second point is especially crucial. In most titles certain words give an indication of what is expected by the lecturer. Let's review some of these, although you will have come across them before.

Our example contains the first point below:

- **Compare and contrast** Demonstrate how two or more issues or theories are similar and then draw upon arguments to show how they differ. Say what you think of the arguments and what the significance of the differences might be.

- **Evaluate** Make an argument for the pros and cons, the usefulness or not of a given issue. Assess the worth of something.

- **Justify** Support an argument with evidence to come to a conclusion about it. Debate the objections of others and say why you made your choice.

- **Summarise** Say what the main points about a subject are.

- **To what extent** This sort of phrase requires you to conclude that something is completely true or false. If you are asked to demonstrate 'to what extent good study skills are important to learning', you need to identify ways in which this conjecture is either true or not true.

- **Examine** This means to look in detail or depth at something.

- **Trace** Following an order of something happening either in time or in a sequence of events.

- **Critically evaluate** In this type of title you are being asked to demonstrate that you are weighing the arguments for and against something and that the theories or models used are being assessed as to their own strengths and weaknesses.

- **Distinguish** You are being asked to draw out the differences between, perhaps, two or more issues or theories.

- **Discuss** Argue for and against a given subject and consider the implications of your findings.

I am fairly confident that your own institution's student guide will also list many more terms you may need to understand and I would direct you to these. They are important in that failure to comply with the correct meaning of the term may result in you failing your assignment. For example, if you are asked to evaluate a given theory and then all you do is provide a description of it, you are not actually doing the task set.

The information you need

The second step is to research the subject matter. This is when you need to start to make sense of all the materials that might be available for you to use.

A good place to start is with what you already know. Perhaps you could mind-map this as in Figure 1.6. We will put our title in the centre and then have four arms from it to start with. You may want to add some more to it later.

Having completed the above you are now in a position to start your research. There are many sources of information at your disposal and you can also check with the specialist librarian in your own institution's library for help with this. This person is really a most valuable resource and it's worth taking time to talk to them to see how they might be able to help you.

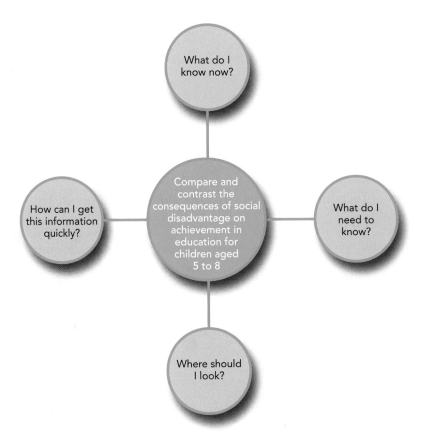

Figure 1.6

You might access the following:

- books
- journals
- abstracts
- reports
- theses
- CD-ROMs
- databases
- internet
- statistics and surveys
- your own lecture notes
- electronic databases.

The catalogues of resources available in libraries nowadays are more often than not in electronic form. These resources can be invaluable to you since they give you the most up-to-date studies and are generally far more accessible. E-books are also becoming more accessible to you and you will find your university library will subscribe to this system more and more. This means that whereas one hard-copy book may leave the library and not be available to others for some weeks, an e-book may be used by several students at once.

The disadvantage to online searching is that it can be very time consuming and can often lead you on wild goose chases as you try to track down material. For example, if you are not specific about what you need to look for and you type in one word such as 'disadvantage', you will get thousands of entries. Narrowing the search by adding one word as in 'social disadvantage' does little to reduce the number of entries, so you must be much more specific about how you search.

Figure 1.7 Data sources

The key words you type in should be used in combination with each other to structure your search. You are advised to go to your student handbook and your library and find materials to help you with such specialist searches, and again the specialist librarian will be most helpful for this activity.

Whatever resources you do find will lead to the generation of a lot of notes and a great deal of useful information, so one of the major things to remember at this stage is:

> Be highly organised!

Organising your information

When you come to write your essay, you will want to use quotes and refer to various writers. Your organisational skills will now come into play and if you have not been diligent in writing down references clearly and organising your notes in an accessible way your task will be a hundred times harder. So, although the reference list and bibliography are the last thing you will compile, by taking time to start them now you will save a huge amount of time and anxiety when your essay is finished.

Another reason to be highly organised and to write down all the sources used is so that you avoid plagiarism. Plagiarism is a serious academic offence but is often avoidable when you are truly organised.

Plagiarism is cheating in that you are using somebody else's work without actually crediting them as your source of information. You might not be doing this on purpose but may just forget to credit where you obtained information from, and in badly organised research there is a real danger of this happening.

It is very important, then, that when you access various pieces of work you wish to use in your writing, you do the following:

- acknowledge the source of the information
- build your own system of referencing, which details the author's name and initial, the date of publication, the title of the work, the page number, the

publisher and place of publication (see Harvard system, below)

■ compile a reference list and bibliography as you read for your essay.

A word here about reference lists and bibliography, which often get confused. In your essay, if you use a quotation or refer to the work of a writer, then you need to include this author in your reference list. If you read something but do not use any quotations or have not directly referred to it in your text, this should be listed in a bibliography. It is work that has helped to inform your own knowledge of the subject about which you are writing but has not been directly quoted.

Compiling your reference list

There are a number of referencing systems but one of the most commonly used is the Harvard system. In this system you need to cite the author's surname and year of publication in brackets in the body of the text, for example (Smith, 2009). On the reference page at the end of the essay the full citation will be shown as follows:

Smith, E. (2009) *Study Skills and How Not to Cheat!* Smithy Press, London and New York.

You are strongly advised to ensure you are using the conventions required in your own institution; these will be found in your student handbook for your own course and faculty or online on the student pages.

Reading efficiently

Having collected the information you want to use, the task now is to read it carefully and make sense of it.

It is possible that you have generated a number of journal articles and books which you now need to review to see whether or not you wish to use the information in your own work. You have a specific reason for reading in this case and can adopt different strategies in order to access the relevant materials for your work.

Before you start, answer the following questions:

1. Do you know exactly what you are looking for in this text?

2. Do you select relevant parts or flick aimlessly through the pages?

3. How do you go about finding relevant information in a text?

4. What do you do as you read?

By asking these questions you are starting to prioritise what it is you need to find out through your reading, and this will help you to read in a more efficient way and not waste time on irrelevant texts. You are becoming an 'active' reader. As you search through the material for the relevant items you need to help you to structure your arguments for your essay, you will find that you learn much more and retain material in a more efficient manner. Passive reading is reading without questioning the text – in other words, merely accepting what the text says, without question.

Having specific goals in mind as you read helps you to identify the information that actually addresses your essay question. You should try to focus on the following (based on University of Worcester, 2007 study skills material):

■ What material is of central importance or relevance?

■ What material is partially relevant, for example background or contextual?

■ What is irrelevant and will take me away from my main focus?

It is possible you have come across the terms 'skimming' and 'scanning', and once you have firmly established goals for your reading it is likely you will adopt one of these to carry out the task.

Skimming refers to the rapid reading of a text with the specific aim of selecting items you need. You may look at the chapter headings and the index or even look quickly at the introduction at the start of the book and this should give you an idea as to whether this is going to be useful for your own work.

Scanning is a more focused activity and in employing this strategy you are fully aware of what you want to find. We scan when we are looking for something specific – perhaps an advert in a newspaper. We go to the relevant section and then scan the columns for the specific material we require. In reading for our essay we will employ the scanning method and look through the text for a term or a word and then read the text when the term has been located.

Two other methods which might be useful are search reading and receptive reading.

Search reading is used for locating key words or phrases that will be of help in finding useful information. We might access the index at the back of the book or journal, find the key words and then read the relevant text. We tend to adopt this sort of search when we use the internet. A word of caution is useful here. Occasionally the words we use may be different from those the author

employs. It is not unusual for terms to be interchangeable, so if you are seeking information on, say, 'child protection', a look at 'safeguarding' may also be needed to get the material you require.

Receptive reading is a more in-depth way of reading and you are now paying a lot more attention to what you are reading. The skimming has revealed a text you think is most relevant and so you take a little more time to read it, making notes and reflecting on what you are reading. In this type of reading you are trying to understand the text accurately and get a good general level of understanding of what has been written.

By using these strategies you can improve your reading significantly.

Let's try an activity to help you with the example essay title.

Activity 1.4

Read the following extract (from Tilmouth, 2008), then answer the questions at the end. Your essay title should be at the top of the page on which you might be writing notes (more on this later).

> Compare and contrast the consequences of social disadvantage on achievement in education for children aged 5 to 8.

Since the late 1970s, there has been a growing concern with respect to a category of youngsters commonly known as NEETs – those who are Not in Education, Employment or Training. Despite the use of a number of initiatives such as youth training schemes and educational maintenance allowance to try to address this problematic area, there are still issues with respect to the numbers of young people falling into this category, and the problems of how to deal with this group remain.

There are also a number of students who, while not falling into the category of NEETs, attend sixth form college, having failed to achieve their target grades of five Cs and above at GCSE.

The prevailing learning culture for some of these young people has been one of time

spent at school disengaged and absenting themselves from the whole system of education for long periods of time.

Many reasons are put forward to try to explain why these particular groups fail to engage with education. First, the population of youngsters termed NEETs may have been alienated from learning because of the experience they have had, which may not have been appropriate for their needs.

The starting point for the literature review began with an online search for information about NEETs. This revealed 1,540,000 citations, all pertaining to this particular phenomenon. Evidently, a wealth of literature exists. All the research through Google Scholar was of recent articles, and 30 articles were read.

One article by the Office for Standards in Education (Ofsted) is called 'Good practice in re-engaging disaffected and reluctant students in secondary schools' (Ofsted, 2008). HMSO seemed to be a useful starting point and highlighted the problem area sufficiently to make a start. This led to a review of work in the area of disaffection and behaviour management and a number of textbooks and articles were reviewed.

From the papers read, a number of themes emerged.

In describing young people who are termed NEETs, disaffection and disadvantage were terms that emerged and therefore require analysis. If these are the reasons for these youngsters not engaging in education, then it would follow that no amount of changes to the education system per se could actually address this. It would need a more far-reaching change in personal and societal influences to address these issues.

The term NEET emerged in 1999 (Nuffield, 2008) but was by no means describing a new category of youngsters. Williamson (1997) suggests that the changing economic and job climate in the late 1970s led to the decline of many low-skilled jobs and an increase in service provision. The lack of skills needed for these jobs left youngsters unemployed and largely unemployable. Recession in the 1970s and 1980s also reduced the number of jobs available. Presumably we will have a similar situation emerging and a possible upward trend of more unemployed due to our current economic downturn.

Despite some decline in the NEETs population at the end of the 1980s there has been a gradual rise in the numbers again since 1999, with a further rise in the period 2003–5 (Nuffield, 2008).

Further, the complex phenomenon of the definition of NEET and of setting targets to try to reduce the population is fraught with difficulty not only due to the way in which the NEETs population is measured but also in the characteristics of the group. These can be summarised as:

- Today 52 per cent of NEETs are aged 18 compared with 40 per cent five years ago.

- Sixteen-year-old boys are twice as likely to be NEETs as 16–year-old girls.

- A higher proportion of young people are not actively seeking employment.

- Of those without GCSEs, 39 per cent are NEETs at age 16 compared with 2 per cent of 16-year-olds who gained five or more A* to C grades.

- Persistent absentees are seven times more likely to be NEETs at age 16.

- Young people who have a learning difficulty or disability are twice as likely to be NEETs.

- An estimated 20,000 teenage mothers are NEETs (EYE briefing paper 3).

These sobering statistics might suggest that the educational system has failed these groups of youngsters and their alienation from education and training has served only to unite them in social and economic disadvantage and underachievement (Williams, 2007; Delors, 2002).

Wakeman (2008) defined disadvantage as 'an inability to participate fully in society' and his main focus was on the correlation with educational attainment.

Material poverty is defined as household income below 60 per cent of median income and the educational disadvantage due to this is supported by statistics, which show that disadvantaged children are up to nine months behind their peers. Those with parents of poor educational background are up to 13 months behind, with the gap widening as they get older.

So the premise put forward by Wakeman (2008) is that the educational system is:

> …failing in its basic task of providing each child with an equal opportunity to succeed, overcoming the effects of an unequal start in life. In facing the difficult challenge of narrowing the gap, rather than allowing it to widen, schools need to note in particular the large jump in social differences early in secondary school. This ties in with the finding that by the end of primary school, many disadvantaged children are starting to become alienated from the school system, and underlines the need for measures to keep them engaged at this age.

Babb's (2003) work appears to support this. The profile of children who are likely to be in this group of underachievers includes those from low socio-economic backgrounds with parents having low or no qualifications.

Living in single-parent households with many siblings seems to compound the disadvantage and has an impact on the child's behaviour.

Disaffection or disengaging with school is manifested in absenteeism, with 50,000 pupils truanting per day (Wakeman, 2008; Harber, 2004).

Poor housing links with illness, overcrowding and lack of study space, and time off further damages the child's chance in education.

A number of reasons are put forward by theorists for the phenomenon of disaffection, including social and financial disadvantage, lack of career focus in year 9 (DfES, 2003) and boredom.

We do well, then, to review literature in the field that is trying to address such issues.

References

Babb, P. (2003) 'A summary of focus on social inequalities', ONS, London.

DCSF (2006) 'Longitudinal study of young people in England: waves one to three', SN 5545, HMSO, London.

Delors, J. (2000) 'Learning: the Treasure Within', report to UNESCO of the International Commission on Education for the Twenty-first Century, UNESCO Publishing, Paris.

DfES (2007) Strategy document online at: http://www.dfes.gov.uk/14-19/documents/NEET%20strategy.pdf

EYE briefing paper 3: Rates of participation of post-126 non-participation in England http://www.nuffield14-19review.org.uk/files/documents195-1.pdf

Harber, C. (2004) Schooling as Violence: How Schools Harm Pupils and Society, Routledge, Oxon.

Nuffield (2008) 'Review of 14–19 education and training, England and Wales'

Ofsted (2008) 'Good practice in re-engaging disaffected and reluctant students in secondary schools', HMSO, London.

Wakeman, M. (2008) Young People from Areas of Disadvantage: Closing the Gap in Educational Attainment, Knowledge and Information Management Services (KIMS).

Williams (2007) 'Personalisation: a NEET approach to policy failure', in Challenging Educational Disadvantage, Solace Foundation Imprint.

Williams, R. and Pritchard, C. (2006) Breaking the Cycle of Educational Alienation. A Multiprofessional Approach, McGraw-Hill, Maidenhead and New York.

Questions:

1. What exactly were you looking for in this text?

2. Did you skim, scan, search or employ receptive reading for this extract?

3. What did you do as you read?

4. Did you think the material was of central relevance, partial relevance or irrelevant and taking you away from your main focus?

Here are some pointers to help you with the above and future text analysis.

Possibly you thought the above text was only partially relevant in that it is dealing mainly with post-16-year-old students. However, the social disadvantage angle has been addressed in the reports focused on in the text and might be worth a further look. Also, a look at the references might interest you and move you to seek out these texts to further develop your knowledge.

Did you chart the main ideas on a notepad? By doing so you may find that certain themes emerge and you can quickly identify the main point that you might be able to use in your own work.

Did you ask questions about what you were reading as you read? By doing this you can formulate your own opinions on what is being said. You might consider that some of the points made are insufficiently supported and therefore unreliable.

Perhaps you want to challenge the writer because of this. Has your reading triggered further ideas of your own?

Did you photocopy the materials and then use pens and markers or margin notes to focus your mind on relevant points?

Did you read with understanding? Or did you merely read it through and pick out a quote you might use later? Did you re-read the difficult parts?

Taking meaningful notes

We mentioned making notes above and now we turn our attention to how this might be done in a more useful way for you. For example, do you make copious notes in lectures and then rewrite them afterwards? Perhaps you make notes and then never read them back or revisit them at all.

If writing notes in the lecture takes your attention away from what is being said,

then perhaps you might consider not writing anything at all.

As our starting point, let's consider what the point is of taking notes.

Activity 1.5

Why do you take notes? List all your reasons.

Did you have any of the following among your reasons?

> It helps me to concentrate on the speaker and keeps me focused.
>
> I note down only important points.
>
> It helps me to revise the materials
>
> It helps me to start my assignment by showing me some ideas.
>
> It helps my memory and reminds me of what the lecture was about.

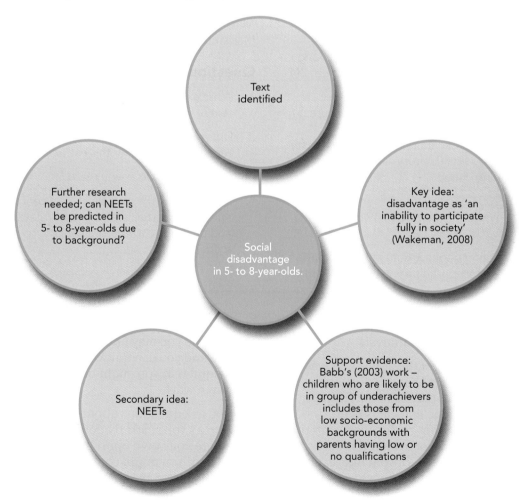

Figure 1.8

Notes remind us about and help us to concentrate on the subject matter – but often they can be a jumble of words that really only serve to confuse us more. Attendance at a lecture or a trip to the library needs to be planned if the notes we take are to be more meaningful for our assignment.

For example, our essay title, 'Compare and contrast the consequences of social disadvantage on achievement in education for children aged 5 to 8', must be firmly in our mind to start with, but to help even further it is useful to set some goals and perhaps detail some questions that attend to what you want to find out.

Here are some examples.

> How should we define social disadvantage?
>
> Is there evidence that achievement is affected?
>
> How is it affected?
>
> What are we comparing and contrasting?
>
> What do we mean by consequences: getting a job or going to university or being unemployed?
>
> Are there major writers in this field?
>
> What are the up-to-date reports on this subject?

Having organised a planned list, you can then be more focused and are unlikely to be sidetracked. I am sure I am not the only person who has spent hours in the library reading something really interesting yet totally irrelevant to my assignment. If you can afford the time, this is fantastic – but working to a deadline means we do not have this luxury.

Armed with a more structured list, you can now use your sources to seek out the answers you need and to write some notes.

There are a number of ways to take notes and you need to find your own preference, but here are a few styles to consider:

> mind maps
>
> headings and subheadings
>
> lists and numbered points
>
> summary of a main point in your own words
>
> diagrams.

Good strategies to adopt include:

- Be brief.
- Be organised.
- Write in your own words.
- Do not copy chunks of text.
- Link up points and colour-code matching ideas.
- Do not spend time rewriting notes to make them tidier.
- Write legibly.
- Always write the source in a reference list.
- Use Post-it® notes to identify relevant pages in books and journals.

Having collated your notes, the next step is to organise them into themes and headings and to start to plan your essay. Look at the summary in Figure 1.09 of the process so far.

Structuring the piece of work

So finally we are ready to put all our notes into the essay.

Having gone through the research process and note taking, you now have a much clearer idea of the structure your essay will take. I have observed students trying to write essays by researching as they go along and this is by far the least efficient way of doing so. The following process is the best way in which to approach this task.

Here we will look at the structure and content of an essay and your lecturer will help you with this by telling you what they expect. Every essay contains the following:

1. Introduction
2. Indicated themes and links
3. References
4. Conclusion.

Introduction

I often write this after I have written the main body of the text but this is a personal preference. What you are doing here is telling the reader what to expect and how you intend to develop the themes. You are also going to say what your ultimate conclusion is likely to be.

A starting point may be to explain what you understand by the title and state why the question is important. You can follow up by defining what the key terms are and then outlining the key themes or arguments that you intend to address.

Indicated themes and links

This is the body of the essay and here you need to do what you have said you will do in the introduction.

It should flow from one idea to another and can be helped if you link ideas. In our essay example you might start by comparing the disadvantaged children in the population in terms of achievement with those who are more privileged. Your writing also needs to show where you are going with the essay and your arguments or where your thinking comes from, so it is useful to use linking phrases to show this – for example: 'Having explored how achievement in lower socio-economic groups compares with that of higher socio-economic groups, I now intend to examine some contrasting views on this by looking at the work of Babb and Williams.' (You will need to check with your tutor about the use of the personal pronoun in your essay).

This indicates a shift in your focus and allows the reader to move smoothly on to the next point.

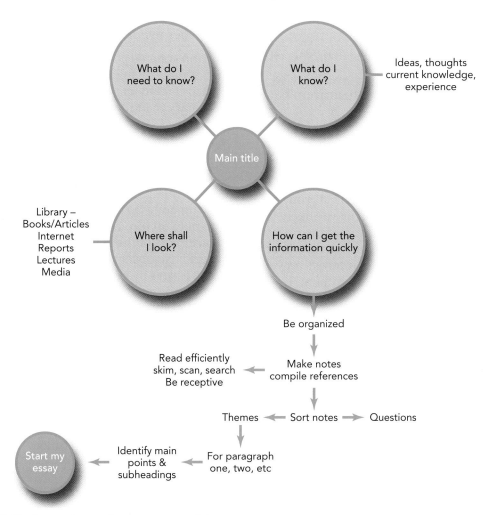

Figure 1.9 Finding and recording source materials

References

As you write, you need to supply references in the text to support your work. Direct quotes must always be credited to the author of that quote and ideas or themes you are exploring in your work should also be cited in the bibliography.

Use the Harvard system if this is the system favoured by your institution, and, within brackets, cite author surname, date of publication and page numbers. You must then ensure that full details (but not page numbers, except for journal articles) should be included in the reference list and also the bibliography if you are requested to supply one.

Conclusion

I often tell students to refer back to their introductory paragraph and relate this to their conclusions. This is the part of the essay when you tell the reader what you have done. In the final paragraph you will be summarising the key points made and linking these back to the essay title. You may also want to state what your own position is in relation to the title – but do not merely state your own personal opinions; you must ensure that your opinions have support from the arguments used in the text.

I remind my students of the following with respect to structure:

> Introduction: tell the reader what you intend to do.
>
> Main body: now do so!
>
> Conclusion: now tell the reader what you have done.

Clear expression in language

In this section we address the actual way we use language in the essay.

A dictionary should accompany you in your writing so that you are not using inaccurate words.

Get into the habit of reading in a critical way. In this way you will be able to determine whether your work makes sense in terms of sentence construction, and you can highlight any poor grammar. If you read the work out loud to yourself you can more easily see whether or not it makes sense.

Avoid lengthy sentences. One or two points per sentence is probably enough.

Do not confuse full stops and commas or use them interchangeably. A full stop finishes a thought or a sentence; a comma merely provides us with a pause. I have often read students' work in which they use a comma instead of a full stop. When I ask them to read the passage in question they find it hard to make any sense of it since the sentences are running into each other.

Avoid repeating words and themes within the same sentence or paragraph.

Critical analysis or evaluation

An ability to organise the concepts and theories we have researched in relation to the ideas and subject matter of the essay, and structure these into a coherent argument, means that we are analysing what we have learned.

A 'critical' analysis means we are able to comment on the strengths and weaknesses of arguments within the subject matter of the essay.

Using your own words

The only way you can demonstrate that you have understood what you have read is to restate it in your own words. So this is an important part of the content part of the essay. It is also a way in which you can reduce the possibility of plagiarism (Northedge, 1992).

The difference between a first class and a third class essay

So the essay is written. How can you maximise your chances of a first class degree? How do you get the A grade?

Here is our example title again:

> Compare and contrast the consequences of social disadvantage on achievement in education for children aged 5 to 8.

For a first class grade you must:

- say what the consequences of social disadvantage are

- make a good comparison and go on to contrast the consequences
- comment upon the theories and draw conclusions about the achievement and how it is defined
- draw your conclusions and analyse the links back to the original title.

For a second class grade you must:

- say what the consequences are
- make a comparison and go on to contrast the consequences.

For a third class grade you must:

- write about social disadvantage and achievement without thinking about planning a coherent essay.

Reading in a critical manner

Critical reading includes identifying key points and constructing defensible arguments.

We have already said how we might read in a more meaningful way and in this final section we look at critical analysis in more detail. We cover this again in Chapter 8 and you will find a checklist there to help you to structure your work. Here is a little more detail to get you started.

When you are carrying out secondary research, you are going to access a number of journal articles as well as books and reports.

The information here will apply to all kinds of articles, but each type may require slightly different questions and we will try to address some of those differences here.

In analysing a journal article your critique must include some basic details of the author's name, the title of the article, the journal, together with the volume number, date, month and page numbers.

You also need to highlight at the outset of your critique what the article is discussing and what the author's purpose, methods, hypothesis and conclusions are.

These are all details you can easily access, but the major part of your critique must be your opinion of what you are reading. This can sometimes be a little daunting. If you merely restate what the article is about and how the research has been carried out, you are doing little more than showing a good grasp of what is already in the text. While it is important to do this, the major thrust of your work has to show a deeper understanding and a more evaluative approach about what has been written.

You can start by reading the article through in its entirety in order to get an overview. Once this is done you can then begin the task of being a little more analytical in how you approach it. You need to read it again, critically. Perhaps you will need to photocopy the article in order to make some of your own notes on it.

There are some standard questions you might want to ask:

- Is the title of the article clear and does it give you a good idea about what you are reading?
- Is there an abstract which specifically highlights details of what the article is about, and mentions the methods used, together with conclusions and results?
- Is the purpose of the article shown in the introduction?
- Are you aware of any errors of fact or interpretation? You may find this difficult at first, but as you become a more seasoned reader and researcher you will become more able to determine when this is the case.
- Is the discussion relevant or does it go off at a tangent?
- Is the literature pertinent to the research or is there a clouding of the issues with texts that are not relevant?
- Does the author write in a clear way?
- Has the author been objective in the discussion or is there evidence of subjective reasoning?

Having read the article, you now need to structure your response. Allow yourself the luxury to disagree if you feel you can do so in a way that supports your own findings. You need to express your argument in an objective and well-reasoned manner.

Be sure to supply a list of acknowledgements for the sources of information you have used in your writing. Doing so will ensure you are not in danger of plagiarism.

Summary

The aim of this chapter has been to assist you in your quest to become an independent, reflective learner. Having identified several intelligences, you may now feel relieved to know that you can bring to your particular year group at university different skills and knowledge. Remember: some people in your group may well be good at mathematics but you might have a very useful creative approach to your studies. Both skills are highly useful and of equal value. Also, by exposing yourself to intellectual pursuits, such as reading around the subject and critically questioning what the writers are saying, you can expect to develop your intellect and the skills you may have struggled with in the past. The content in this chapter and the checklist in Chapter 8 will help you to access literature and evaluate it in a more critical manner.

Reflection is a major agenda item for all universities since the Dearing report (1997), and the importance of personal development planning (PDP) should now be clear to you. Your university education will help you to became more aware of yourself and how you learn and also how you might improve your own personal performance.

The way to approach critical evaluation of articles and the structure of essays have been covered, but you are expected to access other texts to give you a much broader understanding. The importance of organising key texts you have accessed and the need to write an accurate reference list has also been covered here.

Now try Activity 1.6, which links directly into the learning outcomes. No answers are supplied but the activity may well help you with the assignment your lecturer will have prepared for you in this unit.

Sample assignment you may be asked to complete:

> Critically reflect on your personal development and consider the importance of ethical issues relevant to reflection on work-based learning.

Activity 1.6

Write a short summary for yourself about what it means to be an independent, reflective learner and how this links with personal development planning.

Select a meaningful method for yourself of organising your written work and ensure you have a clear understanding of the correct conventions of referencing.

Using the text in this chapter, identify what it means to read an article in a critical manner.

References

Cottrell, S. (2003) *Skills for Success; The Personal Development Planning Handbook*, Palgrave Macmillan, Basingstoke.

Cottrell, S. (2008) *The Study Skills Handbook*, 3rd edn, Palgrave Macmillan, Basingstoke.

Dearing, R. (1997) *The Summary Report of the National Committee of Inquiry into Higher Education*, HMSO, London.

Northedge (1992) *The Good Study Guide*, Open University Press, Buckingham.

Nuffield (2008) 'Review of 14–19 education and training, England and Wales'.

Tilmouth, T. (2008) 'Special study – disadvantage and disaffection in education', unpublished PhD thesis, University of Birmingham, Birmingham.

Worcester University (2007) Study skills advice sheet.

Bibliography

Babb, P. (2003) 'A summary of focus on social inequalities', ONS, London.

DCSF (2006) 'Longitudinal study of young people in England: waves one to three', SN 5545, HMSO, London.

Delors, J. (2000) 'Learning: the Treasure Within', report to UNESCO of the International Commission on Education for the Twenty-first Century, UNESCO Publishing, Paris.

DfES (2007) Strategy document online at: http://www.dfes.gov.uk/14-19/documents/ NEET%20strategy.pdf.

EYE briefing paper 3: Rates of participation of post-126 non-participation in England http://www.nuffield14-19review.org.uk/ files/documents195-1.pdf.

Harber, C. (2004) *Schooling as Violence: How Schools Harm Pupils and Society*, Routledge, Oxon.

Jasper, M. (2003) *Beginning Reflective Practice. Foundations in Nursing and Health Care*, Nelson Thornes, Cheltenham.

2 Interpersonal skills and counselling relationships

Effective interpersonal skills are an essential part of any healthy relationship. Being able to communicate well is extremely important for anyone working in the caring professions. Communication is the basis of interaction; communication skills, in particular listening skills, are essential in health and social care for effective delivery of services and productive teamwork. The majority of therapeutic interactions within health and social care settings are with vulnerable people or their carers. It will sometimes be the case that you are communicating with a person who is feeling upset or going through personal crisis, so the possibility of misunderstandings in communication increases and it is therefore important to get communication right: effective communication is the key to successful working.

We need to be able to put people at ease as soon as we meet them so that they feel able to communicate their concerns. We need to truly understand what it is the other person is saying rather than assume that we understand. As a general rule, we should aim to finish the interaction leaving someone feeling better than they did before we met them. To be truly effective in interpersonal skills we must know ourselves well and be aware of what we bring to the relationship, and how we might impact on the other people we communicate with. Self-awareness and the ability to reflect are essential. This chapter will explore the theory and practice of effective communication and give you the opportunity to reflect on and explore yourself in relation to others.

Learning outcomes

By the end of the chapter you will be able to:

- explain theories of interpersonal communication
- reflect on the concept of self-awareness and personal development, including self-presentation and personal boundaries
- identify factors that help and hinder effective communication
- describe the term 'therapeutic relationship'.

What are interpersonal skills?

Interpersonal skills involve a variety of different types of communication; before exploring these it would be helpful to explore some definitions of communication.

> Communication involves the reciprocal process in which messages are sent and received between two or more people (Bazler Riley, 2008).

Crawford, Brown and Bonham (2006) go further and suggest that 'communication is something we do in our internal world of thoughts and in our external world by speaking, writing, gestures, drawing, making images and symbols or receiving messages from others'.

It is clear from these definitions that communication involves an interaction between two or more people and that it can take any form. It is useful to use specific terminology when discussing different types of communication.

Terminologies used in the study of communication:

- interpersonal communication
- environmental communication
- intrapersonal communication.

Interpersonal communication

Interpersonal communication involves non-verbal, paralinguistic and verbal communication between two or more people.

Table 2.1 Non-verbal communication

Facial expression	Our facial expression communicates emotions unless we train ourselves to mask our feelings. Burnard (1997) argues that it is important to be congruent: if you say you are angry while smiling it gives a confusing mixed message.
Eye contact and gaze	The way we look into another person's eyes during conversation is what is known as eye contact. If somebody can hold eye contact through a conversation it can communicate a level of confidence and willingness to communicate fully. Some of the people we communicate with will have a very low level of eye contact, which might communicate a lack of ease with the conversation or a lack of confidence. It is a good idea to reduce the level of our eye contact to reflect theirs, otherwise it can feel threatening. The appropriateness of maintaining eye contact differs according to culture.
Gestures	Gestures are movements of your arms and hands that accompany speech. Gestures can help communication; for example, pointing the direction a person needs to go can add emphasis to the communication. However, too much gesturing can be distracting. My friend and I gesture a lot during conversation. Once our children decided to tie our hands behind our backs to find out if it affected our conversation. The result was that our communication was stilted and uncomfortable.
Body position, posture and movement	The body position of a client can tell you a lot about how they are feeling. If they are hunched over with arms and legs crossed they are probably feeling quite anxious. Rogers (1990) recommends that we relax and it is important not to appear too formal and distant. However, if we are too laid back in our posture we could appear disinterested. Sitting with our arms and legs crossed can appear closed off and defensive. In some circumstances it may be a good idea to mirror the body posture of the person we are with.
Personal space and proximity	Two to three feet in distance between the chairs is about right for me. However, I have noticed that some clients push their chairs back as soon as they sit down in the prearranged chairs. I assume the space does not feel comfortable to them. People seem to have their own invisible boundaries, which change according to who they are interacting with and how comfortable they feel. Porritt (1990) calls it a bubble that surrounds us.
Clothes	The clothes we choose to wear say a lot about us. Dressing too informally or too formally can alienate us from our clients.
Therapeutic touch	Touch can be a contentious subject. On the one hand, there is evidence of touch having therapeutic benefits; on the other, it can be misinterpreted and seen as an invasion of a person's personal space. Bonham (2004) suggests it may be appropriate and supportive when patients or carers are distressed as it may validate the degree of their suffering. He suggests that appropriate places to touch in this situation are hands, forearms, upper arms and shoulders.

Non-verbal communication

When communicating, 'our attention is focused on words rather than body language. But our judgement includes both. An audience is simultaneously processing both verbal and non-verbal cues. Body movements are not usually positive or negative in and of themselves; rather, the situation and the message will determine the appraisal' (Givens, 2000).

See Table 2.1 for examples of non-verbal communication.

Argyle (1978) argues that non-verbal communication can have as much as five times the impact of words spoken on a person's understanding. According to Barbour (1976), communication can be broken down as follows; a large percentage of the impact is in non-verbal communication:

what you say (the words themselves): 7 per cent

how you say it (volume, pitch, tone, rhythm, etc.): 38 per cent

your body language (facial expressions, gestures, posture, etc.): 55 per cent.

Crawford *et al.* (2006) note that clients in a health and social care setting may have communication difficulties and may not pick up the non-verbal cues communicated.

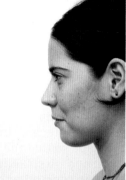

Figure 2.1 **Non-verbal communication**

Paralinguistic aspects

Paralinguistic communication (see Table 2.2) refers to the different ways in which we moderate our speech, for example pitch, volume, rhythm, tone of voice and timing alongside grunts, 'umms' and 'ahhs'. The

way we say things is as important as the words we use and can affect the way our message is perceived. Other forms of paralinguistic communication include: yawning, sighing, coughing, tutting, laughing and groaning. In written, text or email communication, paralinguistic aspects could be communicated by different colours or size of font or the use of capital letters.

Burnard (2005) argues that we must be careful of making assumptions about how someone is feeling, however paralinguistic communication can offer us a clue to how a person is feeling.

Verbal communication

Verbal communication is the spoken language used in an interaction between people and can be complex. The meanings of words alter between cultures and generations, and on their own can be an ineffective form of communication. For example, my sons would use the word 'random' in a different way from me and both my sons and I would use the word 'gay' in a different way from my granny. The words we use alter depending upon the situation and the people involved. A problem in communication is that we cannot be sure that a word has the same meaning for two people (Porritt, 1990). This is particularly important when communicating feelings as the strength of the word may differ between people.

Table 2.2 **Paralinguistic communication**

Tone of voice	Our tone of voice carries information about our feelings. It can add emphasis to the words we use.
Speed of speech	How fast our speech is can indicate whether we are nervous. However, if our speech is slow we may communicate that we are unsure about how we are being received by the listeners.
Volume	How quiet or loud our voice is when talking is important. For example, we may intentionally speak in a low volume so that only the person closest to us hears. A person may mumble a reply when leaving the room so that you know they disagree with you but are unsure what they have said.
Pitch	This refers to how high or low our voice is. Its level may change and indicate that we are unsure of the impact of what we are saying.
Hesitations	'Umms' and 'ahhs' sometimes communicate fear. They can also be used to pick up clues that the other person wants to take a turn in the communication.
Accent	This communicates where we are from. It is important for a health and social care worker to be understood, so we may have to learn to modify a strong accent.

Table 2.3 Linguistic aspects of verbal communication

Choice of words	Some people choose to try and impress the people they are communicating with by using big, unfamiliar words. In health and social care we need to be careful not to use jargon and abbreviations that our clients or patients cannot understand.
Phrases	Euphemisms (which could also be called double-speak) are phrases that we use when we think that more straightforward words may be upsetting – such as saying someone has 'passed away' instead of died.
	Medical jargon and abbreviations among team members may be fine but we should remember that clients may not understand and it puts a distance between us.
	Clichés such as 'Would you like to share something with me?' can sound overused and inauthentic.
Figures of speech	Metaphors are figures of speech, in which we use one object to describe another. They are used to convey feelings. An example would be dealing with anger: letting it 'simmer on the back burner'. Another example is feeling 'under par'. As with the phrases above, such terms may not be understood.

Activity 2.1

Try to come up with as many different ways of saying 'Hello' as possible.

Even such a simple word as 'Hello' can be both formal and colloquial, and words alone are not always sufficient to get our message across. See Table 2.3.

Written communication

Being able to maintain clear and accurate records is an important part of working in health and social care. The use of succinct, clearly written handovers is extremely important in many health and social care settings. Donnelly and Neville (2008) suggest that written communication should be accurate in detail, up to date, non-judgemental and legible so that others are able to read it. Written records should be kept in a safe place and out of view to comply with confidentiality guidelines.

Email and other forms of electronic communication have become important forms of communication and are often used in health and social care. There are advantages and disadvantages to email communication. It is quick and convenient and people can respond when it is convenient to them. It is a written record of a communication which can be accessed afterwards for evidence in a way that a telephone communication cannot. Links to relevant internet sites can be included in the message so that the respondent can click on them and go straight to the information. You can send other documents as an attachment. It is free; unlike letters, you do not have to pay postage. Finally, it can save journey time to and from meetings.

The disadvantages are mainly that it is impersonal and the people communicating cannot pick up paralinguistic and non-verbal signs. I tend to be to the point in email correspondence and sometimes other people think that I am being rude. People may not reply to an important message quickly enough. People also may not reply because they have not fully understood the message. Confidentiality is another important consideration; emails with confidential information may go to the wrong person by mistake or may be accidentally forwarded by the respondent to someone who would not be included by the first writer.

Environmental communication

The way that our environment communicates with us is extremely important. The initial impact of a room or building can have a huge effect on how people feel when they enter and can influence the success of an interaction. For example, it is important to think about the choice of room when someone is being given bad news.

Activity 2.2

Make notes on how the following environments communicate with the people who use them:

- a preschool
- a GP surgery
- a nursing home reception area
- a hospital outpatients waiting room.

Consider how information is conveyed via posters and signs; the use of colour; the lighting; the temperature of the room; the ambient sounds; the state of the decor. An environment for young children might be full of vibrant colours and age-appropriate interactive toys, while an environment for people who are doing a relaxation session might need to be quite uncluttered and with a muted, peaceful decor.

It is important to consider the way a room is set up. Sitting behind a desk may not be appropriate for many types of health and social care interaction as it can be too formal. However, sometimes sitting at a desk with a mutual focus such as a drawing or pictures with somebody who is uneasy with direct eye contact might help the interaction and make it feel less challenging. Other factors including the warmth and lighting in the room communicate important messages.

Intrapersonal communication

Intrapersonal communication is that which takes place within ourselves, or 'self-talk'. We have internal dialogues with ourselves all the time, even when we are in the process of communicating with another person. These internal dialogues can change the way we interact with others and often make our interactions less successful because we are distracted by what we are telling ourselves. But sometimes these internal conversations can be useful because we are picking up non-verbal signals and cues from another person and reacting to them. Intrapersonal communication can inform us if we feel uncomfortable with what we are hearing or

seeing. Our differences in belief systems and values are communicated intrapersonally. This is why it is so important to be self-aware and know how our beliefs and values might affect the way we communicate with others.

Self-awareness

Effective interpersonal skills require you to observe and reflect upon the communication skills you currently have and how best you can develop those skills for working with children, young people, adults, parents and carers to ensure good therapeutic relationships. Being aware of who you are and the impact you have on others demands that you attend to your own personal growth and development.

According to Geldard and Geldard (2003), through development of your self-awareness you can resolve past and current issues.

Donnelly and Neville (2008) comment that being aware of yourself enables you to review your personal values against the professional standards that you are expected to work within.

Before looking at how we can improve our self-awareness, it would be useful to understand more about how the personality develops.

Activity 2.3

How do children develop a concept of self?

Think about how a 0–1-year-old baby starts to develop a sense of who they are.

Think about how a 5-year-old child develops this understanding.

Think about a teenager and what impacts on their self-concept.

What experiences would change an adult's self-concept?

While doing Activity 2.3, you have probably realised that the experiences we have as a child help to form a sense of self. The way that we view ourselves, other people and our world is rooted in our family relationships and interactions, in the environment we live in, in the experiences we have and the people that have helped to shape those experiences. So a child brought up in a warm, caring, supportive family and who does not experience any significant physical or psychological trauma is more likely to develop a strong and positive sense of self than a child who has had negative experiences. The majority of people have a complex mixture of positives and negatives and our level of self-esteem is dependent on how successfully we interact with our significant others and the environment we live in. I have already emphasised how important self-awareness is to enable us to communicate effectively in health and social care settings; in order to become more self-aware, it is useful to understand some of the theory behind personality development and a concept of self.

There are different perspectives of personality development including psychodynamic, humanistic, behavioural, cognitive behavioural and transactional analysis. These frameworks are also theories of counselling that allow practitioners to think systematically about human development and the counselling process. See Table 2.4 (overleaf).

The more you read and understand the different frameworks, the more you realise that although they have different approaches and viewpoints and use different language, there are common strands in their understanding of personality development.

Two theories that I have found most useful in my clinical practice in health and social care settings are humanistic and transactional analysis.

Humanistic theory

Two important theorists in the humanistic theoretical model are Maslow and Rogers.

Maslow's hierarchy of needs

Figure 2.2 (p. 28) shows Maslow's hierarchy of needs and illustrates the humanistic belief that as humans we are all 'self-actualising'. That is, we are able to develop our full potential and make the best of our existence. In order to develop our potential as a person it is necessary for

certain needs to be met. This simple diagram of needs is useful when we consider the people that we are helping. It can be assumed that many of the people who need our help are experiencing problems. In order for them to feel a sense of esteem and self-actualisation they need to have their physiological needs, safety needs and love and belonging needs satisfied.

Carl Rogers

Rogers drew from Maslow when developing his concept of actualisation. He believed that as humans we are all organisms and have a tendency to self-actualise. In order to do so we need positive self-regard and we get this through messages given to us by our environment, particularly people. For example, a baby will feel a sense of positive self-regard when she coos and smiles at her mother and her mother coos and smiles back at her. She feels a sense that she has been recognised and is important – she knows that her smile and coo are welcomed and encouraged.

As we grow, we get verbal and non-verbal message from the people around us. These messages are called conditions of worth. We feel worthy only when we do the 'right' thing, when we 'behave'. When we bend ourselves to fulfil these conditions of worth we get conditional positive regard. For example, a little girl who has managed not to get her dress dirty when playing is told what a good pretty little girl she is for not getting dirty. She will then associate being clean and pretty with being good. We often judge ourselves by the conditions of worth and this is called conditional positive self-regard – we like ourselves only if we meet the standards set by others. In health and social care this will often be the case with the people we are helping – their self-esteem is low because they are not able to meet their conditions of worth.

If all goes well and we are able to self-actualise and feel positive self-regard, we develop a real self. On the other hand, if we are forced to live with conditions of worth that are out of step with our real self and receive only conditional positive regard and self-regard, we develop instead an ideal self – something not real, something that is always out of our reach, the standard we can't meet.

Table 2.4 Psychological theories

Psychological theory and main contributors	Counselling approach
Psychodynamic counselling Key contributors Sigmund Freud 1856–1939 Carl Jung 1875–1961	The counsellor works with the client to uncover and analyse past life experiences and understand their influences on present life events. The emphasis is on the unconscious influences on human behaviour. Analysis of dreams may be a part of counselling. Transference and counter transference are useful concepts to note in the helping relationship. This is when previous relationships in our lives can create barriers to communication and will be discussed more fully later in the chapter.
John Bowlby 1907–1990	Bowlby believed that the first bonds formed by babies with their parents or carers have an enormous impact on psychological health that continues throughout life. According to Bowlby, attachment also serves to keep the infant close to the mother and therefore improving the child's chances of survival.
Behavioural Ivan Pavlov 1849–1936 Burrhus Skinner 1904–1990 John Watson 1878–1958	The counsellor works with the client to change undesirable and observable behaviours. All human behaviour is thought to be learned through classical and operant conditioning and can be unlearned. Positive and negative reinforcements will shape our behaviour.
Cognitive behavioural Aaron Beck 1921– Albert Ellis 1913 – 2007	Derived from the integration of behavioural and cognitive theories. Cognitive behavioural theories are concerned with thought processes and belief systems and how they impact on feelings and change behaviour. Cognitive behavioural therapists work to challenge faulty thinking and analyse irrational beliefs to lessen their impact.
Humanistic Carl Rogers 1902–1987 John Heron 1928 Abraham Maslow 1908 –1970	Human beings have individual potential that needs to be achieved in order to experience satisfaction with life. Rogers drew from other theorists such as Maslow to develop the concept of actualisation which is striving to achieve internal harmony between what we feel and what we experience. Humanistic counsellors work with the client to understand the actualisation process and the need for congruence between feelings and experience to create internal harmony.
Eric Berne 1910–1970	Transactional analysis Personality is structured into Parent, adult and child. We communicate with transactions from these different ego states.

When communicating in health and social care settings, it is important to be aware of our own sense of self and conditions of worth, as they can often be a barrier to effective communication. For example, a very common condition of worth for those who choose to work in health and social care is: 'I must be nice and kind and caring.

I must not complain'. But if we continue to give and not ask for help, either practical or emotional, we can burn out and have nothing left to give. It is also important to be aware that the people we work with will have experienced conditional regard and have deep-rooted conditions of worth. An example would be an elderly man who will

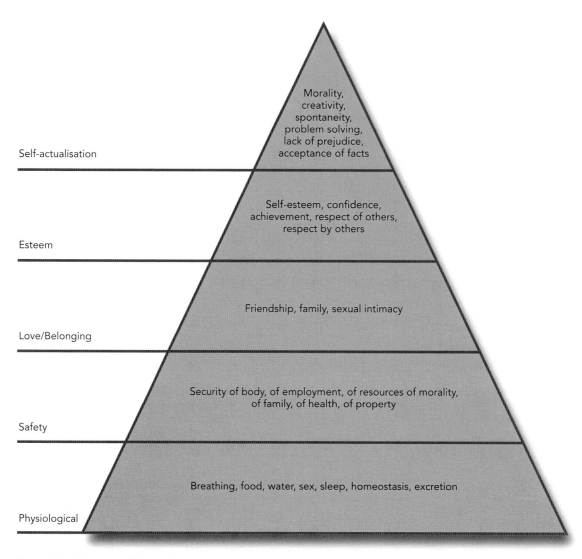

Figure 2.2 **Maslow's hierarchy of needs**

not admit to being in pain because he feels he is weak and unmanly; another example would be a teenage girl who cannot allow herself to be seen without full make-up because she only feels worthy when she's 'pretty'. Transactional analysis can further help us understand self-awareness and personality development. It also helps us explore how we communicate with others.

Activity 2.4

Give yourself some time to think of the main conditions of worth you were given as a child; how do you think these have affected you?

Transactional analysis

Transactional analysis (TA) was created and developed by Eric Berne in the 1950s and 1960s. It became very popular in the 1960s. Transactional analysis offers a theory of how personality is structured in the ego state model. This model also helps us understand and analyse communication and interactions between people. Transactional analysis is a way of looking at what goes on between people – interpersonal communication – and what goes on inside people – intrapersonal communication. It is a way of studying and making sense of intrapersonal and interpersonal relationships. Transactional analysis's concept of strokes has some similarities to Rogers's conditions of worth.

Strokes

TA suggests that all our interactions are made up of strokes. This name came from research indicating that babies require touching in order to survive and grow. A stroke is a unit of recognition. A transaction is an exchange of strokes. A stroke can be verbal or non-verbal, positive or negative and unconditional or conditional. An example of a positive verbal stroke is 'Hello', and an example of a negative verbal stroke is being sworn at. Non-verbal stokes are smiles, frowns, waves and rude hand gestures, I am sure you can guess from the list which ones are positive and which negative. The best type of stroke to receive is positive unconditional. A newborn baby needs positive unconditional stokes. If a baby is lucky it will get an unlimited supply of positive unconditional stokes. It will be picked up and cuddled. Often it will have lots of attention and will receive cooing and smiling. However, as a mother of three children I wonder how any mother can give positive unconditional strokes to all her children at all times. The next-best stroke to get is positive conditional. Our parents give us these strokes when we do something that they approve of: 'Do well at school', 'Eat nicely at the table', 'Dress in a way that we approve of', 'Speak politely'. Negative conditional strokes are given for aspects of our behaviour that are not approved of. 'I don't like your dress', 'Your cooking is too salty', 'You are too shy': these are examples of negative conditional strokes. The final and most negative stroke is the negative unconditional. 'I hate you' is a common example of a negative unconditional stroke. On the whole we prefer to receive negative strokes than no strokes at all – at least that way we know we exist and others know we exist. This is an important factor to note in interpersonal relationships as people will actively seek out negative strokes if they are not getting enough positive strokes.

Personality structure

When people communicate with each other, they do so from three ego states. Transactional analysis calls these parent, adult and child. See Figure 2.3.

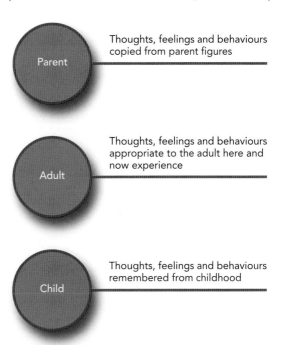

Figure 2.3 **Personality structure**

The parent ego state is described by the Institute of Transactional Analysis (1999) as like a tape recorder, a collection of prejudged, prejudiced codes for living. It develops as a consequence to all the things we have been taught. When I am in parent ego state I hear a voice saying 'Stay strong, try hard and don't give up'. The parent ego state is divided into nurturing parent and controlling parent (Stewart and Joines, 1987): there are positive and negative aspects, which are detailed in Figure 2.4. The adult ego state is logical and able to solve problems. When we are in our adult ego state we are thinking and feeling in an appropriate way for the situation we are in and the child and parent ego states do not interfere with the process. The adult ego state is not divided. In our child ego state we act as we did when we were children. The child ego state is divided into free child and adapted child (Stewart and Joines, 1987). When we are in child ego state we are creative, spontaneous and also naughty; we are most likely to be in this ego state when we are at a party or a sporting event. Throughout the day we can make many shifts from one ego state to another. Berne (1961) calls this a flow of cathexis.

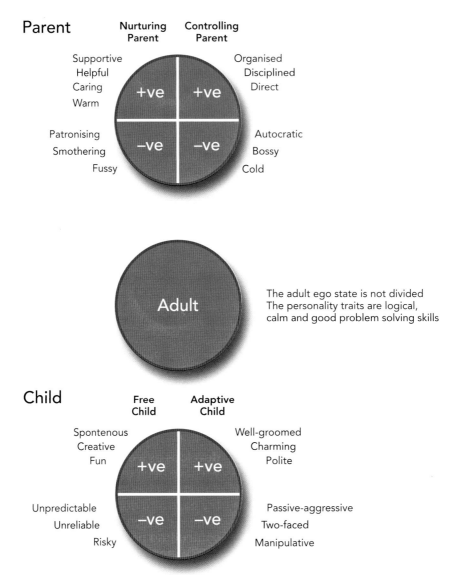

Figure 2.4 **Personality structure in more detail**

Transactions

A transaction occurs when someone opens a conversation and another person replies. The ego state model enables us to understand what goes on during the process of communication. There are three types of transaction:

Complementary From one person's ego state to another person's ego state without crossing. For example: 'What's the time?' 'It's three o'clock'. The first person asks the time from their adult ego state and the second person replies from their adult ego state. It is also very satisfactory to have a parent-to-parent complementary transaction discussing a mutual friend and all of her problems. A child-to-child transaction would involve a lot of fun. Complementary transactions are perceived as predictable and easy to communicate by the people involved.

Crossed These transactions are experienced as uncomfortable by the participants. The first communicator may ask the time, directing the question from their adult ego state to the other person's adult ego state. However, the reply comes back with anger from the other person's parent ego state: 'Buy your own watch!' If you draw a diagram of this transaction, the lines cross.

Ulterior The social-level message is different from the psychological message. The first person says 'I like your dress'. However, their non-verbal communication – frowning and looking the other person up and down – communicates a different message: 'You look dreadful in that dress'. When we receive an ulterior transaction we usually react to the non-verbal psychological message (Stewart and Joines, 1987).

Reflective practice

Reflective practice has been identified as an important way in which we can learn from our experiences and make links between theory and practice (Jasper, 2003). Being able to recognise your strengths, your weaknesses, your abilities and skills provides you with a baseline against which you can measure your development. In understanding yourself you will be able to adapt your behaviour and in consequence change your effect on others. Before reflecting on specific interactions, it is helpful to reflect on the strengths you bring to the workplace and the areas that you feel need further development. A strengths, weaknesses, opportunities and barriers (SWOB) analysis enables us to reflect on our strengths and weaknesses in a focused way. See Figure 2.5 (from Jasper, 2003).

Reflection Point

Do your own SWOB analysis, using the questions in Figure 2.5 as guidance. Focus on yourself in the workplace.

Think back to a recent successful interaction you have had in a health and social care setting. Reflect on the stages of what happened and what you did. What were the things that made the interaction successful? What techniques would you use again in similar circumstances? How did the interaction make you feel?

Now think of an incident where you did not follow through on the course of action that you had decided was needed. Why did you decide not to act? How satisfied are you with the outcome? Do you find that you still think about the incident in a negative way? What do you think about it now? Is it still unfinished business?

Models of reflection

Jasper (2003) explains fully several models of reflection that you can use to reflect upon your learning.

Strengths	Weaknesses
• What are you good at? • What about yourself are you happy with? • How do you get on with other people? • What approaches do you take to life? • What have you achieved in your life so far, what does this tell you about your strengths? • What experiences have you had that provide a foundation for your course/work placement?	• What would I like to change about myself? • What things have not been successful? • What things have I not achieved that I wanted to by now? • What disappointments have I had that affect the ways I think about the future?
Opportunities	**Barriers**
• What is available within the course/work placement to help me? • Who can help me? • What support do I have that will help me?	• What actual obstacles are there to me achieving what I want? For example, time limitations, travel, family commitments, financial concerns • What perceived obstacles are there to me achieving what I want? For example, ideas you have about yourself such as 'I'm bad at writing essays'

Figure 2.5 SWOB analysis

Kolb (1984) developed a cycle of experiential learning and this has led to the development of models of reflective practice. Kolb recommends that we need to recall our observation of an event, reflect on the observations, develop and research some theories about what we saw and then decide on some action as a result of the process (Jasper 2003).

Figure 2.6 A Reflective Cycle
Based on the work of Kolb (1984)

Gibbs (1988) followed Kolb's ideas and developed stages of reflection:

Description You may ask yourself where you were, who you were with, what happened and what the result was.

Feelings Recall what you were thinking or feeling at the start and if the feelings changed during the event.

Evaluation What was good and bad about the experience? How do you judge the event?

Analysis What sense can you make of the situation? How can you break the situation down?

Conclusion What else could have been done? How can you learn from the experience?

Action plan If the circumstances arose again, would you do the same?

Stages of reflection (Gibbs 1988)

There are many ways recommended within the literature of developing a reflective stance in practice, most of which rely on keeping a journal of our experiences, within which we can explore our reactions in depth. However, those who are new to this idea often have difficulty in working out how to reflect effectively on a particular experience. The model by Fish, Twinn and Purr (1991) comprises four strands of reflection:

Factual strand This is where you describe the experience, making reference to procedures and timescale. A critical or important incident may be recorded.

The **retrospective strand** is where you consider the whole experience. Your knowledge and personal experience may be compared with the experiences of others in the group or they may be more individually focused.

The **substratum strand** is where you analyse individual learning, group dynamics, communication or critical incidents from a theoretical perspective. In other words, you must link theory and practice.

The **connective strand** synthesises the material. Here you must reflect on your own learning and identify any changes that need to be made in independent study experiences. Whenever thoughts such as 'What if?' or 'Why?' arise as part of your work, take note of them. Use your reflective journal as an opportunity to pursue this question further, remembering that answers often generate further questions.

How to develop your self-awareness:

▦ Seek feedback from others.

▦ Reflect upon your actions and use a model of reflection in that process.

▦ Keep a diary or journal logging your thoughts and experiences.

▦ Develop a portfolio or extended CV.

It is important to apply the theories that we learn from reading and engaging in discussion to our practice. Reflective practice provides the strategies for us to be able to fully absorb theory and enhance our practice and improves the therapeutic relationship.

Activity 2.5

Choose one of these models of reflection to examine a recent interaction in the workplace.

The therapeutic relationship

A therapeutic relationship is one in which the client is helped in some way. The components of a good therapeutic relationship are trust, being able to talk openly and honestly and being able to work as a client-and-therapist team. There are different types of therapeutic relationship in health and social care. It is important to know what role we are fulfilling in any interaction in health and social care settings. The types of relationships comprise:

1. professional counsellors and psychotherapists; these are individuals with a counselling qualification

2. those with a professional qualification such as doctors, nurses, occupational therapists, social workers and physiotherapists who may use counselling skills but may not have a formal counselling qualification

3. those who use counselling skills as part of their job

4. those in the voluntary sector

5. those who are working in advisory roles

6. informal helpers.

Roles within therapeutic relationships

There are several different types of communication in health and social care. In one interaction we may be:

advising   instructing

welcoming   assessing

observing   informing

counselling.

Approaches to forming a therapeutic relationship

There a different theoretical approaches to forming and interacting in a therapeutic relationship.

Carl Rogers: person centred

We have looked a Rogers's theory of personality development and now we will look at the theories that underpin the helping relationship.

Core conditions

Rogers believed that there were three core conditions that were 'necessary and sufficient' to bring about personality change. It is generally believed in any model of counselling that these core conditions must underpin the relationship if it to be considered therapeutic. They are:

Unconditional positive regard The helper accepts and values the client with warmth and without judgement. If a

Activity 2.6

Imagine that you have a problem and need help.

What are the important factors in a therapeutic relationship that would make you feel at ease?

Think of a situation where someone has been helpful to you. What did they do? What characteristics or qualities did they have?

Here are some ideas:

a friendly warm person

approachable

listens well

someone who is able to put me at ease

a similar age to me or not too young

knowledgeable

same gender

not hurrying me along

someone with life experience

trustworthy

dressed in a smart casual manner

a person who is not fazed by my expressing difficult emotions.

Activity 2.7

Read the extract from Rogers's *A Way of Being* (1980):

I like to be heard. A number of times in my life I have felt myself bursting with insoluble problems, or going round and round in tormented circles or, during one period, overcome by feelings of worthlessness and despair. I think I have been more fortunate than most in finding at these times individuals who have been able to hear me and thus rescue me from the chaos of my feelings, individuals who have been able to hear my meaning a little more deeply than I have known them. These persons have heard me without judging me, diagnosing me, appraising me, evaluating me. They have just listened and clarified and responded to me at all levels at which I was communicating. I can testify that when you are in psychological distress and someone really hears you without passing a judgement on you, without trying to take responsibility for you, without trying to mould you, it feels damn good! At these times it has relaxed the tension in me. It has permitted me to bring out the frightening feelings, the guilt, the despair, the confusion that have been part of my experience. When I have been listened to and when I have been heard, I am able to perceive my world in a new way and to go on. It is astonishing how elements that seem insoluble become soluble when someone listens, how confusions that seem irredeemable turn into relatively clear-flowing streams when one is heard. I have deeply appreciated the times that I have experienced this sensitive, empathic concentrated listening.

What are the important phrases from this extract that describe a therapeutic relationship?

client feels judged by someone who is listening to her, it is very hard for her to be open and honest about her feelings and actions. If we judge our clients by commenting on their actions in a negative way (or sometimes even in a positive way), then they might feel they have to excuse or hide a part of themselves. Sometimes it is very hard not to judge someone or at least dislike what they are saying or doing. For example, I was helping someone who expressed racist remarks full of hatred towards a neighbour. In this case I had to tell him I found it hard to hear him speak like that, that it made me feel uncomfortable and I wondered where those feelings came from. In this way I was able to be honest and show that although I didn't like what he said, I still valued him as a person.

Empathy This is the ability to understand the client's internal frame of reference, to be able to put yourself in their shoes. This is very different from being sympathetic. People are not usually asking for our sympathy, which might make them feel pitied. They do, however, want to be understood and want to know that they have been heard and understood. The active listening skills described in this chapter are the best way to show empathy.

Congruence The helper is genuine, honest and true. Rogers believed that a helper has to be fully present with the client in the moment, the here and now. The helper can only expect the client to be open and honest if he is too. This does not mean sharing every thought with the client; it means being real with them and sharing thoughts and feelings only when they are relevant and would be helpful to the process.

Gerard Egan's three-stage model

Egan's model of helping relationships is based on the key principle that health and social care practitioners help people to become better at helping themselves in everyday lives through the development of a therapeutic relationship: 'Help people become better at helping themselves in their everyday lives' (Egan, 1990).

The model assumes that the core conditions of empathy, unconditional positive regard and congruence will underpin the relationship with the client but it is more proactive in its approach. Egan identifies three stages in the helping relationship:

Stage 1: Exploring

– Beginning.

– Attending, listening and using non-verbal communication.

– Pacing and handling silence.

– Reflection, using questions, summarising.

– Being empathic, accepting.

– Begin to build a trusting relationship with the client; help them to explore thoughts, feelings and behaviour. This involves encouraging the client to tell their story, using active listening skills.

Stage 2: Understanding

– Understanding involves the helper supporting the client to try to identify what they would like to change or do differently.

– It uses skills to help the client reach a clearer understanding of the problem.

– Information sharing.

– Deeper empathy.

– Confrontation.

– Self-disclosure.

– Immediacy.

– Imagining.

– Setting goals.

Stage 3: Action planning

– Action involves the helper supporting the client to make the changes they have identified. The client will be encouraged to set goals and to explore the things that might hinder or support them.

– Helps the client use strengths to cope more effectively with the problems by making appropriate decisions.

– Brainstorming – writing down all of the ideas without censoring them.

– Sorting pros and cons – the good things and the bad things about making the change.

– Force field analysis – strengthens the forces supporting a decision, and reduces the impact of opposition to it (Mindtools, 2010).

– Teaching.

– Making contracts.

Activity 2.8

Rogers believed that the core conditions were 'necessary and sufficient' to bring about changes. Egan believed that the core conditions were 'necessary' but not 'sufficient'. What do you believe? Think how your learning so far has impacted on the way you interact with the clients you work with. Do you agree with Rogers's approach or Egan's?

Skills for helping

In order to understand your clients and communicate your understanding, you will obviously need to listen to them and use active listening skills to show that they have been heard. Here are the most important skills:

– Acknowledging and reflecting feelings

– body language

– restating

– paraphrasing

– summarising

– questioning

– coping with silence

– immediacy

– disengaging from the communication.

Acknowledging and reflecting feelings

- repeating back to the client a word, phrase or sentence that they have spoken

- to show attention

- to invite further detail

- to allow the client to hear the words that they have used

- to validate.

Activity 2.9

List all the feeling words that you can think of.

The website http://www.psychpage.com/learning/library/assess/feelings.html has many feeling words listed under these 16 headings:

open	angry
happy	depressed
alive	confused
good	helpless
love	indifferent
interested	afraid
positive	hurt
strong	sad

If you examine the feeling words closely, you may notice that they can be reduced to four main feelings:

- angry
- sad
- afraid
- happy

See Figures 2.7 to 2.10.

Think of the main colours in an artist's palette. What colour would you associate with each primary feeling?

Use the appropriate coloured pen to circle each of the feelings in your list.

It is beneficial for people to know what emotion they are feeling and expressing feelings is important for a healthy mental life. There are so many feeling words that we should not be surprised when people say 'I feel confused'.

You have probably noticed that many of the words in your list in Activity 2.9 have more than one colour around them. If you examine the word 'jealous', what primary feelings does it contain? It may contain anger: you may be angry that someone has got something or someone that you want. However, if you analyse the feeling a little more, you may find that it contains some sadness and fear too. So jealousy is a complex feeling that contains three other primary feelings. Frustration may only contain anger at first glance, but it is anger that does not seem to be expressed. On closer analysis, it may be fear that is preventing expression of anger and therefore turning anger into frustration.

When we feel angry we feel hot and our heart starts to beat faster. When we feel angry we feel an energy force that naturally pulls us forward to tell someone how we feel or push us into action. The first response is to attack. However, it more often solves the problem if we state we are angry and try to negotiate ourselves through the conflict. For more information, see Chapter 9 on team working. We may have angry thoughts initially and then immediately follow with thoughts about what may happen if we express the anger. For example: 'If I tell my boyfriend how annoyed I am he will leave me'. The feeling that may follow this thought is fear and therefore the anger does not get expressed.

When we feel sad we feel heavy inside. Our movements may be lethargic and we may get a lump in our throat and feel like crying. The energy force pulls us down. We feel like hiding away and withdrawing from our problems. One of the problems is that we

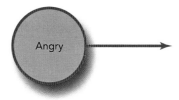

Figure 2.7 Primary feeling: anger

Figure 2.8 Primary feeling: sad

are often encouraged to hide away our sadness. The people who have been most affected when someone close dies are often the people who have to arrange the funeral.

When we feel afraid our breathing increases and feels shallow, our heart races and we feel sweaty and often have a dry mouth. The energy force in fear makes us feel that we want to take a step backwards; this is a good thing in many situations as it allows us to reassess the danger. However, if the fear is unrealistic we may increase the problem by avoiding it.

Figure 2.9 **Primary feeling: afraid**

When we feel happy our body feels energetic and weightless. Our face lights up with a smile. The energy force pulls us up and we become more active and engage in interactions and actions more positively.

Sometimes our feelings are straightforward: a teenage girl is grounded for a week, she shouts at her mum, slams the door, refuses to speak for a day and rants about how she hates her family. There are action and movement in this anger, she expresses it and processes it.

Figure 2.10 **Primary feeling: happy**

Sometimes our feelings are more confused. The same girl is grounded but as well as that her mother is violent and beats her up. She is scared; she retreats

and takes the punishment silently. Here the feelings of anger and fear are confused and cause the girl to remain static, unable to process her feelings.

Sometimes we don't know what we are feeling, we feel 'bad' but we can't identify the feelings because they are so confused: happy and jealous, sad and angry.

Being listened to and having the space to explore confused feelings with someone who isn't going to tell us to stop feeling angry or sad or afraid can help us to process our feelings and feel better about ourselves.

Heron (1977) suggests that there are four emotions that are commonly suppressed or bottled up:

> anger
> fear
> grief
> embarrassment.

Very often bottled-up emotion is a mixture of all four. The expression 'bottled-up emotion' is helpful in that it allows the person to be clearer in his thinking once he has released it.

Body language

Egan (1990) used the acronym SOLER to help us remember the importance of body language and how to use our non-verbal communication to create a therapeutic relationship. See Table 2.5.

Restating

Restating involves repeating back to the client either single words or short phrases that they have used. For example:

> Client: I felt so punished.
> Helper: Punished?
> Client: Yes, I put thought and effort into that essay and the feedback was so cutting. I felt really down. I thought I deserved a higher mark too. I don't trust my judgement any more.

Restating can show the client that he has been heard and understood. It can also encourage further exploration without being too intrusive. Restating can also maintain focus in a session.

Table 2.5 **SOLER**

S	sit squarely	Sit slightly opposite the other person so that you are either side of an imaginary corner. This allows you to see all aspects of non-verbal communication that you may not see if you were sitting side by side and is less threatening than sitting face on. When working in a mental health setting I was encouraged to take my personal safety seriously: it is advisable to arrange the seating so that you have easy access to the exit.
O	open position	Sit with uncrossed arms and legs; this conveys to the client that you are open and not defensive.
L	lean slightly towards the client	Leaning slightly towards the client shows that you are interested and want to understand their problem.
E	eye contact	It is important to get the balance right. The client will feel uncomfortable if you stare and will think that you are not interested if you do not look at them at all.
R	relax	If you are relaxed, you can concentrate on listening rather than worrying about how to respond to the client.

Paraphrasing

Paraphrasing is the skill of rephrasing what you understood to be the core message of the client's communication. It is a way of showing that you understand their concerns from their point of view. In using this skill you will communicate the core qualities of acceptance and empathic understanding and start to build a trusting relationship. You will be able to check your perception of what the client has said and gain information about how clients see themselves and their concerns

You need to be accurate when paraphrasing, and sometimes you might get it wrong. If you are not sure, you can offer the paraphrase tentatively, using phrases like 'It sounds like …' or 'It seems that …' or 'I'm wondering if I've got that right'.

An example of paraphrasing would be:

Client: I get so angry whenever I talk to my dad, it's like he doesn't listen to me at all. Then I go to school and my friends get on my nerves. I lose my temper, I take it out on them and they start to ignore me.

Helper: It sounds like it's hard to contain your anger and that ends up with you being ignored by your dad and your friends.

Summarising

This is gathering together the client's statements to identify their specific thoughts and feelings:

- to focus on the main problem
- to manage a multiplicity of problems
- to facilitate movement.

An example would be: 'I understand from all that you have said that your main concerns are … and that you are feeling …'.

Summaries are longer paraphrases and enable you to bring together the important aspects of what the client has said in an organised way.

They can:

- clarify content and feelings
- review the work
- end a session
- begin a further session
- prioritise and focus
- move the helping process forward.

The summary might come at the end of a session when the client has talked at some length about the issues that concern him. For example: 'You've talked about how hard it has been to deal with the changes in your life, particularly losing your home and independence. You've also talked about your feelings surrounding your children. I'm wondering which of these issues you'd like to focus on …'.

Here are some guidelines for paraphrasing and summarising (Bond Culley, 2004):

■ Be tentative and offer your perception of what the client has said.

■ Avoid telling, informing or defining the client.

■ Be respectful, do not judge, dismiss or use sarcasm.

■ Use your own words; repeating verbatim may seem like mimicry.

■ Listen to the depth of feeling expressed and match the level in your response.

■ Do not add to what the client says, evaluate it or offer interpretations.

■ Be congruent and don't pretend you understand.

■ Be brief and direct.

■ Keep your voice tone level. Paraphrasing in a shocked or disbelieving tone is unlikely to communicate either acceptance or empathy.

Questioning

An important part of building a therapeutic relationship involves asking the client what is happening in their lives and how they feel about it. Questioning is an essential skill but too many questions can make the client feel pressured or even interrogated. It is therefore important to use questions thoughtfully and sensitively. There are two main kinds of questions: open and closed.

Open questions are questions that often begin with 'What', 'Where', 'How' or 'Who'. These are the most useful kinds of questions as they involve the client more and encourage exploration and thoughtfulness. Try to avoid 'Why' questions as they put pressure on the client to justify his position.

Closed questions invite the client to answer 'Yes' or 'No'. They are non-exploratory and tend to shut the client down.

How to ask questions:

■ Directly – avoid waffling.

■ Concisely – be specific and brief.

■ Clearly – say precisely what you mean.

■ Share your purpose – 'I'd like to be clear. What did happen at home this morning?'.

■ Paraphrase your client's response to check that you understand before asking another question.

■ Link your question to what the client has said with a bridging statement: 'You mention feeling very hurt. What did your friend actually say to you?'

Reflection Point

Think of a situation where you might be asking a client questions about his situation. Write a series of open questions that would elicit exploration of the issues.

Listening to silence

There are different kinds of silences:

■ thoughtful silence, which is often comfortable and gives the client space to process her thoughts

■ angry, tense silence, where the client is processing thoughts but which can be hard to bear for any length of time.

It is important for the helper to know what kind of silence it is and to allow the client space to feel and process her thoughts or to help her out by breaking the silence.

Sometimes the client will signal, through eye contact or body language, that the silence is uncomfortable, in which case the helper might assist her by saying something like 'I'm wondering what's going on for you now'.

Sometimes the client might really appreciate being given the space to think about difficult stuff without having to share it – the presence of the helper might be necessary as a sort of safety net, to help contain difficult thoughts that the client might not be ready to share.

Immediacy

Immediacy means focusing on the here and now of the conversation. It is often more obvious when there is a mismatch between what the client is saying and what seems to be behind the words. To point this out can help the client to explore feelings she might not have realised she had. It can help the client to explore other relationships in her life. For example: 'I hear you saying that you feel that you've resolved the argument with your mum but your voice is sad and you're wringing your hands and I sense there is some unresolved feeling there. What do you think?'

Or alternatively: 'I notice how uncomfortable you seem to be whenever I mention your mother. You seem to close down and avoid eye contact with me. I'm wondering what's going on for you there' (Bond and Culley, 2004).

Disengaging from the communication

It is important to end the communication with the client sensitively, which can be hard if the issues you have been talking about have been difficult and emotionally charged. Here are some things to consider when ending the communication:

- Give some warning that the session will end in five minutes and summarise what you have talked about in the session.

- Ask the client how they are feeling and acknowledge that the session brought up some difficult issues. It is important to start to decrease the intensity towards the end of the session so as to keep the client emotionally safe when they leave you.

- Go over any action that you might have agreed upon and give details about what and who it involves.

- Be encouraging without being patronising.

Blocks and barriers to effective communication

There often times when we feel that we are not communicating well and when it seems impossible to develop a therapeutic relationship.

Activity 2.10

Make a list of all the factors that make listening difficult. You should consider both external and internal factors. Discuss which are obvious and easily noticed and which are more difficult to pick up on. Discuss how these factors can be avoided or dealt with. See Table 2.6.

Figure 2.11 illustrates what goes on behind the scenes in any interaction and shows how easily communication can become blocked and barriers appear.

Table 2.6 External and internal factors

External	Internal
Tiredness	Difference in culture and values
Hunger	Negative feelings towards the client
Feeling ill	Trying to hypothesise
Noise	Working out what you're going to say next
Inappropriate environment	Getting upset about what the client is saying
Client's personal hygiene	Trying to find solutions
	Feelings of inadequacy
	Difficulties in your life
	Feeling unsafe

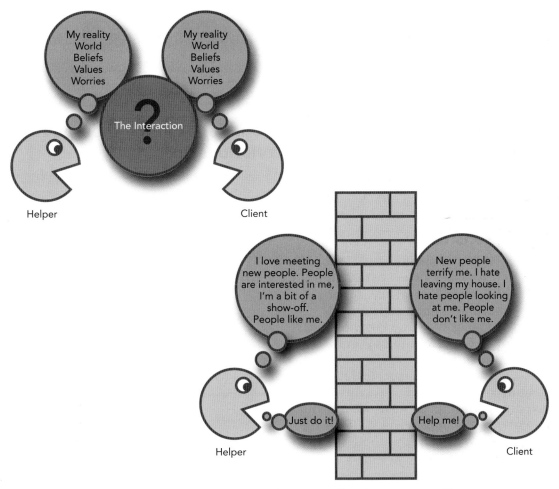

Figure 2.11 Behind the scenes in an interaction (by Lee Badham), University of Worcester

Activity 2.11

Think of a time when you know that you have found it hard to listen to a client or friend:

■ What was going on for you at that time?

■ How did it affect the way that you interacted with that person?

■ What do you think was going on for them at that time?

■ How could you have approached and managed that situation in a different way?

How to deal with blocks

■ Self-awareness: it is essential to be aware of your own 'stuff' so that you can avoid responding to the client from your own frame of reference.

■ Use active listening skills; avoid trying to fix, just listen.

■ Always beware of the client's frame of reference – you can show empathy without having to agree with or like what the client is saying.

■ Recognise your limitations – it can be hard to carry around someone else's pain and anxiety.

'Discussing your concerns with a colleague or line manager (within your confidentiality agreement) can be very helpful as they can offer you support, ease isolation and perhaps make suggestions that you have overlooked' (Donnelly and Neville, 2008).

■ Know when and how to refer on. You need to recognise when another person, agency or organisation is better placed than yourself to offer support.

■ Be congruent. Share your concerns with your client. Sometimes relationships can seem stuck and by bringing this into the open you might be able to address issues that have not previously been talked about.

■ Allow the block to remain unresolved – trust the process and stay with the block. 'Sometimes, the longer we can stay confused about where the relationship is going, the more successful the outcome' (Burnard, 2005).

Cultural sensitivity

In Britain we live in a multicultural society and therefore it is important to be culturally aware in our interpersonal interactions. Miller (2006) points out that defining culture is complex. While acknowledging race, we often confuse ethnicity and culture. Ethnicity, gender and social class are relevant and Miller suggests that we could add religious beliefs, sexuality, rationality, migration patterns, skin colour and experience of oppression. Culture therefore, is always changing and it is impossible to predict or completely understand a person's culture. It is suggested by Miller (2006) that we develop a respectful curiosity about the beliefs and practices within all service users' lives.

Transference and counter-transference

Transference takes place when the client transfers to the helper feelings and attitudes that they once associated with important figures such as parents or teachers in their early life.

Counter-transference refers to the feelings the counsellor develops for the client. This will often be in response to the feelings projected onto the helper.

It is important for the helper to have the self-awareness to notice when transference and counter-transference are happening and to stop them blocking the communication. Often it can be useful to share the observation as the quality of the client–helper relationship can inform the client about other relationships in his life.

Activity 2.12

What boundaries do you need to be aware of in a therapeutic relationship?

Boundaries in the therapeutic relationship

Boundaries need to be discussed and negotiated at the beginning of the relationship as our feeling can often cause complications. Sometimes transferred feelings can blur the boundaries for the client and the helper.

Confidentiality

The relationship between health and social care staff and service users should be one of trust. Health and social care staff are required to maintain confidences obtained via their work. For example, a client's HIV status. However they may break confidence in public interest;

■ to report or prevent a crime

■ to report malpractice

■ to report suspected child abuse

■ to prevent suicide

■ to report professional misconduct.

It is important not to talk about patients or clients in a public place where you can be overheard. Make sure that patient records are kept safe and can not be seen by anyone outside the team. A breach of confidentiality can be met by disciplinary action by an employer and/or legal action by clients for damages.

Summary

In this chapter we have explored and given examples of interpersonal skills. The importance of self awareness in communication is explained and models of reflection introduced to encourage the reader to increase self awareness. The chapter goes on to discuss the therapeutic relationship and different skills involved in forming a therapeutic relationship. The chapter ends by discussing some of the barriers and blocks to effective communication.

Summary assignment

Reflect on a recent event demonstrating your effective interpersonal communication in order to develop a therapeutic relationship.

Write a reflective piece that explores the communication and connects to theory of effective interpersonal communication and the development of a therapeutic relationship.

References

Argyle, M. (1978) *The Psychology of Interpersonal Behaviour* 3rd edition Penguin Harmondsworth.

Alton Barbour, A. Koneya M. (1976) Louder than words: nonverbal communication Columbus, Ohio : Merrill.

Bazler Riley, J. (2008) *Communication in Nursing* Missouri: Mosby Elsevier.

Berne (1961) *Transactional Analysis in Psychotherapy The Classic Handbook to its Principles.* New York: Grove Press.

Bond T, Culley S (1991) *Integrative Counselling Skills in Action.* Sage, London

Bonham, P. (2004) *Communication as a Mental Health Carer* Cheltenham Nelson Thornes

Burnard, P. (1996) *Acquiring Interpersonal Skills A Handbook of Experiential learning For Health Professionals* 2nd Edition London Chapman and Hall

Burnard P. (*1997*) Effective Communication Skills for Health Professionals Nelson Thornes Ltd.

Burnard, P. (2005) *Counselling Skills For Health Professions* 4th Edition Cheltenham Nelson Thornes

Crawford, P. Brown, B. Bonham, P. (2006) *Communication in Clinical Settings* Cheltenham Nelson Thornes.

Donnelly E & Neville L (2008) *Communication and Interpersonal Skills* Reflect Press. Exeter.

Egan, G. (1990) *The Skilled Helper: A Systematic Approach to effective caring* 4th Edition Brooks Cole Monterey, California.

Egan G.E. (2002). *The Skilled Helper.* 9th edition Brooks and Cole, California Fiedler, F.E. (1950) The concept of an ideal therapeutic relationship *Journal of Consulting Psychology* 14 239–45.

Fish, D. Twinn, S. Purr, B. (1991) Promoting Reflection: The Supervision of Practice in Health Visiting and Initial TeacherTraining. West London Institute Press, London.

Geldard K & Geldard D (2003) *Counselling Skills in Everyday Life.* Palgrave Macmillian London.

Gibbs, G. (1988) *Learning by Doing: A guide to teaching and learning methods.* Further Education Unit, Oxford Brookes University, Oxford.

Givens, D.B. (2000) Body Speak: What Are You Saying? Successful Meetings (October) 51

Heron, J. (1977) *Catharsis in human development,* Human Potential Research Project, University of Surrey.

Hough M (2002). *A Practical Approach to Counselling* 2nd edition Person Educational. London.

Jasper M (2003) *Beginning Reflective Practice.* Nelson Thornes. Bucks.

Koneya, M. Barbour, A. (1976) *Louder Than Words Nonverbal Communication* Merrill. Ohio.

Miller, L. (2006) Counselling Skills for Social Work Sage Publications London

Mindtools 2010 http://www.mindtools.com/pages/article/newTED_06.htm accessed 27.11.10.

Murgatroyd S. (1994) *Counselling and Helping Psychology in Action* BPS Routeledge. London.

Porritt, L. (1990) *Interaction Strategies An Introduction For Health Professionals* 2nd Edition Churchill Livingstone. London.

Ramjan L. (2004) Nurses and the Therapeutic Relationship; Caring for Adolescents with Anorexia Nervosa. *Journal of Advanced Nursing* 45; 495–503.

Rogers C (2002) *Client Centred Therapy.* Constable London.

Rogers C (1980) *A Way of Being.* Houghton and Mifflin Company New York.

Rogers, C.R. (1957) The necessary and sufficient conditions of therapeutic personality change *Journal of Consulting Psychology* 21, 95–104.

Stewart, I. Joines, V. (1987) *TA Today* Nottingham: Lifespace Publishing

3 Diversity and inequality in health care work

This chapter links with Chapter 5 and starts to address our values and attitudes towards the individuals we meet in the course of our daily work.

The need to practise in a non-judgemental and anti-discriminatory way towards people requires us to have an awareness of our own prejudices, values and beliefs.

By exploring values and issues of prejudice, discrimination and inequality and discussing and reflecting on these things you will be introduced to diversity and equality and what these mean to the care professions and those who use their services. The social exclusion of groups as a result of discrimination or simply isolation will also be addressed.

Learning outcomes

By the end of the chapter you will be able to:

■ demonstrate how beliefs and values impact upon relationships in health care

■ explore how discrimination and social inequalities impact on the health and general well-being and welfare of individuals in the UK and lead to social exclusion

■ describe how health and social care professionals practice in an anti-discriminatory manner to counteract discrimination and inequality.

Values and beliefs and their impact on relationships in health care

Have you ever told somebody that you value their opinion? Or perhaps you want to sell your car, so you take it to the garage to have it valued. Perhaps you have come across the term 'care values' and 'value systems'. These are just a few of the ways in which the word 'value' is used. It describes a monetary value but at the same time can be used in a personal way – how can you price the value of somebody's opinion?

The whole concept of 'valuing' is about having a preference for something; it also links in with choice.

The *Oxford English Dictionary* (2001) defines 'value' as:

the worth, desirability or utility of a thing, or the qualities on which these depend …

It defines 'values' or 'valued' as:

having a high or specified opinion of; attach importance to …

The term 'belief' can also be used interchangeably with 'value' since what we believe to be important is usually the same as something we value.

If you value something, you give it high priority and ascribe importance to it. A 'value system', then, refers to values that are felt to be important in the way you conduct yourself in society; but, as we shall see, not all societies or groups share the same values and occasionally this leads to conflict.

Working in the health service is a privilege. We are caring for vulnerable groups of people who, disabled by illness, find themselves in less than satisfactory circumstances. If you have ever been seriously ill and in need of expert help you will appreciate this point. Being at the receiving end of care can be quite distressing and may be made all the more so if the person delivering the care is less than sympathetic and does not appear to 'value' us. What is it about this particular 'carer' (and in such instances even this word seems out of place) that makes them treat others without respect? We shall look more at this later on in the chapter.

Roakeach (1973) defines value as an 'enduring belief' and a value system as 'an enduring organisation of beliefs concerning preferable modes of conduct … along a system of relative importance'. (Beckett and Maynard)

But how do we come by these values and beliefs? How did our carer come about his or her system of values and beliefs? Why do societies and individuals within them behave the way they do? On what basis do we take important life decisions?

Our behaviour is a direct result of our own personal values that we hold and which guide us. The decisions we make are based upon knowledge, morals and ethics. The values we have learned throughout our lives become a part of our personality and make-up and when we are faced with a decision or have a choice to make about something we will always look to what we value the most in the making of that decision. If we value comfort over fashion, then we may choose the more sensible shoe when deciding what to buy. That's a simple example. Things become a little more demanding when we are making more important life decisions.

Think for a moment about a personal value you hold and try to trace it back to your very first experience of it. How did you acquire it?

As you can appreciate from Figure 3.1, the way in which we are introduced into the world by our family and our upbringing, together with the experiences we have had in life through our education and work, all help us to formulate our personal system of values and beliefs. We learn through our parents and through observation of what is happening around us about what we feel is 'good'. We are taught how to behave in a manner that is polite and acceptable to others in the family and wider society. As we grow older, the influences increase and our friends become more important to us. One of the things you may find at university is that as you learn, meet new people and experience newer things, you could well find some of your personal values being challenged and changed to incorporate new thinking.

Our value system has developed over a long time and all sorts of influences affect our learning. We may acquire our values in a conscious or unconscious way. We are taught certain things by our parents and teachers and even by religious instructors but occasionally we are subject to more subtle influences that become part of our value system. For example, in the course of my teaching I have come across many children who do not seem to value their education. They constantly truant or take time off from school, claiming sickness. They do not engage with homework and rarely participate in lessons. One never gets to meet the parents, who seem not to have any contact with the school. When I have spoken to these children about their behaviour it becomes apparent that the family does not consider education to be

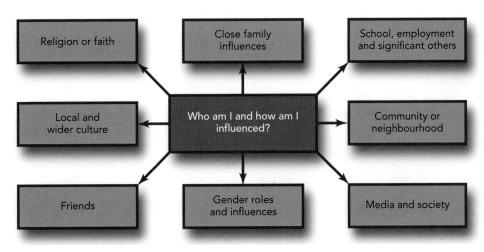

Figure 3.1

useful or something to aspire to. The opinion that 'education never did me any good' has been passed on to the value system of these children, who perpetuate the same view. A similar situation can arise in the learning of prejudiced attitudes. While we may not overtly teach our children our own prejudices, the way we behave can lead them to model that behaviour.

Bandura (1977) followed up on the work of earlier psychologists and posited the theory of social learning. This suggests that prejudice is learned in the same way as we learn other attitudes and values – through association, reinforcement and modelling:

- **Association** We learn to associate a particular group with bad traits: for example, skinheads portrayed as thugs (some may be but not all are), or elderly people as weak and senile.

- **Reinforcement** Taking part in the telling of racist or sexist jokes just because others laugh and think it's fun.

- **Modelling** Children may simply imitate the prejudices of their family and friends.

This process of learning is known as socialisation and it occurs throughout our lives. The socialisation that occurs within the family is referred to by sociologists as 'primary socialisation' and it is within this close-knit group that you are likely to learn the values your family hold.

As we grow and start to mix with more people outside our family we come into contact with more influences. This process – 'secondary socialisation' – begins at school and continues throughout our lives, shaping our thinking and often causing us to question our values and beliefs.

Figure 3.2 **We learn values through education and mixing with others**

Activity 3.1

List some examples of personal values you may hold and think back to the first time in your life you were aware of them.

You may have responded with some values like the following:

- Perhaps you believe that all humans are equal – or that men are superior to women.

- Perhaps you value your health to the extent that you believe that you are responsible for it and need to reduce risk and keep yourself healthy.

- Alternatively, you may have a firm belief that what will be will be and you are subject to whatever fate brings you with respect to your own health. In other words, you take the view that there is no point in giving up smoking since you may well be subject to another condition anyway.

- Some universally accepted values highlight honesty and respect for others.

- You may have been brought up in a particular religion and therefore hold certain views about how you should live your life.

- Or perhaps you have started to question those particular views and values and may be changing your outlook with respect to those family views.

What you are doing in this process is starting to question the things you have learned and as a consequence are developing your self-awareness. By paying more attention to how you feel about something, or by reflecting upon experiences and being truthful to yourself about how you feel, you can start to become a more self-aware person. This process can then help you to start to choose your own values rather than merely reflecting those of others and those you have learned in child hood.

You may actually experience this sort of process at university. Although having your values and beliefs challenged is not always a comfortable process, it can be very liberating.

Case study

John, an undergraduate, grew up to believe that homosexuals were 'dirty' and had some form of mental illness. His views were never challenged at school and he avoided all contact with anybody he considered to be 'dodgy' or 'that way inclined'. His parents reinforced his views throughout his life and jokes about 'gays' were commonplace.

At university he shared a flat with Sarah and they were interviewing for another flat share. After seeing and talking to David , a lad on the same course as Sarah, John told Sarah that no way would he be getting the room because 'He's gay, isn't he?'.

Sarah's response – 'And your point is?' – stopped John in his tracks and made him consider his views. He found he could not respond in a reasonable way as to why David should not have the room and after discussion with Sarah was deeply embarrassed at his previously held views. These views, he realised were based on nothing more than ignorance and untrue stereotypes and he started to re-evaluate his stance.

What are your views on the Case study and is there anything you have had to re-evaluate as a result of previously held views? Write a reflective account about this for your personal development journal.

Figure 3.3 Different values and beliefs

Values, ethics and conflict

A value system is a set of guidelines passed down through generations by which we live and by which our actions are informed.

John's value system included a negative view of homosexuality, based upon ignorance and possibly fear. When faced with the need to make an important decision, this system helps us to evaluate the right and wrong ways to approach the issues or the pros and cons of the outcome of any action we may take. If challenged, as in the above case, we may need to question our views and rethink our values.

Values and beliefs, then, guide us when we are taking some decision in our lives; but because we are individuals and are subject to all sorts of external influences, there will not be a common set of values, so we may meet with conflict at certain times in our lives.

Conflict of values occurs when our own sets of beliefs fail to match those of our clients, friends or colleagues. This can affect relationships and the process of care. Dealing with conflict can be difficult and requires you to be aware of your own values and at the same time respect those of the other person. It is as well to try to understand the reasons for the person's behaviour before reacting to a situation in an inflammatory way.

There is also the issue of acting in an ethical way and we need to determine how ethics and values are linked. Is it possible, for example, to hold a value which might be ethically wrong?

Let's look at an example. On visiting your GP one day, you note that he is eating his breakfast while he discusses your treatment. The behaviour you are observing is wrong in the context in which it is happening. It is not how you would expect your health professional to behave. However, could the actions here be considered to be ethically or morally wrong? No, of course not – but on what have we based this view?

In judging any action or behaviour, we need to draw upon several points of view. The legal aspects of the action, codes of conduct, political stances and even religious codes can all be used to evaluate whether behaviour is right or wrong.

The study of ethics refers to the moral values we hold. Integrity, commitment and truth are part of these values and help us to make ethical decisions. They also aid us in judging whether an action is right or wrong. As care workers we need to operate within an ethical framework, the standards of which can be judged as right or wrong, good or bad.

Organisations are guided by a set of their own core values and these are usually presented to the workforce as codes of conduct and standards. The care profession has a set of care values to which all care workers should adhere. The values shown in the section below override your own personal values since they form the basis of anti-discriminatory or anti-oppressive practice and as such represent the entitlement of individuals who access our care provision. Based upon legal requirements and ethical considerations, these care values may cause some tension with your own personal values. Let's look more deeply at an example to demonstrate this point.

Let us suppose that as a result of your upbringing and religion, you have strong beliefs about the access to termination of pregnancy for women. You believe it is morally (ethically) wrong to abort a pregnancy. During one shift at work you are asked to prepare and escort a young woman to theatre for just such a procedure. This would be a difficult situation for you since you know you are to undertake your duty and respect the rights of the patient

but feel loath to do so and this may affect how you deal with the patient.

Activity 3.2

Reflect on this for a moment. Have you had occasion to question your own beliefs with respect to care you may have had to carry out?

Write a short piece to say how you felt about this and say what you learned from it.

Good practice demands that the patient should expect good-quality treatment despite how you feel about the procedure, and this is the sort of conflict you may come across. You do, however, have a choice. You can choose to compromise your own values out of respect for the patient's views and for the sake of your work, in which you are duty-bound and expected to undertake this sort of procedure, or you can leave this particular job and take one which does not deal with this sort of procedure.

As the former Central Council for Education and Training in Social Work sums up for us (CCETSW, 1976):

> A value determines what a person thinks he *ought* to do, which may or may not be the same as what he wants to do, or what is in his interest to, or what in fact he actually does. Values in this sense give rise to general standards and ideals by which we judge our own and others' conduct.

Care values and codes of conduct

The care value base comprises three main values that are based upon the rights to which we are all entitled in health care. We show that we 'value' our clients by promoting these rights and leaving our own personal values at home. We are duty bound to act in the best interests of our clients and patients, and by applying the care values in our day-to-day work we can assure clients and patients of good-quality care.

Figure 3.4 **Ethics require integrity, commitment and truth**

You may have met these values before (Fisher *et al.*, 2006):

■ promoting service users' rights

■ fostering equality and diversity

■ maintaining confidentiality.

Within this chapter we will look in depth at the equality and diversity part of the care value base. Rights and confidentiality are covered in other chapters within the book.

Codes of ethics and conduct constitute a profession's commitment to the public who use the service. They generally reflect the way in which the member of that profession is expected to behave. For example, the Nursing and Midwifery Council (NMC) has a code of conduct and expects nurses and midwives to uphold the professional standards laid down therein. Failure to do so can result in the member being excluded from practice. See opposite.

The British Association of Social Workers (BASW, 2000) highlights five care values:

■ human dignity and worth

■ social justice

■ service to humanity

■ integrity

■ competence.

As a result of such guidelines the public, who use the service, can expect to receive a standardised service that is committed to excellent practice and quality care. When we talk about standardising something we refer to the fact that the standards, or in this case guidelines, apply wherever you might be in the health care system. So for example, the code of conduct laid down by the NMC will ensure that *all* nurses in the UK adhere to the standards. In this way the care we can expect to get in one county should be similar to care obtained at the other end of the country.

The codes of conduct of any profession or organisation reflect the institutional values of those institutions. In accepting a job of work in an organisation we are saying we commit to that value system as outlined by the code of conduct.

NMC code of conduct

Standards of conduct, performance and ethics for nurses and midwives

■ Make the care of people your first concern, treating them as individuals and respecting their dignity.

■ Treat people as individuals.

■ Respect people's confidentiality.

■ Collaborate with those in your care.

■ Ensure you gain consent.

■ Maintain clear professional boundaries.

■ Work with others to protect and promote the health and well-being of those in your care, their families and carers, and the wider community.

■ Share information with your colleagues.

■ Work effectively as part of a team.

■ Delegate effectively.

■ Manage risk.

■ Provide a high standard of practice and care at all times.

■ Keep your skills and knowledge up to date.

■ Keep clear and accurate records.

■ Be open and honest, act with integrity.

■ Uphold the reputation of your profession.

The concept of our own personal and professional values, then, does impact on the sort of care we give to our clients and patients. As we pointed out above, occasionally this causes conflict between our own personal values and those of our employer, and can lead to 'moral distress' (Burkhardt and Nathaniel, 2002).

As we can see from the Case study on the next page, the new head teacher may have been justified in making changes but these caused conflict with the staff since the new regime went against their own values and beliefs about education. The more business-orientated model being operated by the new head teacher, while not wrong, seemed to undermine the educational values of the existing staff.

Case study

Tanya's job as a classroom assistant underwent change when a new head teacher was appointed. Prior to the appointment, Tanya enjoyed her work and the school ethos fitted well with her own values and beliefs about education. The school valued the rights of children to be treated with respect and care. The easy-going nature of the previous head teacher meant that the children enjoyed a freer atmosphere and were able to access a large number of extracurricular activities. Each child was afforded the opportunity to learn to play an instrument and school funds were diverted to this purpose. There were many trips to various theatres and activity centres, all paid for by the PTA and school funds. The children and staff were happy and Ofsted was impressed with the progress of the school, which was graded as a two. The SATs results were satisfactory and attendance was very good.

When the new head teacher came to post it became apparent that change was on the agenda. Cuts to funding at a county level required a restructuring in some of the posts. The governors also introduced a performance-related pay scheme for the head teacher; one of the criteria for a bonus was the achievement of a grade one at the next inspection.

Tanya was aware that redundancies were possible and that the head teacher's plans to reduce spending meant that the music opportunities and school trips were at risk. The children were increasingly being coached in SATs to improve their scores and teachers were being asked to do more to ensure the children performed in a more academic way.

Tanya noticed a change in the culture of the school and experienced colleagues becoming dissatisfied, angry and frustrated at the new regime.

Activity 3.3

Access a copy of your own code of conduct for your particular workplace and analyse it in terms of the values it shows. How do they fit with your own personal values?

Our values change as we progress through life as a result of new experiences and the occasional challenges to our beliefs. Anti-oppressive and anti-discriminatory care depends upon congruence between our values and those of our clients or patients and the institution in which we work. In the next section we will address the consequences that conflicting values have on society as a whole.

How discrimination and social inequalities impact on individual health and general well-being

Society is unequal and this fact alone has a major influence on life chances for various groups and even on their mortality and morbidity. As care workers, we must understand the ways in which this inequality in terms of treatment leads to disempowerment of individuals, and the resulting lack of respect towards certain groups, denying them their dignity. Poor practice leads to oppression and social exclusion of vulnerable groups in society.

We often hear the term 'equality and diversity' – in fact, it is one of the care values we are expected to foster – but what does it actually mean?

The Nursing and Midwifery Council comments in this way:

> The NMC values the diversity of our staff, nurses and midwives and the wider community we serve. Our passion and drive are for this diversity to be reflected in everything we do …

Valuing diversity is:

- valuing people
- recognising them for their skills, experience and talent

■ treating them fairly irrespective of race, disability, age, sexual orientation, religion or belief and gender.

While there is no mention of equality you will see how the two link together in the following discussion.

If you ask somebody to define 'equality', it is likely the response will be: 'treating everybody the same'. However, this is not strictly accurate. What would be good for me may not fit well with you. As individuals we are unique in the way in which we view the world and as such in a care or welfare setting we are likely to require and respond to different approaches. As health care professionals we are more interested in creating equality of opportunity, thus recognising the differences in all people but providing equal access to services and opportunity in, for example, work and education. The link here is to value the difference people have but treat them fairly and equally.

Diversity refers to the differences in our experiences, beliefs and values (again), which all require recognition in order to ensure we are afforded equal access to various provisions in terms of health and social care. These differences are the various characteristics that mark people in groups as being different, but it is those differences which lead to oppression of some groups and discrimination. Rather than having a positive view of diversity and celebrating the richness of the varying cultures in our society, the differences shown by various groups has been a basis for unfair discrimination and has led to disadvantage.

Race and ethnicity, social class, gender, disability and age are some of the ways in which groups in society differ. You may well be able to identify others but we shall look at these in more detail here.

The issues surrounding diversity have been of significance in developing policy in the care sector for the last 40 years. A range of initiatives including anti-sexist and anti-racist campaigns designed to address the prejudice and discrimination that had come to light were put in place to develop a more equal service in terms of access to care and participation.

However, one of the features of any society is the fact that the differences amongst various groups lead to problems with respect to access to wealth, influence and power (Alcock and Erskine, 2003) and it is appropriate to trace the effects of this now. In the next section we will introduce the groups named above and demonstrate briefly how they are affected.

Race and ethnicity

Racism has had a long and complex history in the UK and continues to prove difficult to deal with. The visible differences noted in groups in society lead to assumptions being made as to their abilities, behaviour, trustworthiness and worth in general. The terms 'ethnic' and 'ethnicity' are used to denote groups of people who share a culture of values and beliefs, national origins, and customs and traditions. On the other hand, the term 'race' implies biological differences. This carries with it the inherent belief that white races are superior to black races and this has come about as a result of years of oppression and enslavement of black groups and ethnic minorities. Racial or ethnic diversity has often been viewed as a 'problem' within health and social care settings.

The definition supplied in Thompson (2006) by Burke and Harrison (2000) is a good one:

> Racism is a multidimensional and complex system of power and powerlessness; it is a process through which powerful groups … are able to dominate. It operates at micro and macro levels, is developed through specific cognitions and actions, and perpetuated and sustained through policies and procedures of social systems and institutions. This can be seen in the differential outcomes for less than powerful groups in accessing services in the health and welfare, education housing and legal systems.

So rather than being just a reflection of personal values – and prejudiced ones at that – this definition shows a more complex set of issues at play, including the perpetuation of racist behaviour through institutional policy.

Such behaviour at organisational level has come under scrutiny and the term 'institutional racism' has been applied to the failure of organisations to address the way in which their structures and systems discriminate against people of different ethnic or racial origins. For women and black staff in particular, this has been a reality in health and social care settings in the past and researchers have shown many areas of discrimination (Baxter, 1997; Doyle *et al.*, 1980). During the migration of people from the Caribbean in the 1950s and 1960s, studies showed that the ancillary and auxiliary jobs within the NHS were more likely to be offered to black women. When they applied for training, the opportunities were limited to the less-senior state-enrolled nurse (SEN) courses. A result of this was to limit the career opportunities of these women.

We seem to have moved away from this sort of overt racism nowadays and through various initiatives have addressed some of these issues. The Race Relations Act 1976 has made discrimination on racial grounds unlawful and this has had enormous impact on the treatment of ethnic minority groups in the UK.

But we may still be guilty of racist behaviour at a more unconscious level. If we fail to challenge racist comments by ignoring them and hoping they will stop, or if we disadvantage people just because of cultural differences, then we covertly discriminate. Atkins and Rollings (1996) comment upon the way in which some carers view the care of Asian people. The notion that these families 'look after their own' and therefore require no help from the system is unintentionally racist since the outcomes for these people are lack of help and subsequent isolation. This is just one example of allowing a stereotype to condone our lack of action.

Activity 3.4

Think about ways in which you may have been guilty of this type of behaviour. Are there any stereotypes that perpetuate your views on racially different groups? Discuss with other students.

As a closing remark we should comment here about the terms we have used, namely 'race' and 'ethnicity'. The usefulness of these has long been debated. The term 'ethnic minority' has come to mean 'different' or, more negatively, 'inferior'. We automatically think of ethnicity as black, Asian or other physically different groups, yet a look at Storkey's (1991, cited in Thompson, 2001) definition of ethnicity belies this:

> … all the characteristics which go to make up cultural identity: origins, physical appearance, language, family structures, religious belief, politics, food, art, music, literature, attitudes towards the body, gender roles, clothing, education.

So ethnic groups in our society should also include other groups who are excluded from the mainstream society simply because of the culture and way of life they adopt. One such group would be travellers, who have suffered discrimination for many years and therefore are at a disadvantage in terms of the services they can access.

Social class

Another of the major divisions in the UK is that of social class. We aspire to being a 'classless' society yet are said to be particularly class conscious (Beckett and

Figure 3.5 Nurses from NHS of Caribbean descent

Maynard, 2005). For example, accent, dress, where we live and the job we do all lend themselves to providing clues about a person's social class.

I very quickly learned that my Essex accent would have to change if I were to be taken seriously in some of the higher-paid jobs in education and nursing. Sad but true. In order to fit in I needed to change.

Our need to measure and define social class in our society has had a major impact on service provision, health and welfare, and affects policy development. Recognition in the last 50 years or so of the poor health in those from lower socio-economic groupings has led to better housing, improvements in social security provision and health care.

One thing that needs to be recognised, however, is the impact of where we fit into the social class system and how this has a major effect on our health and well-being. A major effect of class is the link to poverty and the impact this can have on our well-being.

But what is it like to experience poverty and how does it affect individuals in our society?

Poverty: absolute and relative

Absolute poverty refers to the minimum level of subsistence a person requires to survive. In 1995, the United Nations listed basic human needs such as water, food, health, shelter, sanitation, education and

information; if these needs are not met, the individual is deemed to be impoverished (Spicker, 2007).

In determining relative poverty we need to look at the standards of living that the majority of people in a given society enjoy. In the UK we compare level of income with the average throughout the country, and if it is less than 60 per cent of that average then the individual is said to be living in poverty. Of course, this level will change depending upon the society we are looking at. For example, some people live without access to good sanitation or even fresh water, but in our society we take these for granted and our relative level of poverty may well be measured with respect to access to three meals a day.

One of the major contentions with respect to measuring poverty in our country is the relative ease with which families have access to mobile phones, computers and TVs. Can a family with these consumables said to be impoverished even though they are living below the 60 per cent criterion?

However we view poverty, the fact remains that it has a major impact on our health and well-being despite the efforts of governments and health professionals.

Activity 3.5

Browse The Poverty Site on http://www.poverty.org.uk/35/index.shtml and look at the national statistics online to access more information on the effects of poverty on health and well-being. Write a reflective account of your learning.

With respect to heart disease and lung cancer, there is a dramatic increase in those dying in the poorer communities.

A study carried out between 2005 and 2006 by researchers at the University of Sheffield, Sheffield Hallam University, the University of Essex, the London School of Hygiene and Tropical Medicine, and Social Action for Health explored the relationship between long-term health conditions and

Figure 3.6 Class division

Table 3.1 National statistics socio-economic classifications

	Analytic class	Examples of occupations
1	Higher managerial and professional	Senior officials in national and local government, directors and chief executives of major organisations, civil engineers, medical practitioners, IT strategy and planning professionals, legal professionals, architects
2	Lower managerial and professional	Teachers in primary and secondary schools, quantity surveyors, public service administrative professionals, social workers, nurses, IT technicians
3	Intermediate	NCOs and other ranks in the armed forces, graphic designers, medical and dental technicians, local government clerical officers, counter clerks
4	Small employers and own account workers	Hairdressing and beauty salon proprietors, shopkeepers, dispensing opticians in private practice, farmers, self-employed taxi drivers
5	Lower supervisory and technical	Bakers and flour confectioners, screen-printers, plumbers, electricians and motor mechanics employed by others, gardeners, rail transport operatives
6	Semi-routine	Pest control officers, clothing cutters, traffic wardens, scaffolders, assemblers of vehicles, farm workers, veterinary nurses and assistants, shelf fillers
7	Routine	Hairdressing employees, floral arrangers, sewing machinists, van, bus and coach drivers, labourers, hotel porters, bar staff, cleaners and domestics, road sweepers, car park attendants

Office for National Statistics 2001 Census, mid-year population estimates, death registrations, ONS longitudinal study

poverty across a diverse population. The findings revealed that poverty was:

broadly conceived and covered three domains: financial hardship, lack of participation in employment and limited social participation.

It further showed that individuals suffered from multiple conditions and thus health problems were often clustered. Often, ill health was related to work, in particular being linked to participation in lower-paid employment and low pay. People with long-term health conditions experienced a range of barriers to employment, despite wanting to work. Additionally, claiming disability benefits was perceived as stressful, and making ends meet had a poor effect on health and on household well-being. (Salway *et al.*)

Of interest is the link to the effects of limited social participation and the effects on individuals. Not only is poorer health a factor for these groups but social isolation also has major impact upon well-being and we will look at this in more detail later.

Gender

Despite advances in addressing sexism, this division in society remains a sticking point for women. Women continue to be paid less than men. They still undertake the major share of housework in the home and continue to be over-represented in low-paid work. They also rate highly as the most likely to become the carer of elderly parents or relatives.

In health and social care services there is evidence to suggest that inequalities based on gender are still an agenda item for reform. The majority of workers in care services are women, yet it is men who are in positions of authority. The medical profession, which continues to a lesser extent nowadays to be a male-dominated profession, still tends to be a more powerful profession than that of nursing. What this means is that women continue to be excluded from decision making in terms of policy and change mechanisms in the workplace.

We appear to still be part of a male-dominated world, which raises issues for anti-discriminatory practice.

One of the major issues for women and how their position in society affects their health was highlighted in a study by Brown and Harris (1978). The incidence of depression in the female population was identified as being due to a number of factors, one of which was low self-esteem. This seemed to make women more vulnerable as a group. The multiple roles women take on in the family, particularly with respect to the care-giving role, further limits their opportunity in employment. They are the first to take on the child-rearing role, with its subsequent effect on their careers.

Disability

Oliver (1996) wrote:

> Certainly it is true that disabled people have been systematically excluded from British society; they have been denied inclusion into their society because of the existence of disabling barriers.

The disabled person in our society has to contend with personal prejudice, which may manifest itself in treatment and can range from simply ignoring the person to patronising them and offering help out of sympathy. Our society is also geared towards able-bodied people and certainly in the past access to various venues was virtually impossible for disabled people. This negative treatment led to the development of popular stereotypes of disabled people as victims and misfits in our society and the group became marginalised.

Through the legal system and the development of the Disabled People's Movement there have been major advances to address the effects of disadvantage for this group. One of the major changes has been in the way which disability is viewed in society. Historically disabled people were either destined to spend their lives in institutions or

Figure 3.7 Disability

were viewed as poor unfortunates who needed help. A major cultural and societal shift has now turned this situation on its head. The Disability Discrimination Act (1976, 1995, 1998) brought major changes to housing provision, education and employment for disabled people. It made it possible for disabled people to fully participate in society by addressing the services provided with respect to transport, access to public buildings and employment. Thus disability began to be viewed as a problem of society and its failure to provide services for a group who had previously been excluded, rather than failure on the part of the disabled person.

Age

A stereotypical representation of elderly people as being redundant and somewhat worthless in society has led to discrimination against this group.

Activity 3.6

Think for a moment about the assumptions you may have about elderly people.

In your work placement, focus on how the elderly are treated by other care workers and make a comment in your reflective journal about how this links to stereotypical views.

Neil Thompson (2001) highlighted the following 'assumptions', which have led to the use of the term 'ageism':

- old = useless
- old = childlike
- old = ill
- old = lonely
- old = asexual
- old = unintelligent
- old = poor.

These were just some of the points he made and it might be useful for you to read his comments relating to these. Perhaps you shared some of these views. What is happening here is the dehumanising of a group in our society by implying that age makes the person different in some way – and not necessarily in a good way. This negative view of an ever-increasing group of people in our society has made it much easier for us all to ignore this group and to express these views by marginalising the group.

Again there is some evidence of change occurring and the raising of the retirement age may go a long way to addressing some of the issues.

The need to move to retirement homes to access full-time care may lead some elderly people to be treated as burdens on society and in this way they are discriminated against as a group. As a carer in this setting, then, the challenge is to recognise that age does not reduce the person's ability to make choices and to manage their own care.

Stereotyping and prejudice

The groups shown above are some of those in society who are more likely to be subject to discrimination and disadvantage. We might also include those with mental health problems as being disadvantaged when it comes to accessing health services.

The 'differences' all these groups manifest lead us to make certain assumptions about them as groups and this we acknowledge as stereotyping or labelling.

You will have come across the term 'stereotyping' before. Simply put, this is

sets of beliefs we hold about groups of people based upon the characteristics they have. These beliefs are often inaccurate, yet they do help us to make sense of our world and help in health care work to organise services. In organising a youth group in a local area, for example, it would be necessary to assume what the young people have in common as a group and this may require some stereotypical views about youth and their characteristics. Similarly, with elderly services, we do need to look for common characteristics of this group in order to get some idea about what might work in structuring a service for them; this requires some assumptions to be made. The problems with stereotyping occur when we assume that *all* members of youth and elderly groups, racial or religious groups are likely to act in the same manner or possess similar traits.

As Shah (1995) puts it:

> In short, stereotypes lead persons who hold them to ignore important differences between unique individuals.

Unfortunately, stereotyping can lead to the oppression of and subsequent discrimination against groups, based unfairly on certain characteristics.

Prejudice can arise out of stereotypical views and is an attitude we may hold based on beliefs, born of ignorance, about a group of people.

Baron and Byrne (1991) define prejudice as:

> an attitude (usually negative) towards the members of some group, based solely on their membership in that group.

An unfortunate trait of the prejudiced individual is the inflexible way in which they view the object of prejudice and the inability to make a change based upon new knowledge. In other words, prejudice is an ingrained attitude and one that is difficult to change. When it leads to discrimination, the prejudiced group can become marginalised in society and this can lead to oppression.

Discrimination, while often used interchangeably with prejudice, is not the same thing at all. It refers, rather, to acting upon prejudiced beliefs. In other words, we may have a prejudiced attitude towards a group but discrimination only occurs if we act upon this and treat the group in a less favourable way.

Do you hold any prejudices about particular groups?

Activity 3.7

Can you think of ways in which the following groups are discriminated against or oppressed in some way in our society?

gays and lesbians

black groups

elderly people.

On a personal level we see such groups being treated disrespectfully by being verbally abused or criticised. We may make assumptions about their lifestyles simply because of the stereotypes we are aware of. There may also be avoidance of the group simply because they are different from us. If we are apt to judge people because of stereotypes and behave differently towards them or treat them differently, we are being discriminatory. Our actions can take many forms. We may simply decide to ignore the group, such as the way in which we may steer clear of people with mental illness. I noticed a distinct form of this when I was out with my niece, who has Down's syndrome. I was aware of many people we knew crossing the street as soon as they noticed we were walking towards them. Their embarrassment or fear of the condition was certainly a discriminatory action although I wonder whether they might view it as such. Another way in which we might act in a discriminatory manner would be to exclude the group by restricting their membership to jobs or clubs simply by making the entrance criteria impossible to meet for certain groups. At a societal level covert discrimination or oppression also occurs.

For example, the beliefs and policies in institutions may consistently reduce opportunities for certain groups simply because of the rules within that organisation. Women in the past have been discriminated against in the workplace and the issue of child care and the break in service for women who required maternity leave often meant they were unable to sustain employment in some cases or rise to higher levels in others.

Also, the difficulty in adopting children for same-sex couples is only just being addressed in a more tolerant way today and has been an object of discrimination to these groups in the past.

Ageism refers to the way in which some people act towards elderly people in our society. As health care improves year on year, we are finding that there are many more elderly people in our society. Ageism with respect to the job market has led to some elderly people being unable to find work despite being perfectly fit and able to work.

These are just a few examples of discrimination and oppression which led to changes in the legal system to try to address the situation. In addition, disability and gender differences can lead to unfavourable treatment and leads to the oppression of women in particular as well as those who are disabled in any way.

Such treatment leads to the marginalisation of groups. This term 'marginalisation' describes the way in which discriminated groups are excluded from society. These are the groups we as a society have a tendency to forget since they are no longer part of mainstream society.

As care workers we have a duty to ensure that such people do not remain invisible when it comes to accessing care services and welfare. Rather than allowing them to be viewed as problem groups in society, we need to be able to provide such individuals with a voice to afford them respect.

Often the term 'oppression' is used and a further definition might be useful. Like the terms 'marginalise' and 'excluded', use of this word implies that a person or a group is being disadvantaged in some way. It seems to be a powerful word in that it may conjure up images of slaves and people being downtrodden in some way; but it aptly describes the treatment of some groups in our society who experience hardship and injustice simply because they have been excluded from the mainstream of society or because they are suffering from discrimination due to a medical or mental condition or to the fact that they belong to a particular group.

Thompson (2001) aptly noted that oppression could be defined as:

> ... inhuman or degrading treatment of individuals or groups; hardship and injustice brought about by the dominance of one group over another; the negative and demeaning exercise of power. Oppression often involves disregarding the rights of an individual or group and thus is a denial of citizenship.

This oppression of certain groups can lead to victimisation and powerlessness, and certainly denies some specific human rights. However we view the term 'oppression', and whether or not we like it, it remains the case that certain groups in our society live in substandard housing, have poor incomes, and are stigmatised in a society that is clearly intolerant. While not all people in these groups are necessarily financially deprived, some have health problems that can lead to oppression due to the attitudes of others in society who may fail to understand the impact of their conditions.

One of the more far-reaching problems with the issue of oppression is the way in which the oppressed person views themselves. An abused child may well believe they deserve the treatment they get simply because they are worthless individuals. They have internalised the treatment and come to believe it is all they can expect. This can only leave the child with a very poor self-image and low self-esteem. The child, then, has taken on the oppressor's view and virtually agrees that they deserve the treatment they are getting. What we are seeing here is the powerless accepting their state and adopting the oppressor's view. They begin to believe the way in which they are treated is acceptable in some way and start to adapt to it accordingly. As care workers we may also allow this self-image to perpetuate by encouraging the person to become

dependent on us helping them in some way, and thereby assuming the person is the 'victim' who requires our help and support.

Without doubt our own personal values impact upon the manner in which we treat others in our society. We all hold prejudiced views and may even have been guilty of acting out those views, thereby discriminating against some individuals in our care. It is up to us now to reflect on this and to determine how this might have affected the person or group in question.

Activity 3.8

Consider an example of how you may have acted in a discriminatory manner towards a client, leading to oppression of that individual. Reflect on your account and determine how you would deal differently with it in the future.

Anti-discriminatory and anti-oppressive practice to counteract discrimination and inequality

Time after time government agendas include the need to address the inequality in health care across the UK. This has led to various initiatives to introduce anti-oppressive and anti-discriminatory practice. We shall trace the development of such initiatives.

Since the publication of the Black report in 1980, the link between poverty and ill health has been a major area of concern for governments. Unfortunately, the groups described above are more likely to find themselves living in poverty and are therefore subject to the ill health this can lead to. For example, ethnic minority groups are more likely to live in poorer areas of the community and may find it harder to find work. Those in lower socio-economic groups, if in work, are more likely to be in low-paid work and are therefore prone to experience higher levels of stress and depression. People in unemployed households and lone parents with dependent children also show higher levels of drinking than those in the wider population. So too with smoking behaviour in disadvantaged households: 45 per cent of lone parents with dependent children, 39 per cent of people living in households dependent on state benefits and 38 per cent of people in workless households smoke; more than those in the wider population (National Statistics online).

Despite moves to address these inequalities, there was little to celebrate. In 1997, one of the first things the incoming Labour government did was to commission an inquiry into inequalities in health to be carried out by Sir Donald Acheson. Recommendations made in this report led to the 'Saving lives – our healthier nation' white paper, which was published in 1999. The programme set out to save lives, promote healthier living and reduce inequality in health. It recognised that actions on the part of government would only be sustainable by working in partnership with local communities and individuals.

Following this, the publication of the NHS plan in 2000 emphasised the importance of tackling health inequalities by extra public investment directed at improving and modernising the National Health Service (NHS). Access to NHS services, especially primary care, improvements in child health, and nutrition and reduction in smoking were to be given particular emphasis to address inequality.

As we can appreciate, government policies for health and welfare have gone a long way to improving the lot of disadvantaged or oppressed groups in our society. We will examine this further in Chapter 5.

Social exclusion

People are excluded when they have few links to social networks such as education, employment, family and friends, due to ill health, mental illness and unemployment.

The impact of a lower income on a child in a family can mean the difference between access to holidays, school trips, books and even new clothes, and this can immediately restrict the child's inclusion in society.

People who are socially excluded in this way cannot maintain relationships in the same way as you or I and lack opportunities to engage in activity in the community; the education of the child suffers. In this way the socially excluded become powerless to make changes to their state and are oppressed. As we touched on in the previous section, this oppression has both personal implications as well as societal and health ones.

We made the statement earlier that society is unequal and, because of this, vulnerable groups are subject to the effects of poverty and ill health due to oppression and discrimination. This sort of treatment leads to social exclusion and a perpetuation of inequality in health care. Although UK governments have worked hard to try to rectify these effects by introducing welfare improvements, the service we deliver as health care workers can have a far-reaching effect on the client's self-esteem and will go a long way to improving the treatment of these groups.

We often use the term 'dignity' in care work, and it is important that all people we care for are treated with respect. In this way, good practice demands that we protect our clients and patients from discrimination and oppressive practices. Recognising the diverse nature of practice and the fact that some individuals are disadvantaged just because they are different has led to the terms 'anti-discriminatory practice' and 'anti-oppressive practice'.

Writers cannot really agree on which is the better term to use and while we know that discrimination and oppression do not mean the same thing, the two terms are often used interchangeably.

In practising in an anti-discriminatory manner we challenge the unfair discrimination some of the more vulnerable groups experience. To practice in an anti-oppressive way we try to minimise the power relations in society that disempower our clients and lead to social exclusion.

With respect to the definition, Thompson (2001) makes a rather useful point:

… it has become the practice in recent years for some commentators to distinguish between anti-discrimina-tory practice and anti-oppressive practice … Anti-discriminatory practice and anti-oppressive practice are therefore presented here as more or less synonymous.

We agree with this. It is possible at times to act in a discriminatory manner and thus oppress somebody. Alternatively, we may oppress somebody simply because we hold a stereotypical or discriminative view about what is acceptable for that group and can therefore rationalise our behaviour.

Let's look at examples of this. Beckett and Maynard (2005) cite slavery and colonialism as oppression that has been justified by discrimination. Using the constitution of the USA, which upholds the right to 'life, liberty and the pursuit of happiness', they questioned the slavery of millions of black people. By reasoning that on the basis of having a black skin a human being is inferior to those with white skins, it becomes perfectly acceptable to allow such atrocities to occur. Hitler is also noted as having similar discrimination against the Jews and thus being able to wipe out millions and justify his oppression on spurious grounds that such groups were not really human.

These are very extreme examples but you might come across discrimination in your workplace, which, though less grave, is oppressive nonetheless.

Activity 3.9

Read the following scenario and say what you think the discriminatory attitude is.

Two widowed residents in a residential care home have become very close and have expressed a desire to move into a double room with each other. The carers are not happy about this and ignore the request.

What is the discriminatory thinking here?

In Activity 3.9, could it be that the carers believe that elderly people do not have sex? In the last section we cited an assumption that elderly people are asexual. This is an example of the oppression of an elderly couple to carry out an act they feel is completely natural, but the ignoring of it by the carers has been justified on the grounds of stereotypical views of elderly groups.

Other examples of this are the comments we note frequently in the media about the belief that gay couples cannot be good parents and therefore should not be able to adopt. The belief that two men will be unable to fulfil certain roles for children is discriminatory and so oppresses the right of the couple to fulfil a desire.

One of the things clearly lacking in this sort of behaviour is respect. To deny somebody their basic human rights or not allow them to have their own views or lifestyles is to oppress them and will affect their self-esteem.

It is apparent that the way in which we approach our practice and the sort of attitudes we display will be important in establishing effective anti-discriminatory and anti-oppressive practice.

By challenging oppression you will be acknowledging the rights of clients in your care and respecting their right to control their own lives.

People who use the health service are more often than not in a vulnerable position due to ill health and are therefore dependent upon service providers. The person providing the service should respect the client's values and act towards them in a non-discriminatory manner. But to develop a health care service that is truly anti-discriminatory is a complex matter. The fact that there is a vast number of ways in which people in our society are discriminated against, and often these ways are subtle, can make this process a difficult journey.

The following are useful pointers to how we might change our practice:

- Acknowledge the impact a group's difference has on their lives. We talked about the child who was abused and how they feel about themselves. But what of the experience of the elderly client and the assumptions made about their intelligence? How does that make them feel? By starting to understand how such groups acknowledge these differences and stereotypes we can start to process the ways in which they need to be treated.

- Challenge existing structures and practices. Institutional racism, sexism and even disablism need to be challenged by looking closely at how services operate and may discriminate by virtue of the way in which services are structured.

- Adopt anti-oppressive approaches that challenge the ways in which current practices disadvantage, either directly or indirectly, patients or clients from different vulnerable groups.

- Challenge inequality by being self-aware and thinking and reflecting on the differences and their positive aspects.

- The need to practice in a non-judgemental and anti-discriminatory way towards people requires us to have an awareness of our own prejudices, values and beliefs.

- By exploring values and issues of prejudice, discrimination and inequality and discussing and reflecting on these things, you will be introduced to diversity and equality and what these mean to the care professions and those who use the services. The social exclusion of groups as a result of discrimination or simply isolation will also be addressed.

Summary

This chapter links with Chapter 5 and you would be wise to use that alongside it when addressing your final activity.

By addressing our personal values and attitudes towards the individuals we meet in the course of our daily work we can begin to understand how we need to

practise in a non-judgemental and anti-discriminatory way. Good practice requires us to have an awareness of our own prejudices, values and beliefs and to challenge the negative ones.

By exploring issues of prejudice, discrimination and inequality and discussing and reflecting on these things, we are in a position to engage with practice that appreciates and celebrates diversity and ensures our clients or patients receive equality of opportunity. If we continue to challenge underlying stereotypical assumptions, we can address the social exclusion of groups and the isolation they experience.

Summary assignment

Write a reflective piece that explores the change in your own awareness of values, attitudes and inequalities; drawing on theory, discuss the potential impact of the selected issue on a service user.

References

Ahmad, W. I. U and Atkin, K. (eds) (1996) *'Race' and Community Care*, Open University Press, Buckingham.

Alcock, P., Erskine, A. and May, M. (2003) *The Student's Companion to Social Policy*, 2nd edn, Blackwell Publishing.

Atkin, K. and Rollings, J. (1996) 'Looking after their own? Family care-giving among Asian and Afro-Caribbean communities', in Ahmad and Atkin (1996).

Bandura, A. (1977) *Social Learning Theory*, General Learning Press, New York.

Baron, R. A. and Byrne, D. (1991) *Social Psychology: Understanding Human Interaction*, 6th edn, Allyn and Bacon, Boston.

Baxter, C. (1997) *Race Equality in Health Care and Education*, Bailliere-Tindall, London.

Beckett, C. and Maynard, A. (2005) *Values and Ethics in Social Work: An Introduction*, Sage Publications, London.

British Association of Social Workers (2000)

Burke and Harrison (2000) in Thompson, N.(2001) Anti-discriminatory practice, 3rd Ed. Palgrave, Basingstoke.

Burkhardt and Nathaniel (2002) – Ethics + issues in Contemporary Nursing. 2nd Ed. US. Delmar.

Brown G.W. and Harris T. O. (1978) The origins of Depression. London, Tavistock.

Central Council for Education and Training in Social Work (1976) Paper 13, 'Social work curriculum study' CCETSW, London.

Doyal, L., Hunt, G. and Mellor, J. (1980) 'Migrant workers in the NHS. A report to the Social Science Research Council', Department of Sociology, Polytechnic of North London, London.

Fisher, A., Blackmore, C., McKie, S., Riley, M., Seamons, S. and Tyler, M. (2006) *Applied AS Health and Social Care*, Folens.

Oliver, M. (1996) Understanding disability: from theory to practice, Macmillan, Basingstoke.

Oxford English Dictionary, Oxford University Press (2001) OUP, Oxford.

Rokeach M, (1973) 'The Nature of Human Values. NY: Free Press.

Salway, S., Platt, L, Chowbey, P., Harriss, K. and Bayliss, E. (2007) 'Long-term ill health, poverty and ethnicity', Sheffield University and Social Action for Health.

Shah, R. (1995) *The Silent Minority: Children with Disabilities in Asian Families*, National Children's Bureau, London.

Spicker P. (2001) The idea of Poverty, Bristol: Policy Press.

Storkey, E. (1991) cited in Thompson, N. (2001).

Thompson, N. (2001) *Anti-discriminatory Practice*, 3rd edn, Palgrave, Basingstoke.

4 Healthy living for individuals and communities

Defining health is complex. We all have our own ideas and experiences of health and the way in which it is promoted. The aims of this chapter are to show the dynamic nature of the subject and focus on the different perspectives that feed into it. Attempts to define the strategies for improving the health and well-being of the nation and public health promotion is a core feature of this particular chapter.

The chapter will debate the complex nature of public health promotion and education and will provide a comparison of the models of health promotion and their purpose.

Learning outcomes

By the end of the chapter you will be able to:

- define and analyse health and the role of health promotion

- compare and contrast models of health promotion and delivery and evaluate the political influence on the public health agenda

- debate positive and negative influences on health with respect to race, ethnicity and gender

- debate why some individuals do not conform to advice

- compare health promotion campaigns and evaluate their impact.

Define and analyse health and the role of health promotion

If we are to promote health in our clients and patients, we require a definition of the term. You have undoubtedly been down this road before and I would suggest that at some point in your studies and your work you have been asked to provide your own definition of health. Not easy, was it? Perhaps as a result of further work and study you may have changed your original view. Why would this happen?

As we become more knowledgeable about life and the interests we have, we may change our opinions and values and this may well have had an effect on us personally and on our own concept of health. Certainly as I get older I find my own definition of health is changing. I feel healthy if I can get up without my usual backache or if I can walk my dogs without getting too breathless as I trudge up the hill!

Perhaps, though, you find it easier to define illness. Illness, after all, is easy to recognise. You don't feel well, and you may have signs and symptoms, such as a temperature, a rash or a headache. What of the patient or client who has an undiagnosed condition? They may feel well but would you say they were healthy? Let's explore this in more depth.

Health and illness are subjective experiences in that only we can say how we feel about what is happening to us. It is a personal phenomenon and as such the experience of feeling ill is not always

Figure 4.1 Health and well-being

matched by an objective reality. For example, we may visit our GP with vague symptoms of feeling 'not quite right' or of just feeling tired all the time and this may be viewed less than sympathetically if the doctor can find no tangible reason for these 'feelings' or reported symptoms. It does not, however, mean we are not ill. The converse is also true. We may feel really well and not be concerned about our health but an underlying condition that has yet to reveal itself by becoming symptomatic may negate that view. It is possible to feel well only to have a routine screening examination throw up a diagnosis of cancerous changes occurring in parts of the body. The matching of our subjective feeling of wellness is therefore at odds with the diagnosed disease and we become officially 'ill' or not healthy.

So health is a difficult concept to get to grips with and numerous tomes have been written about the subject. We will, in this chapter, try to come to some consensual opinion in order to make the task a little more palatable.

The definition of health is a contested one and we all have our own views.

Activity 4.1

Think for a moment about how you define health. Now write that definition down and collect five more from other students. Analyse the differences and see if you can put them into themes.

In Activity 4.1, did you notice how some definitions had negative connotations while others were positive? This is a good starting point. The negative definitions are the sort that describe health as simply 'the absence of illness or disease'. Townsend and Davidson (1982) provide us with 'freedom from ascertainable disease'. This is certainly one legitimate view and we will look more closely at it when we examine the medical model.

A more positive definition is one that describes health as a more holistic notion. You will recall the World Health

Organization's definition of health as being 'a state of complete physical, mental and social well-being and not merely the absence of disease and infirmity' (WHO, 1946).

This definition has been upheld as a more favourable description of health, with its multifaceted view combining the social and the physical aspects of health. Critics have pointed to the problems there are with measuring and achieving this definition simply because it encompasses the whole of the human race. As you will have noted from Activity 4.1, you have six definitions, all of which may be different. How much more will definitions differ when we approach the many different societies around the globe with their different values, attitudes and norms? So the critics make a fair point and in response the definition was revisited by the WHO some years later. In 1984 they came up with:

> the extent to which an individual or group is able, on the one hand, to realise aspirations and satisfy needs; and, on the other hand, to change or cope with the environment. Health is, therefore, seen as a resource for everyday life, not an object of living; it is a positive concept emphasising social and person resources, as well as physical capabilities.

What emerges from this last definition is just how multifaceted the concept is. As Ewles and Simnett (1999) have stated, holistic health incorporates several different facets, including:

- physical
- intellectual and mental
- emotional
- social
- spiritual
- sexual.

Let's just briefly define each of the terms.

Physical health refers to bodily functions and fitness, and describes the ability of the body to function in an efficient way.

Intellectual and mental health concerns the sense of purpose we have in life and the ability to feel good and to cope. If we can think clearly and coherently, then we are more likely to be intellectually healthy. It also deals with the need to grow and learn and our capacity to become self-actualising. Self-actualisation is worth mentioning since it is a term much used by psychologists. Kurt Goldstein (1878–1965) and Carl Rogers (1902–87) referred to this as a 'basic drive', and one that would enable us to reach our full potential. Maslow's hierarchy of needs (1975) has 'self-actualisation' at the apex of the pyramid and refers to creativity, motivation and problem solving as well as lack of prejudice as notions associated with this ability.

Emotional health is about our capacity to love and feel loved, and to be able to voice our emotions in a responsible manner in order to maintain relationships with others.

Being involved in these sorts of relationships and having a sense of support in our lives is all about **social health**. Our ability to make friends and to be involved in activities with others is incorporated here as well.

Spiritual health is often a difficult one to recognise since not all of us have a belief in a god or a religion. Some individuals have a strong need to belong to a group or organised religion and feel they are not complete without a belief of this kind. But spiritual health can also be about our moral principles and the way in which we live and have purpose in our lives. For these people

the concept of a god or a need to be part of a religion is unnecessary; they just want to live 'good' lives.

Sexual health is about how we accept and express our own sexuality.

All of the above represent our individual dimensions of health but clearly we are also affected by external influences. For example, the wider society in which we live, where we live and the sort of environment we live in will all have influences on our health and well-being. This is referred to by the WHO and other writers in the field as the social determinants of health, or 'the conditions in which people are born, grow, live, work and age' (WHO).

The social model of health as described by Dahlgren and Whitehead (1991), and cited in Moonie shows the layers of influence on health. Their social ecological theory of health maps the relationship between the individual and their environment and disease.

At the centre of this particular model is the individual with their own attendant set of genes, which will have an influence on that individual's experience of health. However, surrounding them are influences on health that can be changed to a certain extent. For example, the first layer describes personal behaviour and ways of living that can promote or damage health – such as choosing whether or not to smoke.

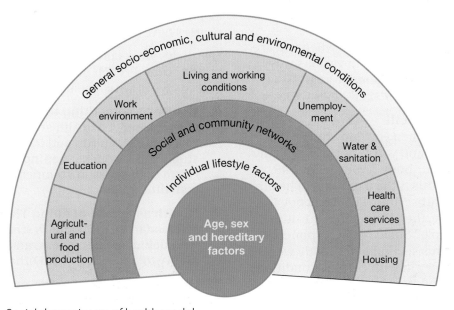

Figure 4.2 Social determinants of health model

The next layer refers to the influences imposed by our social and community lives.

If there is support for members of the community in unfavourable conditions, then this will have a positive effect on individuals. Lack of support would evidently work the opposite way and have a negative effect.

The third layer includes structural factors such as housing, working conditions and the services and welfare systems in place to support us in our society.

As we can see, there are social, economic and environmental conditions that influence the health of individuals within our society and these are all shaped by government policy as well as the distribution of money, power and resources at global, national and local levels. The link between the social determinants of health and health inequalities is a fairly strong one, as we will further explore.

To promote health in a society where there are so many different interpretations and definitions of it, we need to determine what the public's definition of health might be.

Sociologist Mildred Blaxter, an eminent writer in this field, undertook research in an attempt to do just this. Her study on 'lay perceptions of health' asked the question 'What is health?' of 9,000 people. Her findings were much as expected, namely that 'a single all-purpose definition of health is impossible' (Blaxter, 1983).

Her question 'What is it like when you are healthy?' was answered in various ways and Blaxter made a thematic analysis of these responses. Her six themes were:

Health as not ill
'Health is when you don't hurt anywhere and you're not aware of any part of your body': woman aged 49. Perhaps this is the definition of health to which I subscribe. If I haven't got a backache, then I'm not ill! Or is it really that simple? Some of the respondents within this section of the study were clearly very ill with chronic conditions and disability yet still described themselves as healthy.

Health as physical fitness and vitality
Age was a major factor in the different descriptions. Young people tended to talk about strength and athleticism whereas older people focused on energy: 'Health is when I feel I can do anything … nothing can stop you in your tracks': man aged 28.

Health as social relationships
Women tended to use this definition more than men and good relationships with family and friends were cited as examples of being healthy.

Health as function
This tended to be an overlap of the above two definitions and was linked to being able to carry out tasks despite advancing years. For example: 'Health is being able to walk around better, and doing more work in the house when my knees let me': woman aged 79.

Health as psychosocial well-being or health as a psychological concept
'Health is to feel proud – when you can go out and you can hold your head up, look good. You don't have so many hang-ups and you think straight': computer operator aged 25.

Health as leading a healthy lifestyle
In this theme individuals referred to lifestyle choices as a demonstration of health.

As we note from Blaxter's work, individuals' definitions of health are indeed diverse and can be somewhat contradictory. Other writers have also supported this notion.

Herzlich's work (1973) on lay beliefs in middle-class French people highlighted three ways in which health was described:

- **Health as something to be had** This concept showed health and being a reserve of strength, and the potential to stop illness from happening usually as a result of the person's temperament or constitution.

- **Health as a state of doing** This referred to an individual's strength, well-being and happiness, and the ability to get on well with other people.

- **Health as a state of being or the absence of illness**.

Calnan's research (1987) revealed similar notions to those above; differences between the social classes were also noted. Four different concepts of health were shown:

- **Health as never being ill.**

- **Health as being able to get through the day** – to carry out routines.

- **Health as being fit** – being active, taking exercise.

- **Health as being able to cope with stresses and crises in life**.

They do show similarities with Blaxter's work but there were differences in the responses according to social class. For example, working-class women were more likely to quote the first two concepts, whereas middle-class women seemed to opt for the third and fourth options as their preference.

Seedhouse (1986 and 2001) posited five theories as to health definitions:

Health as an ideal state

Although criticised for being too idealistic and therefore potentially unattainable, this theory provides a holistic view of health. A person who is free from physical illness may be socially isolated and is therefore not in an ideal state. One who may be feeling well and yet have an undiagnosed illness again fails to be in an ideal state. This theory then relates to the relationship between all facets or dimensions of health being met.

Activity 4.2

Using the diagram below, add further examples to each of the definitions.

Access Blaxter's work and read Chapter 1, 'How is health defined?'.

Identify where Herzlich's and Calnan's researches overlap with Blaxter's findings.

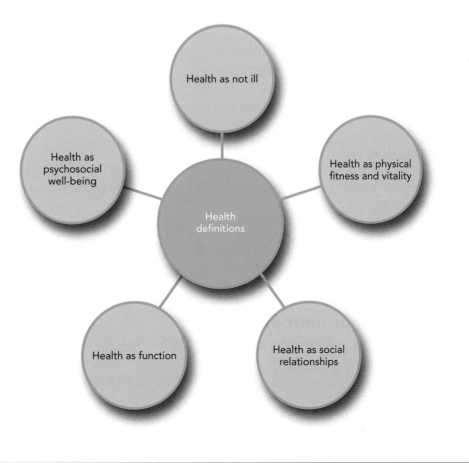

Figure 4.3

Health as mental and physical fitness

Talcot Parsons (1951) (see also Chapter 5) suggested a functionalist perspective when viewing health. This theory suggests that health is when people can fulfil certain functions in society and so excludes those who have a disability. If you are unable to perform your normal social roles in society, then this theory deems you unhealthy.

Health as a commodity

This implies that health can be bought and some individuals in society subscribe to the view that paying for their health care privately will guarantee a better service and better-quality care.

Health as a personal strength

Derived from Maslow's hierarchy of needs (1970) and the need to self-actualise and move towards discovery, this view tends to encourage an individual to define their own health but fails to address the social environment that is most important in reaching our goals.

Health as the basis for personal potential

This theory links to the desire to attain self-actualisation and corresponds with the views of Rogers and Maslow.

As we can see, health is a much contested concept and different attempts to describe it have led to various models and beliefs emerging to try to address this conundrum. In the promotion of health the definitions do not end there. We might expect there to be numerous definitions as to the ways in which health professionals will approach the promotion of health. Surely it depends upon their definition of health? We will now look at some of the beliefs and models that address this.

Models of health promotion and delivery; political influence on the public health agenda

There are a number of ways in which we can approach the promotion and delivery of health and the models we shall look at do indeed reflect how health is defined.

The aim of health promotion is to ensure our societies remain healthy and to prevent disease, but the way in which we achieve this will be a reflection of the different ways in which different professionals work. To understand health and illness behaviour, there has been a great deal of research to construct models and to address the way in which the power relationships between health professionals and the users have evolved. The dominance of the position of the health professional started to be questioned and there was a resultant change to the way in which health care was viewed. As a consequence, various models have been described over the years and some are now favoured over others.

Models or theoretical frameworks simply describe a means of approaching a task, in this case how to deliver health promotion. They are not guides as to how to do this but help professionals to describe the aims and strategies within each approach. Eisenberg (1977) describes models as 'means of constructing reality'.

Models differ in the way they seek to understand health, illness, the body and the roles of clients and health professionals.

No single approach is held as being better than another although it is clear that some have come under scrutiny and have evolved as a result of political action and ideology with respect to health care and its impact globally.

The approaches we shall look at are:

- the medical approach (also known as the biomedical model or disease prevention approach)

- the behaviour change approach

- the educational approach

- the client-centred or empowerment approach

- the radical or social change approach.

The medical approach

In its broadest sense, health promotion can be described as enabling individuals to control and improve their own health.

From a disease prevention or medical point of view, health promotion is seen as having three strands: primary, secondary and tertiary prevention.

This, however, might be seen as a rather negative way in which to promote health. Sometimes referred to as the medical model of health, this approach looks to prevent deaths and disease by applying medical interventions as shown below.

Primary prevention concerns the avoidance of disease by immunisation and screening, thereby detecting those at risk of disease and addressing the onset before it happens.

Secondary prevention refers mainly to dealing with the disease once it happens and educating the individual to shorten the disease episode by showing them how to deal with the symptoms. For example, the person who has had a myocardial infarction will be treated and will then be counselled with respect to his cigarette smoking and diet and lifestyle to effect a change, thus preventing a further episode.

Tertiary prevention is the attempt to improve the quality of life once the disease has taken hold and the individual is faced with a chronic condition or disability.

The aim of health promotion in this type of definition seems to focus mainly on the effects of ill health and how to deal with them to prevent a worsening of the condition and this is why I (and other writers) refer to it as negative.

In this model the knowledge of the practitioner is viewed as professional, expert and scientific, as opposed to lay beliefs, which are generally devalued and believed to be ill-informed. The focus is on objective, measurable signs and symptoms that enable the professional to make

diagnoses. Critics of the model subscribe to the view that this has led to a reductionist approach to care in that the individual is thus viewed merely as a set of symptoms.

But it is not without its successes and followers. The status afforded it due to the scientific approaches it uses to measure and influence disease make it very attractive. In addition, prevention is certainly better than cure in terms of cost. As it is led by the medical profession it has a certain amount of authority and expertise to support it and its success in terms of eradication of some diseases worldwide is also noteworthy.

One major criticism of the model is that it seemingly fails to address the actual social causes of the condition in the first place. It does not look to what risk factors the individual may find themselves facing, which may be unavoidable by them, and makes the assumption that all is equal and readily available to all. It also relies on the uptake by the individual of vaccinations and screening to prevent certain diseases. The re-emergence of measles as a life-threatening condition has caused alarm and is related to the downturn in uptake of the MMR vaccine following erroneous information in the 1990s.

In this model, being healthy is viewed as having no disease – the model subscribes to the view that health is the 'absence of disease'. So if something in the body goes wrong it can be 'fixed' with medicine or surgery. By targeting and treating the pathogen that has invaded the body, the disease can be cured. This heavy reliance on the specific aetiology of the disease and the identification of the bacteria or viruses causing the disease led to criticism that this oversimplified complex disorders that have many factors causing the body to fail.

Figure 4.4

Figure 4.5

There are conditions that are not amenable to the medical model explanations. Mental health conditions such as stress are not caused by pathogens and this is an example of the limitations of the medical model. We will look more closely at these criticisms later in the chapter.

The behavioural change model

Amidst the dominance of the disease orientation of the biomedical model a sea change occurred and a different approach emerged. The biopsychosocial model (which we return to in another chapter) came to prominence and began to show that illness cannot be treated in isolation from the social environment. This model revealed that biological, psychological and social effects all have an impact on our health.

This change in focus was reflected in research priorities and the more far-reaching view of governments that illness and health had to be everybody's priority.

In 1976 the publication 'Prevention and health: everybody's business' by the Department of Health made it clear that a behavioural approach to health was the way forward and that individuals should be responsible for choosing healthy lifestyles.

In the words of the publication: 'it is clear that the weight of the responsibility for his own health lies on the shoulders of the individual himself' (DoH, 1976).

Further papers followed in which individuals were encouraged to change lifestyle habits such as smoking, drinking, risky sexual practice and poor eating leading to obesity and malnutrition.

The emergence in health promotion practice of the behavioural change model was a move towards a more client-focused model, although it fell short of fully devolving responsibility, as we shall see.

The clear message within this model, then, is to adopt healthy lifestyles and to be responsible for your own health. It endeavours to persuade the individual that change in behaviour is necessary to ward off unwanted effects of disease and illness and to be responsible for their own health.

Like the medical model, there is an expert-led bias to this model, with the health professional educating the lay public about what is good for their sustained health and the avoidance of disease.

Campaigns to address issues with smoking, alcohol consumption and healthy eating are

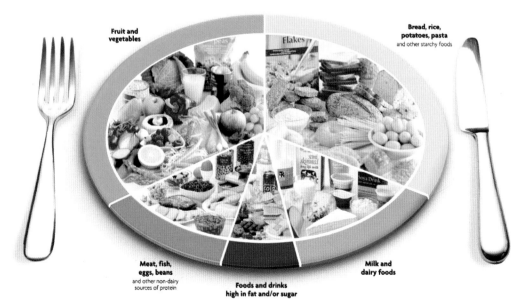

The eatwell plate

Use the eatwell plate to help you get the balance right. It shows how much of what you eat should come from each food group.

FOOD STANDARDS AGENCY
eatwell.gov.uk

Fruit and vegetables

Bread, rice, potatoes, pasta and other starchy foods

Meat, fish, eggs, beans and other non-dairy sources of protein

Foods and drinks high in fat and/or sugar

Milk and dairy foods

Figure 4.6

Figure 4.7

The 'Quit smoking' educational programme

Young people were given several sessions detailing the effects of smoking on the body. They engaged in group activities in which they were shown pictures of what smoking might actually do to their bodies. They talked about how they might quit and what that would mean for them in terms of health and finances. All avenues were explored.

They left the group with every good intention to quit smoking. Yet at a follow-up clinic after a six-month interval, fewer than half had quit.

How would you explain the poor take-up in the programme?

abundant and we are familiar with the ways in which the media and health professionals guide us to effect changes in our lives. But criticism of this approach lies in the belief that essentially what is happening is the development of a blame culture. In other words, if the person does require treatment or gets ill, then clearly it is the fault of their lack of willingness to change their risky behaviour.

It seems simple. Health professionals tell us what to change in order to lose weight or to give up smoking, we do it and we remain healthy. We are all aware that smoking increases our risk to many forms of cancer and respiratory problems and yet still we see a rise in this behaviour despite government's and health professionals' efforts to address the issue. Clearly other factors are in play here and we will look at these later and address the reasons why people do not conform to health advice.

The educational approach

This seems similar to the behavioural change approach but takes the stance that by giving the person more knowledge and information, the outcome will be to widen the choice of the individual to enable them to make more informed choices about how they can be responsible for healthy living. The intention is that education in this sense will enable the individual to undergo a change in their attitude towards a health behaviour and that this will lead to change

in that behaviour. A cognitive behavioural approach is therefore advocated in that individuals are provided with information that they then discuss and put into practice through role plays or group activity, leading to changes in the way they view the problem and subsequently a change in the behaviour.

As you may be aware, attitudes are notoriously difficult to change and despite having a negative attitude to smoking some of the individuals in Activity 4.3 may still be smoking. People respond in a variety of ways to information and educative programmes. Some may be concerned about what they have learned and make the change required; others may simply cut down on their intake; others may deny they have a problem and completely ignore the advice. An increase in knowledge and even an increase in the desire to change are not sufficient to enable behavioural change and there are clearly other factors at play here. We will look in more depth at why people do not conform to health advice later on in the chapter.

The client-centred or empowerment approach

The term 'empowerment' has become something of a buzz word in health and social care and refers to the choice and control afforded to the individual over their own life and well-being. In the health promotion context the health professional takes on the role of a facilitator who puts into place resources and strategies to enable the individual to take control of their own lives and health. As an example, let's apply this to our smoking scenario.

The individual would identify their own need to give up smoking and approach the health professional for help. The health professional would put into place a number of strategies to which the individual might turn. They might suggest treatments such as hypnotherapy, support groups or patches and gum. They would then allow the client to make the choice based on the information. The health professional then takes a back seat as the individual undertakes their own chosen route.

In a target-driven world we would be hard-pressed to evaluate how far the changes to the person's behaviour are due to the intervention of the health professional. A change in behaviour here will be difficult to specify since we can never be sure of the factors that may also have played a part.

Of the four models so far, all rely on the individual to seek treatment to address a disease or condition, or make a change in their behaviour, or become more knowledgeable and educated, or take the power on board to make the change. None of them, however, seems to address the influence of external factors on the health of the individual and the fact that despite the best effort of individuals, sometimes change is not achievable due to other factors (think back to Dahlgren and Whitehead's social model described earlier in this chapter).

The medical model, as we have seen, relies on the influence of the health professional to treat the disease, but this has been criticised for its failure to recognise external influences on health.

One critic, Thomas McKeown (1979), disputed the role of medicine as being the only explanation for good health and made some interesting comments to support his view. He showed the link between the improvements in social conditions in the 1800s and 1900s and the decline in TB. In the 1800s, 80,000 people died of TB. In 1880

the bacillus causing it was identified. But it was not until the 1950s that a vaccine and treatment were found to prevent and treat it – yet already the decline in cases was significant. In the 1940s cases amounted to only 4,000.

McKeown's explanation was that the reduction in TB was as much due to the lifestyle changes that were happening at the time, with improvements in housing, cleanliness and sanitation, as the medical advances with the advent of antibiotics and treatments.

This was only one such case in which a decline in disease was noteworthy following the changes to social and environmental conditions and not due to medical advances. While medical techniques are useful in treating illness, non-medical factors do, in fact, have a huge impact on the mortality of the nation (Blaxter, 1983; McKeown, 1979). The reductionist and mechanical nature of the medical model, in which disease required correction by repair or replacement, was clearly in need of a radical overhaul and the move to a more holistic view of health and illness was being proposed.

This recognition that housing, education, the way we live our lives, and poverty all have an impact on our health is a view that has gained in popularity and led to the development of more holistic models of health.

The three remaining approaches – behavioural, educative and empowerment – while all recognising the role of the individual in eliciting change, do not adequately address the social issues that may prevent the necessary change.

The increasing awareness that some individuals are unable to effect such changes due to the influence of poverty and other factors on health led to further initiatives and a concerted effort to tackle the inequalities in health that were becoming more and more prevalent.

The radical or social change approach; influence on the public health agenda

The social determinants of health have become an increasingly popular agenda item for governments not just in the UK but globally.

Following the conference in 1977 when the WHO called for a broader health agenda worldwide in order to achieve 'health for all by the year 2000', the whole context for approaching health promotion was changed. Lifestyle improvement was just one part of the global strategy, with environmental conditions and health care, as well as peace, freedom and equality of opportunity, being firmly established as minimum requirements in the quest for good health.

There followed numerous conferences and in 1986 the WHO in the Ottawa Charter published five key strategies for the promotion of health, in order to place 'health on the agenda of policy makers in all sectors and at all levels, directing them to be aware of the health consequences of their decisions and to accept their responsibilities for health' (WHO, 1986).

The development of healthy public policy (HPP) emerged as a major initiative from this paper and one of five strategies. The others included supportive environments, the development of personal skills and coping strategies, strengthening the sense of community and social support networks and, finally, reorientation of health services away from treatment and towards improving access to services.

While the HPP is nothing new, having its origins in the 19th-century sanitary reforms through to the Poor Laws and the rise of the Public Health Acts of 1848, 1872 and 1875 and on to today (see Chapter 5), it has brought together the main features of the values that seem to underpin good-health-promoting practice and is likely to have a global effect.

One of the impacts of HPP was to address the way in which health promotion was carried out by recognising not just the disease process but the external influences as well. This approach was referred to as an 'upstream' one, which incorporated the preventive or medical approach but at the same time addressed the social, economic and political determinants of health.

This upstream approach is analogically referred to by many writers as the rescue and subsequent treatment of an individual only to find a similar case falling in upstream. The doctor providing treatment is so busy doing so that he has no time to see what is causing other cases to fall in upstream in the first place. Let me give you an example. For years as a nurse I remember a gentleman who would be admitted with bronchitis to the hospital in which I worked. It was always during the winter and he referred to it as his annual holiday! We would duly fix his condition and send him on his way with the knowledge we would see him again next time. We sent him back to his damp, cold and wholly unsuitable home, with his poor diet and his cigarettes, without actually addressing the cause of the condition. Had we arranged for some form of social help with respect to his housing, we might have seen him less. Of course, we *educated* him with respect to his smoking ('You really shouldn't, you know – have a leaflet') but did we actually help him much? The point here is that his quitting smoking may have had a small effect on his health, but, as Blaxter's work (1983) goes on to reveal, it is the circumstances in which we live that have a more significant effect on our health than any of the behaviours we indulge in. For somebody who is living in poverty the choice of eating more healthily is often beyond reach simply because it really does cost more to do so.

So the focus for health promotion in this instance is somewhat more far-reaching, suggesting that merely addressing behaviour change as a way to good health is to blame the person for the circumstances in which they find themselves. What this approach advocates is to focus on the social and economic factors surrounding the individual and address those. Returning to the example above, in terms of preventing the annual recurrence of our gentleman's bronchitis, it would have been much more useful to look at how and where he was housed, perhaps to address the area in which he lived and to have tackled the emissions from the local factory which churned out pollutants. It therefore requires political and public input to raise awareness of local issues as well as individual change.

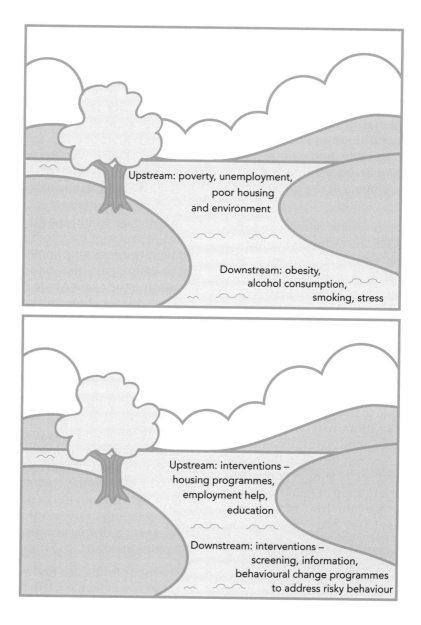

Figure 4.8

Activity 4.4

How might Jamie Oliver's campaign to revolutionise school meals be an example of the upstream approach?

In Activity 4.4, you may have included some of the following points. His interest in obesity in children and healthy eating led him to look at schools' food programmes. His findings, you may recall, showed some very poor food being consumed. His campaign was to change this and by engaging with schools, parents and the government, he did much to move the

healthy eating agenda along in schools and we now see vastly different practices in place as a result.

More theoretical frameworks for health promotion

The different approaches to health promotion provide us with some good descriptions about what health professionals actually do, but to analyse how these all work for the health of society we need to look at the more in-depth models of practice, namely the theoretical frameworks. Theory helps us to predict and organise our knowledge into a more usable format so in this respect we can expect a theory of health promotion to analyse practice, plan for the future and help us to identify the sorts of interventions that are working in practice.

Such models and theories, as we might expect, come from very different stances with respect to the terms used and the ways in which they have been influenced by political ideology and values. Caplan and Holland's (1990) and Beattie's (1991) both models cited in Naidoo and Wills provide a structuralist approach and therefore derive material from a sociological and social policy perspective.

Caplan and Holland (1990)

Using two dimensions – the 'nature of knowledge' and the 'nature of society' – four perspectives of health are suggested. See Figure 4.9.

The nature of knowledge, if viewed as a continuum, ranges from subjective to objective views of health in which the objective view is the 'absence of disease'. The vertical dimension shows society in terms of radical change and social regulation. When these are seen together, the model resembles four quadrants each containing a 'paradigm' or perspective of health promotion.

The interesting part of the model is that each quadrant represents views about society, health promotion and the problems within each view. Let's take this a little further:

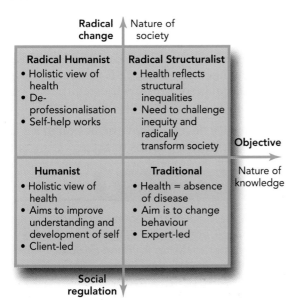

Figure 4.9 Caplan and Holland model

Traditional perspective This represents the expert-led knowledge base, and information giving is emphasised here. So the aim in this view is to change behaviour.

Humanist perspective The education of individuals is seen to be the best approach in this perspective, and a holistic view of health is proposed. Personal skills and resources dominate here as being the best way to develop healthy lifestyles.

Radical humanist perspective This is influenced by the empowerment model in which the emphasis is on the personal issues being explored and individuals being encouraged to support each other through networks and organisational groups. There is a move away from the professional-help route to a more self-help-orientated stance.

Radical structuralist perspective In this view the causes of health problems are viewed as the social inequalities that exist in society, and health promotion's role is to address this. By working towards a more equitable society, this perspective believes that health can be achieved.

Beattie (1991)

Similarly, Beattie offers four paradigms or perspectives of health promotion in his model.

Again two dimensions are adopted, the first being the 'mode of intervention', this ranges from the top-down expert-led view to the bottom-up, negotiated or person-centred view on a continuum. On the horizontal axis the continuum Beattie offers is the 'focus of intervention', this going from the individual who is responsible for their own health to the collective view in which the roots of ill health are the main focus.

The four quadrants resulting in this model give a framework for practice by allowing us to choose the perspective we value the most and the role the health professional feels is the most appropriate. It highlights the strategy and the choices available when choosing a health promotion programme and links well with various political ideologies.

Figure 4.10 Beattie model

This is illustrated as follows:

■ **Health persuasion** In order to *persuade* or encourage the population to adopt healthier lifestyles, the health professional is the expert and gives advice and guidance. This matches a conservative political ideology.

■ **Legislative action** To *protect* the population by making healthier choices more available, the health professional takes on the role of 'custodian' of the nation's health and employs policy work and lobbying to get the job done. This links with a reformist political ideology.

■ **Personal counselling** From a humanist political ideology this perspective *empowers* individuals to gain the skills and confidence to take control over their health. The health professional adopts the role of 'counsellor' working with people's self-defined needs, and uses counselling and educational approaches.

■ **Community development** In this perspective groups and communities are emancipated so that they are encouraged to recognise what they have in common and how social factors influence their lives. This radical political ideology puts the health professional in the role of 'advocate'.

Community development and action are used to empower groups to act.

Activity 4.5

Show the sorts of strategies you might put into place, using Beattie's model to address drug taking in young people.

In Activity 4.5, perhaps you wrote something like this:

- health persuasion – school nurses and youth workers encouraging young people to 'Say no to drugs' or to use them sensibly and safely

- legislative action – lobbying parliament to endorse tighter drug controls; Acts of Parliament addressing the classification of drugs

- personal counselling – health workers working with young people to give them the skills to deal with drug issues; to work with youngsters who have defined a need

- community development – work with parents to address local issues and to form support groups to address issues in their own communities.

Tannahill's model of health promotion (1996) (cited in Naidoo and Wills)

A popular model, the three spheres shown in the diagram show how each concept links and works together:

Health education In this sphere, communication with individuals or groups is aimed at improving knowledge and attempting to change attitudes and behaviour to improve health. Its link with health promotion will be the following-up of education in terms of changing policy and law. An example might be seen in the 'Quit smoking' campaigns. First, the educative process addresses knowledge and attitudes to smoking, and the need to stop. The promotion sphere puts no-smoking policies in place in workplaces or lobbies parliament for a ban on smoking in public places. The prevention sphere will use nicotine gum as a preventive aid.

Prevention This involves interventions aimed at preventing disease, such as immunisation and identifying risk as in screening procedures. Where it is not possible to stop the disease from occurring through these means, treatment is aimed at reducing the effects of the disease process.

Health protection Tannahill defines this as: 'Legal or fiscal controls, other regulations or policies, or voluntary codes of practice aimed at the prevention of ill health or the positive enhancement of well-being'. Health protection in this model, then, refers to the societal activities that need to be undertaken since health protection in this instance is beyond the scope of the individual.

Positive and negative influences on health with respect to race, ethnicity and gender

As we can see, the approaches and the subsequent frameworks and theories for practice have shown how we need to look at health promotion in a collective way. As McKinley (1992) pointed out, 'individual characteristics and behaviours, as well as environmental and occupational exposures, are correlated with and may indeed cause illness, disability and death'.

This, as we know, has led to efforts by numerous governments to improve health and well-being through the implementation of various policies for health and welfare.

One of the major areas for the last 200 or so years has been the need to address the overwhelming effects of poverty on health and the so-called class divide that results in individuals from lower socio-economic groups being disadvantaged in terms of health and mortality.

The development of a more structured welfare state and the birth of the NHS

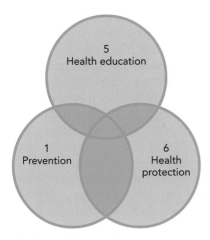

Figure 4.11 Tannahill model

went a long way to addressing these issues. However, 30 years ago a more definite link was found by Sir Douglas Black and his committee, and poverty, ill health and the relationship with social class entered the political arena as a major health challenge. Have a look at the following chronology, which traces the developments since that time:

1979 The Black report; Conservative government; inequality between classes, income and access to health services.

1980–90 Health gaps widen even more.

1986 WHO publishes in the Ottawa Charter five key strategies for the promotion of health.

1986 Development of HPP initiative.

1992 Publication of 'The health of the nation', Conservative response to widening gaps in health inequality.

1997 Labour government returns; commissions Sir Donald Acheson to carry out an independent inquiry into inequalities in health; findings show a decrease in mortality rate across all social groups but health gap has widened still further due to poverty.

1997 Publication of 'Saving lives: our healthier nation', which built on 1992's 'The health of the nation'.

1998 Introduction of health action zones in areas of deprivation, to address the causes of ill health.

2001 Health inequalities named as one of seven priorities in the 2002 Comprehensive Spending Review.

2002 Consultation document 'Tackling health inequalities' published.

2004 Publication of 'Choosing health: making healthy choices easier'.

2005 Department of Work and Pensions report on link between poverty and social class.

2007 Office for National Statistics reports on low-birth-weight babies and the link to mortality in mothers from lower socio-economic groups.

Since these reports there has been an emerging picture from writers in the field of health inequality that shows extensively that gender, geographical location within the UK, social class and ethnicity all have an impact on how long an individual lives and how healthy they are.

Far from being just a combination of our genetic make-up and lifestyle (though these are important), our health or ill health is linked to social characteristics (health inequality is discussed further in Chapters 3 and 5).

Inequality amongst women and the relationship to their social class have been reported by Brian Johnson and Ann Langford in *Health Statistics Quarterly*, Summer 2009, 42, 6–21. They reported the mortality rates in women aged 25–59 in 2001–3, revealing that those in the least advantaged socio-economic group were twice as likely to die at a younger age than women in the most advantaged class.

In addition to gender differences, where we live in the UK also brings inequality. The variation between rates of 'not good health' between government office regions in England shows a clear north–south divide, with the lowest rates of 'not good health' in the South east and East (6 per cent) and the highest in the North east and North west (10 per cent).

The Acheson report of 1998 further highlighted how ethnic groups also suffered from inequality with respect to health. The report suggests that there is a link with social class and the socio-economic status of these groups, the higher incidence of unemployment in these groups compared with the white population as being a major contribution. Income and poverty again provide a striking link to inequality. In addition, racism has been cited as a cause of unequal access to health services, together with differential treatment by staff. This has come under scrutiny in the last 20 years or so. With the promotion of anti-discriminatory practice and developing awareness of the need for equality and diversity in the public services, this has led to the oppression of marginalised groups being challenged and a tranche of policies and laws to empower such groups has become more widespread (see Chapter 3).

There have been numerous efforts by the WHO and UK governments to address inequality and, as a result, health promotion is a firm fixture in the quest for improving health. The fact that it remains on government agendas as a target for reduction would seem to imply that we are losing the battle and we would do well to address some of the reasons put forward for this.

Reasons for nonconformity to health advice; the link to the health locus of control

There is overwhelming evidence that a number of lifestyle choices we make with respect to smoking, drinking and whether or not we exercise carry with them enormous risks to our health. Yet we continue to meet individuals, either in a social or a professional capacity, who fail to heed advice. Why is this?

It is important to try to understand the reasons for nonconformity in order to structure the way in which health promotion will have to be delivered. As individuals, we all learn and approach life in individual and unique ways and our beliefs about health and lifestyle are no exception.

At the outset of this chapter, we acknowledged that an individual's concept of health is shaped by their beliefs and the interpretation they place on their feelings and experiences, and the way we behave with respect to our health can be negative or positive. If we believe we can have a certain amount of control over our health, then we may make more of an effort to make changes to reduce our risks. This positive view of health means that such individuals will take up the screening procedures on offer and will take responsibility for their own health. Their positive attitude towards controlling those factors that are within their power will go a long way in preserving their health. On the other hand, if some individuals adopt a fatalistic attitude to health and believe that external factors are more potent than any change that can be made, this can lead to a negative attitude with respect to health behaviour. You may have come across individuals who refuse to give up smoking despite having breathing impairment simply because they 'might get run over by a bus tomorrow'.

This is referred to by Azjen and Fishbein (1991) as the locus of control and describes the extent to which they feel responsible for their own health, or the extent to which an individual feels their health is influenced or controlled by others or fate or 'God's will'.

Matarazzo (1984) referred to these as 'health protective' and 'health impairing' behaviours. In any such behaviour our beliefs about what is likely to happen to us will be central to the way in which we behave, and in order to find effective ways of altering those beliefs the health models we have looked at in the first part of the chapter go a long way to addressing this. Further research has tried to understand why people behave in this way. For example, a willingness to change behaviour is influenced by whether or not we fully accept responsibility for that behaviour. Weinstein (1984) proposed the term 'unrealistic optimism' as a reason for why individuals continue to practise unhealthy behaviours and this is due to inaccurate perceptions of the risk.

Some of the points made in this theory follow in Activity 4.6.

Activity 4.6

Weinstein determined that 'unrealistic optimism' was due to the following experiences and belief:

- lack of personal experience of the problem
- the belief that the problem is preventable by individual action
- the belief that if the problem has not already appeared it is unlikely to in the future
- the belief that the problem is an infrequent occurrence.

You have a client who is overweight and at risk of developing blood pressure problems and diabetes. She has experienced shortness of breath and palpitations and you are concerned that this might be the development of health problems. Using the four statements above, what sort of responses might she give you as a reason for not losing weight?

Figure 4.12

In your answer to Activity 4.6, possibly you had something along these lines:

- **Lack of personal experience of the problem** 'A lot of my friends are overweight and they have never experienced this' or 'All my family have had weight problems due to glands but they were okay'.

- **The belief that the problem is preventable by individual action** 'I will just have to take it easy when I exercise in the future'.

- **The belief that if the problem has not already appeared it is unlikely to in the future** 'It was just a one-off and I am sure it will disappear as quickly as it came'.

- **The belief that the problem is an infrequent occurrence** As above or 'If it happens again I will try and change my diet a bit'.

The health belief model (Becker, 1984) makes the suggestion that the individual's own analysis of the cost and benefits of changing will influence whether or not they do so. For example, if change is to occur the following factors need to be in place:

- There must be an incentive to change or a perceived gain.

- The individual feels threatened in some way due to experience of ill health at the moment and the seriousness of the ongoing condition.

- The individual believes that the change will be beneficial.

- The individual feels able to carry out the change.

Attitude and behaviour change is difficult to achieve and with respect to health behaviour can be a source of consternation for many health professionals.

The dependence upon so many factors needs to be taken into account if any health message is to be effective. For example, the influence of peers, the media and advertising as well as how the person views their own health are all powerful influences on whether change will occur.

The cultural and social world the person inhabits will have a marked effect on whether or not a health message is going to be successful but, as we saw previously, any strategy adopted needs to take a holistic view of the issue.

Appealing to the individual to change needs to be strengthened by activity to support the change, factual information about costs and benefits, and a skilled strategy to actually ensure the message is put across in a meaningful way.

Health promotion campaigns and their impact

Health promotion campaigns can so easily fail if the method used to communicate the message is received poorly or poorly delivered. Mass media are used widely in an effort to get the message to the greatest number of people. For instance, you will be aware of the campaign to 'Quit smoking' that bombarded TV and billboards with messages highlighting the risk of this behaviour. Our screens were filled with people dying from smoking-related disease. In addition, there was a move to ban the advertising of cigarettes in cinemas, and cigarette companies' sponsorships of various sporting events were reviewed. Primary health care workers worked towards the government target to reduce deaths from smoking by engaging with smoking-cessation methods such as clinics, support groups and aids such as patches and gum being offered for those who seriously wanted to quit. Health campaigns in schools addressed the problem amongst young people and the message about the effects of smoking was clearly delivered via leaflets and posters and in GP surgeries and hospitals.

Everywhere we looked there was something to remind us of the need to quit, and finally a ban on smoking in public places was enforced. But what has been the impact of this campaign on the health of the nation?

The Times on 1 July 2007 reported a fall in heart attack hospital admissions since the smoking ban. Researchers estimated a 2.4 per cent reduction in heart attack emergency admissions to hospital (or 1,200 fewer admissions) in the 12 months following the ban. Billed as a 'well-conducted study', the report hails a clear association between the smoking ban and a decrease in admissions due to heart attacks, although it makes the point that it is not possible to say how much is due to people giving up smoking or due to less exposure to second-hand smoke.

We fully understand the associated risks of smoking and the link to heart attacks, although we need to exercise caution. There are additional reasons for a person to be at risk of heart attack such as poor diet and being overweight. But changes to lifestyle and diets can reasonably reduce that risk.

The study carried out by researchers from the University of Bath was funded by the Department of Health's Policy Research Programme and published in the *British Medical Journal* (Sims *et al.*)

The results show that between 2000 and 2008 there was a decrease in the number of emergency admissions for heart attacks and this decrease accelerated from around 2002 with a greater reduction in older age groups.

The conclusions put forward were that the rates of hospital heart attacks have been falling since 2000, and since the smoking ban the rates have fallen by an estimated additional 2.4 per cent. The researchers suggest that it has shown a clear association between the smoking ban and a decreased rate of hospital admissions. They suggest that further research to ascertain the long-term effects of the smoking ban and quitting be undertaken.

The inference from this study is that the approach by the Department of Health and the government to ban smoking has had an effect on reducing the number of heart attacks due to smoking. We can take this a little further. Our extensive knowledge about reduction of osteoporosis in older women through the link to exercise is well known. In addition, we know that if we reduce our weight we can have more impact on lowering our blood pressure. This information links well with HPP, and the information that is made available to us through health promotion guidance provided by health professionals. But is it that simple? What proportion of these figures (in the case of the reduction in heart attacks) and of the lowering of osteoporosis and blood pressure can be attributed to individual choice as much as government intervention? The HPP agenda can make available a number of changes in social and environmental arenas but we do need to consider that the individual does have a choice ultimately as to whether they actually avail themselves of that change.

As Fuchs in Terris (1980) stated, 'The greatest potential for improving health lies in what we do and don't do for ourselves. The choice is ours'.

This may well be true but as we showed earlier, sometimes it is the whole issue of choice or the lack of it that makes it impossible for some people to make a change to the healthy option.

Health promotion, then, is as complex as the attempts to define health. Looking further than just individual choice and behaviour to individual circumstances with respect to deprivation in terms of environment and economic factors is the key to improving health. We are aware that while personal choice is a major factor in health promotion, the implementation of healthy public policy and the means to reduce inequalities in reducing ill health are also crucial. A range of interventions, modifications and access to health services is a way forward with respect to empowering individuals to make the right informed choice.

Summary

In this chapter we have addressed the concepts of health and showed how the number of ways in which we define health and explain ill health have led to a number of models emerging. The models or approaches – medical, behaviour change, educational, client-centred, empowerment, radical or social change – provided us with some good descriptions about what health professionals actually do, and the more in-depth models of practice – namely the theoretical frameworks that emerge from these approaches – can help us to predict and organise our knowledge into a more usable format.

The chapter addressed the ways in which government has been reducing health inequalities and promoting health, and you are asked to look at Chapters 3 and 5 for more on this. The connection between health and poverty has informed much of what is termed HPP or healthy public policy and is of global concern.

The encouragement of individuals to look to ways of reducing ill health by addressing lifestyle issues and making changes, and the difficulties inherent in these changes due to external and internal influences, were also highlighted. As health professionals we are aware that health promotion is about choice but also about the social responsibility of the welfare system to make that choice easier for individuals who are disadvantaged.

Summary assignment

Produce a resource for your work placement which includes the following:

■ the role and purpose of public health promotion

■ statistics to evidence the positive and negative influences on health and the relationship between social inequalities and health.

Using a range of appropriate bibliographic sources, research an area of public health promotion and present to your peers a small-scale health promotion campaign.

Evaluate the outcomes and the success of your campaign.

Set aims and objectives in a written report in order to measure the extent to which your audience has learned.

Justify and rationalise the models of health and health promotion you are using to deliver your campaign.

References

Acheson, D. (1998) *Independent Inquiry into Inequalities in Health*, HMSO, London.

Azjen, I. and Fishbein, M. (1980) *Understanding Attitudes and Predicting Social Behaviour*, Prentice-Hall, New Jersey.

Becker, H. M. (1984) *The Health Belief Model and Personal Health Behaviour*, Slack, New Jersey.

Blaxter, M. (1983) *Health*, Polity Press.

Calnan, M. (1987) *Health and Illness: the Lay Perspective*, Tavistock, London.

Department of Health and Social Security (1976) *Prevention and Health: Everybody's Business: a Reassessment of Public and Personal Health*, HMSO, London.

Eisenberg, L. (1977) 'Disease and illness. Distinctions between professional and popular ideas of sickness', *Culture, Medicine and Psychiatry*, **1**(1), 9–23.

Ewles, L. and Simnett, I. (1999) *Promoting Health: a practical guide to health education*, 4th edn, Harcourt, Edinburgh.

Helman, C. (2001) *Culture, Health and Illness*, 4th edn, Arnold, London.

Herzlich, C. (1973) *Health and Illness*, Academic Press, London.

Johnson, B. and Langford, A. (2009) 'Social inequalities in adult female mortality in 2001 and 2003 by the National Statistics socio-economic classification', *Health Statistics Quarterly*, Summer, **42**, 6–21.

McKeown, T. (1979) The role of Medicine: Dream, Mirage or Nemesis. US Princeton University Press.

McKinley, J. B. (1992) 'Health promotion through healthy public policy: the contribution of complementary research method', *Canadian Journal of Public Health*, supp 1, March–April, 811–19.

Matarazzo, J. D. (1984) 'Behavioural immunogens', in B.L. Hammonds and C.J. Scheirer (eds), *Psychology and Health,* American Psychological Association, Washington DC.

Moonie, N. (2005) AS level for OCR Health and Social Care. UK Heinemann

Naidoo, J. and Wills, J. (2009) Foundation for Health Promotion. UK Bailliere Tindall.

Seedhouse, D. (1986 and 2001) *Health. The Foundations for Achievement,* 1st and 2nd edns, John Wiley and Sons, Chichester.

Sims, M., Maxwell, R., Bauld, L. and Gilmore, A. (2010) 'Short-term impact of smoke-free legislation in England: retrospective analysis of hospital admissions for myocardial infarction', *British Medical Journal,* **340**, 2161.

Tannahill, A. (1985) 'What is health promotion?' *Health Education Journal,* **44**(4), 167–8.

Townsend, P. and Davidson, N. (eds) (1982) *Inequalities in Health. The Black Report,* Penguin Books, Harmondsworth.

Weinstein, N. D. (1987) 'Unrealistic optimism about susceptibility to health problems: conclusions from a community-wide sample', *Journal of Behavioral Medicine,* **10**, 481–500.

World Health Organization (1946) 'Constitution: Basic documents', WHO, Geneva.

World Health Organization (1977) 'Health for all by the year 2000', WHO, Geneva

World Health Organization (1984) 'Health promotion: a discussion document on the concept and principles', WHO Regional Office for Europe, Copenhagen.

World Health Organization (1986) 'Ottawa Charter for health promotion', WHO, Geneva.

Sociology, politics and policy of health care

The emergence of the term 'empowerment' has come about due to changes in law and policy- and decision-making processes within organisations. This has led to a more client-centred approach being adopted. Students of health and social care need to appreciate how legislation affects the provision of services and their practice. This chapter will show how sociological frameworks have an effect on the legislative framework and the policy-making process. The links to empowerment and informed choice in decision-making processes will also be addressed. This will be accomplished through a historical overview of the work of early sociologists and the development of the welfare system.

Learning outcomes

By the end of the chapter you will be able to:

■ show how early sociological theorists' work has led to the development of the social welfare system

■ show how social policy is made and driven by the legal process and politics

■ demonstrate knowledge of welfare and health care service reform through history from Poor Laws, charity organisations and through Beveridge to today

■ start to apply law to practice in health and social care and demonstrate how clients are empowered in this process.

Early sociological theory and its impact on the development of the social welfare system

As a student of health and social care you will inevitably meet with various types of legislation under which you are bound to work and function. This has come about through various changes over the years to social policy and welfare. The impact of the legislative framework and policy-making process are all the result of studying the way in which our society functions and we shall look at this first by making the distinction between what we understand sociology to mean and how that differs from the term 'social policy'.

Simply put, if we think about the discipline of sociology, then social policy is actually a subject under that umbrella.

As a scientific study, sociology explores the experience of human social life in groups and societies and starts to address questions such as the 'What?' and 'Why?' of how society works. Social policy, on the

Figure 5.1

other hand, addresses the questions of 'Why?' and 'How?' of society and government. In a study of social policy we are interested in the responses of governments to the needs of society and the solution of social problems and ills.

So we might say that social policy draws from sociology an understanding of welfare in a social context. In trying to make improvements to lifestyles and society we need to understand how societies function and this is where we draw upon the scientific theory available to us.

Activity 5.1

Take a look at this picture and write down what you see.

Figure 5.2 What do you see?

Now ask for others' views of the picture.

Chances are that some may have seen a picture of a rabbit while others have seen a picture of a duck. If you are familiar with the picture and have studied it before, you may well see both. What the activity is trying to get you to see is that there are several ways in which we can look at things and we should never take anything for granted. Sociology is like that. It looks in detail at the things we tend to take for granted and attempts to explain those things and find other meanings.

What are the sorts of things we do take for granted?

When you got up this morning, perhaps other members of your family greeted you. You may have settled down to breakfast and then got ready to take the bus or train to college or work. You may have taken your younger sibling or your own child to school and maybe stopped at the supermarket. That's all normal, isn't it? Family life, education, work and the way we obtain our food are all acceptable arrangements for how we live and are 'normal'. Well, think about this for a moment.

Not too far from you there are people who live alone and not in a family group. Others may not have enough to eat and there may be some who perhaps do not go out to work because there are no jobs for them to do.

Figure 5.3 Family

That's just in your neighbourhood. What about when we look at the way in which people live in other parts of the world? You may have seen the advertisements on television asking us to give just £2.00 per month to help a child in another country to have fresh water or an educational opportunity. For these children, collecting water by walking for miles each day is 'normal'. Education is not a given and many children miss out on this opportunity.

In other countries, family life is set up in different ways. In communes, for instance, children 'belong' to the whole group and not just to their biological parents. In a kibbutz, children are more likely to be independent of their parents and live separately from them in age-grouped rooms.

Figure 5.4 Poverty

What emerges for a sociologist studying the differences in behaviour of various groups are the differences in beliefs, values and what is considered to be normal or the 'norm'. The things we believe and value in our own society such as the importance of education and family life are not necessarily shared in other societies.

What it is like to live in our world and the decisions made about how we all should live may differ according to where we live and the circumstances in which we live. We cannot take anything for granted.

Beliefs, values and norms

You have probably come across the word 'culture'. One definition of culture is a way of life. It is a view of how we ought to live in a society and varies across the globe. Within a culture we share a set of beliefs, values and norms (see Chapter 3 for further information on this).

Cultures are not fixed entities and change over time, and in larger societies there are likely to exist 'subcultures'. Think about our own society, for example. Young people share beliefs, values and norms with respect to dress, language and music that may be very different from those of their parents.

What are beliefs, values and norms? Lets remind ourselves.

Beliefs are the opinions we hold about the nature of the world in which we live. For example, they give us guidance as to how we are expected to treat others.

Figure 5.5

Values define something as being good and important and worth striving for. It is an idea that helps us to shape our behaviour. So in our society, achievement in education may be seen as a thing worth having and of value to us.

Norms, on the other hand, are the ways in which it is socially acceptable to behave and are linked therefore to values. The child in school who misbehaves, truants and generally does not respond to the education environment is seen not to value education and there are laws in place to deal with this behaviour. Our legal system has seen fit to make schooling compulsory, such is the strength of that value.

In this way the norms by which we conduct ourselves directly reflect the values. However, norms and values differ in societies around the world and somebody from another culture or society may not necessarily share what we value, and this then accounts for the differences we have in our opinions and views on certain things.

Sociologists believe that norms and values act as the binding force for societies and that shared norms and values are essential if societies are to function efficiently and cooperatively. What would it be like to live in a world where groups in a society decided that the value of life was not as important as the acquisition of property and started to kill their neighbours to gain access to homes and belongings? There would be disorder and chaos, and we have experienced this in some societies where political unrest occurs.

Alongside beliefs, norms and values we also have social roles and identity. We believe that people in society should act in a specific way, and deviation from that way is not expected. For example, if I were teaching you and spent all my time filing my nails and allowing the class to act in an unruly manner you would rightly be somewhat aggrieved. As a teacher I am expected to behave in a manner commensurate with the given norms and values of that role. We occasionally see newspaper headlines about mothers who have left their children alone while they holiday abroad or go out clubbing at night. As that does not meet with our expected role of a mother we are shocked by this. We all have a number of different roles in our lives and most of the time we work around these in a successful manner. However, sometimes we reach a crisis point or a role conflict and there is a clash. In this case we may find we need to choose our course of action and determine which role is the most important. If I am working and my child is ill do I go home and care for the child or is my work more important? My values and norms are likely to come into play here.

How does this fit into the study of sociology and why should we bother with it? Let's recap:

■ Sociology is about the study of the world and the various societies and their functions within it.

■ The way in which sociologists study the world is by looking at the beliefs, values and norms within cultures.

■ The different cultures and subcultures within societies share beliefs, values and norms and act in social roles accordingly.

■ Social roles sometimes conflict, causing us to choose a course of action that may identify clearly how much we value something.

Societies have guidelines that determine ways of behaving and provide us with information about how we need to act in

certain situations. These guidelines are made up of the beliefs, values and norms that we have learned through a process of socialisation.

Activity 5.2

Read the following examples, then answer the questions.

At the end of a school day you observe two children with adults. The first child smiles when she sees her mother and talks in an animated way about her day at school. The mother takes hold of her hand and then offers to carry her bag. She hands her a drink and they walk off together, talking and laughing and waving at other children as they leave the school playground.

The second child by contrast is not greeted by the adult. The child merely sidles up to the parent, who then barks an order about being 'quick'. They march off the premises with no comments and the child is then reprimanded for being late out of school. You notice the child is not smiling and the parent is walking ahead.

1. Describe the differences between the two scenes and hypothesise as to the type of adults the children will be when they grow up.

2. What sort of behaviour is the second child learning from the parent.

Of course, our examples are simplistic ones. You may have said you might expect the second child to grow up to be intolerant and short-tempered. They may have little time for the niceties of life, whereas the first child may prove to be happier and possibly better adjusted. We might also expect her to do well at school since it appears her parent does take an interest in her. This form of learning from one's parents is termed 'primary socialisation', and those who are close to us will give us our first set of guidelines as to behaviour. Later a secondary process takes place when, at school and through the media and peers, we learn about social rules and how our own society expects us to behave.

We all go through this learning process and it is a powerful way in which societies can operate on a level that is functional and non-chaotic.

We learn by copying the behaviour of those we see in the society around us and by adopting the beliefs, values and norms of those we live with. When we behave in a way that does not conform to society's expectations, then we have to expect consequences and sometimes punishment. We may indulge in a criminal act or just behave oddly; in either case, society deals with us in a way that ensures control is maintained.

Social control may be either formal or informal. Formal social control is maintained by the penal system in a country or society and rules and laws are laid down and enforced when criminal acts occur.

Informal social control refers to the expectations of behaviour that may incur the disapproval of others should we break the code in some way. For instance, it is not a legal requirement to wear black at a funeral but failure to do so may be regarded as disrespectful by some individuals.

The study of sociology, then, has helped us to recognise that the world in which we live cannot be taken for granted and that we learn how to behave in various cultures by adopting the beliefs, values and norms of those around us. Failure to do so results in control measures being taken, in order to ensure the society can continue to function in a stable and non-chaotic manner.

Sociological perspectives

Let's now turn our attention to some differing perspectives about how the world should be studied. For simplicity we shall focus on two opposing forms of theory generation. (For more information on sociological theory you are advised to access texts such as those suggested by your lecturer or in the reading list at the end of the chapter.)

Functionalist sociology: the structural approach

The term 'sociology' was first used by Auguste Comte (1798–1857).

He approached the study of society in a 'scientific' way and believed that it could be compared with the study of the human body. He was therefore interested in examining the parts of society – the family, education, the economy, religion and other structures – in order to determine how they all contribute to maintaining that society. The terms used to describe this perspective is 'functionalism' but you may also see it referred to as 'structuralism' or 'positivism'.

From Comte's point of view, society resembled a jigsaw puzzle with interdependent sections working and fitting together and fulfilling a variety of the functions necessary for the survival of society. The rules and regulations helped to organise society and its members by providing guidelines for behaviour in terms of roles and norms. Institutions such as family, the economy, the state and education were all seen to be central to the structure of society. The unity of the society could only be sustained when all the members within it subscribed to the value system of that society. Without it the society would cease to function.

A most interesting theory with respect to the function of illness was put forward by the sociologist Talcott Parsons (1902–79). (Cited in Lawson et al.) His theory analysed sickness as a social role that needed to be managed if society was to function in an ordered way. If too many individuals declared themselves sick, then they would be unable to fulfil their usual roles for the good of society and this would lead to a 'dysfunctional' society, a society that was disrupted. The person who took on 'the sick role' would need to have this role legitimised by the medical profession and this would then lead to them being released temporarily from their usual societal roles. The 'sick person' would also have to commit to the medical profession's treatment and get better quickly. So, according to Parsons, this was a regulatory role, and one in which the function of the role was to ensure that not everybody opted to undertake this role.

Activity 5.3

What are your views on the 'sick role'? Can you see any difficulties with it?

Whatever your own view of this, there has been criticism of this role. Some believe that conflict between the medical profession and the patient may make this role a more difficult one to get into. We trust the medical profession here to act in the interest of the patient, which may not always be the case. There is also a difficulty with long-term and chronic sickness. When the person is not going to recover, where does compliance with the sick role and the regulations about commitment to getting better fit in this case? Finally, the power of the medical profession to legitimise the illness has been criticised. We are saying here that in order to be sick we need a medical practitioner to say we are.

Simply put, functionalism views society as a collection of interrelated parts that make up a unified functioning society. This unified whole is based upon shared beliefs, values and norms of the individual within it.

This perspective further makes the following points:

■ The various parts that make up the world have a cause-and-effect relationship; for example, we might say that poverty is caused by unemployment.

■ Social reality can be measured by using scientific methods such as experimental research, surveys, historical sources and statistics.

■ Behaviour is observable and predictable since it is governed by underlying causal laws.

The last point is an interesting one. We all believe we have choice and act according to that choice. However, what this sociological school of thought believes is that our behaviour is regular and can be predicted to a certain extent.

Let's think about choice of partner. In our society the individual makes the choice about who they will spend time with and perhaps marry. In other societies the choice

is taken away from the individual and marriages are arranged. But sociologists who have studied this particular choice have found that individuals choose their partner from a limited, select few people. Both will probably have very similar backgrounds, and in terms of education they will perhaps be of a similar type and have the same values and attitudes. In other words, choice is fairly limited.

Comte's theoretical perspective then describes a way of piecing together the society in which we live by testing the structures, such as the family, employment, education and welfare, and showing how all these all work together as a whole and function to make a society.

Émile Durkheim (1858–1917), like Comte, also believed that society could and should be studied with the same scientific detachment as scientists studied the natural world.

He created the term 'social facts' to describe phenomena that are not bound to actions of individuals but which exist in and of themselves. He believed these social facts were external to the individual but had constraining influences on individuals. Such constraints are not recognised as such since, as we mentioned earlier, we assume we are acting out of choice rather than coercion – for example, punishment for crime, rejection for unacceptable behaviour. In essence what Durkheim was saying was that there is more to any society than the actions of the individuals who make up that society. His interest was in what 'glued' society together and prevented it from dissolving into chaos. Durkheim was, in fact, one of the first sociologists to explain the existence and quality of different parts of society by addressing what function they fulfilled.

The perspective first posited by Comte and developed by Durkheim and others shows how society and the rules or laws in which they operate constrain and control individuals and maintain social stability. Just as the parts of a body work together for the good of the individual, society serves a similar purpose, with the structures within it all working together for the good of the society. The functionalists consider order and stability of society as the normal state of things and this can only be achieved through shared goals and direction.

Positivism in brief

Just as the body is made up of parts, so too is society, and the parts all function together to form a coherent and working whole.

Large groups rather than just individuals are examined to find out how they function.

There is a cause-and-effect relationship with how we function.

Society is a giant jigsaw puzzle and we all play a part or have a role in that puzzle.

Individuals are passive in society and shaped by it.

The social action theories

At the other end of the perspective we have sociologists who view society and the study of it in a different way. They baulk at the use of the 'scientific method' to study and understand social behaviour and individuals, and have thus come up with different ways of researching society. They believe that the positivistic approach to sociology and its assumptions that society shapes the behaviour of individuals through socialisation is too simplistic. Rather they view the individual's personality with its unique experience as

being an important entity in how society is structured. They emphasise the importance of underlying meanings in order to understand social interaction.

Their preferences are to look at how people act in society in order to understand why they behave in the ways they do, so a preferred method of study would be interviews and questionnaires that can get to the heart of what people think and feel. There are a number of theories under this particular 'umbrella' of social action, namely symbolic interactionism, ethnomethodology and phenomenology. We shall look at the first two.

Symbolic interactionism posits a simple set of assumptions about how we come to know about social phenomena. These sociologists cannot agree that social interaction can be studied in the same way as we would study natural sciences since we are not dealing with inanimate objects but living, thinking beings. These living beings have a consciousness and are unique in their actions and the way they interpret what is happening to them. They cannot merely be observed and then have meaning attached to what has been seen. There needs to be a deeper level of study in order to understand why the person carried out the action they did in the way they did it. Let's look at an example. We all know that smoking damages health and can kill us or at least seriously damage the quality of our lives due to respiratory problems. So why do individuals continue to smoke when there is such a lot of help to quit?

Graham's (1993) study of women from a low socio-economic background showed a high level of spending on cigarettes in young mothers. From a positivist point of view such behaviour could be viewed as irrational simply because it goes against health advice and also good economic sense.

But by adopting a symbolic interactionist stance, Graham was interested in interpreting these women's actions according to their beliefs and meanings. The findings revealed that smoking offered the women 'time out' and a way of coping with their lives, 'a way of temporarily escaping without leaving the room'

Figure 5.6 Smoking and Graham's study

(Graham, 1993). Rather than an irrational act, the smoking provided the women with an opportunity to carry on with their caring roles in a way with which they could cope. The economic loss and the health issues were secondary to the need to find ways of carrying on in a daily role in the best possible way for these young women – and, in fact, for their children. Rather than being irrational, there was a meaning attached to their actions.

The focus in this perspective, then, is on the individual and not on society as a whole. The meanings attached to behaviour are what the person says they are and not what we assume them to be.

The actual term 'symbolic interactionism' refers to the use of the symbols by which we convey meanings. If we understand the symbols, we can understand the meanings conveyed by the 'actors' or the members of the society in which we are involved.

The assumptions in this theory are that:

1. The individual and society are inseparable because we are only human in the social context.

2. Humans act on the basis of meanings that we give to objects and events that happen rather than simply reacting to external stimuli. We are active and not passive.

3. All meanings come out of interactions and are not simply present at the outset. So meanings are developed and changed within interactive situations rather than being fixed.

4. The methodology of symbolic interactionism means that the sociologist must become part of that which they seek to investigate. So they need to grasp the actor's view of social reality. This is achieved through the use of observational methods and participant observation studies.

One of the major theorists of symbolic interactionism was G. H. Mead (1863–1931), an American philosopher who reflected on language and meaning. Key to the process of interacting is the 'symbol' – something that stands for something else. Words are symbols; non-verbal gestures are symbols. Mead was interested in the way in which we rely on symbols to make sense of all interactions between humans.

Any interaction involving an exchange of symbolic content was seen as a means of both creating and maintaining society and societal institutions.

Mead's work focused on the socialisation of children and the way in which they learn by imitation and then by acting the roles they see, finally coming to a sense of self and how this self differs from others. You will be aware of how influential this work has been in the education field.

Max Weber (1864–1914) is also considered influential here. Although he subscribed to the notion of the presence of social structures, he argued that they were created through social actions. Weber's approach was an attempt to try to bridge the views of positivist sociology and what he considered to be the extreme forms of interactionism.

According to Weber, what we experience as social reality is characterised by the presence of consciousness and because of this we ascribe meanings to the situations around us. The meanings we attach to what we experience will influence our behaviour. Thus what I experience about an event may be vastly different from your experience because it will depend a lot on my own beliefs and values and how they might differ from yours.

Figure 5.7

Meanings therefore are partly determined by cultural norms and shaped by personal experiences of the people involved. This means that to understand social behaviour, observation is fine but it is not the whole story. We need to interpret the underlying meanings and motives. Weber's approach introduced the method of 'empathetic liaison', in which the observer tries to place himself in the actor's position. You may have heard the expression 'walking in somebody else's shoes' – this really was what Weber was trying to establish with his 'verstehen' (meaning: 'to understand') approach.

For social action theorists, the social order of society is dependent upon people behaving in a common-sense way. Ethnomethodologists, however, take this a step further back. For them the aim of sociology should not be merely to identify and record the meanings that people give to situation but to understand how they came to generate those meanings in the first place.

Harold Garfinkel and Aaron Circourel are influential ethnomethodologists who have developed this idea. Garfinkel, in fact, coined the term. They are interested in the process of how meanings are developed and the ways in which people in society come to view their world. They studied the speech exchanges in which the participants are involved in trying to make sense of what others are trying to say. In this way it is possible to come to an understanding of how people in interactive situations come to see what the other person is meaning. One of the things Garfinkel did was to describe and show the underlying assumptions about social interaction that we take for granted and to expose the 'rules' of such interaction of which we may have been unaware.

Have you ever answered the telephone and then not been able to hear the person speaking at the other end? It makes for an impossible situation and in the end you may get so exasperated you slam the receiver down. What are the rules of using the telephone? Social interaction when you

---

Activity 5.4

When you ask somebody 'How are you?' are you then surprised if they go on and tell you in great detail about their ailments and aches and pains?

Think about this. We usually expect nothing more than 'Oh, I'm fine,' the unwritten rule being that the purpose of the question is to interact rather than necessarily to find out the answer. It is merely a common nicety.

Now think about the following:

■ using the telephone

■ why some people may not like using email or speaking to an answerphone

■ speaking to somebody who will not answer you or respond to you in any way.

Discuss these with colleagues and try to determine what the unwritten rules are in these situations and how they might be broken.

---

cannot see the other person means you adopt certain tones and general responses such as 'uh-huh', 'umm', 'yes', 'okay' to indicate that you are still listening. In a face-to-face conversation you might nod – but that cannot be seen on the telephone. We take these things for granted but nevertheless they are important in gauging our understanding of the person and the meanings they are trying to convey to us. This is what Garfinkel was trying to get us to understand.

In terms of email and answerphone, the lack of response may make it difficult for some to engage with this form of interaction. You are talking to a machine and in the absence of the niceties of normal conversation it can sometimes prove quite difficult to speak.

Finally, what about the person who merely stands and looks at you when you are speaking to them? Social interaction requires that we are acknowledged in some way, and an uncomfortable situation occurs when the other person is not 'playing ball' and 'batting back' the conversation occasionally. It can prove to be an embarrassing non-exchange of views.

Garfinkel's work showed that interactions are governed by rules that are usually not written or are unstated, and this makes the whole world of interaction somewhat 'precarious'.

Social action theories in brief

Society is studied through the individuals within it.

Social phenomena are explained from the perspective of the 'actors'.

These actors are motivated by human consciousness that is unique to each individual.

The meanings attached to actions cannot merely be assumed but must be interpreted.

Sociological theory seeks to identify the nature of how society and individuals exist in relation to each other. The beginning of social science has been one of the major developments of the 19th century, and the history of 19th-century politics, industry and trade is about the efforts of human beings to address the ills of the times.

We have looked somewhat cursorily at just a couple of perspectives with respect to the world of sociology but it is necessary to look further if we are to make the link to social policy and how these theories come to shape our society and the way in which we deal with the issues and problems that arise.

How social policy is made and driven by the legal process and politics

Through the study of sociology we can gain an appreciation of how social structures such as health and welfare, care, religions, the family and education systems all work together and function. Sociology can help us to shape social policy by engaging in research to address some of the social ills.

For example, sociologists study health, family and education, all subjects of interest within social policy. The difference lies in the focus of the study. Sociologists are more concerned with exploring society for its own sake, whereas the social policy researcher determines the impact of policy on how people live.

Alcock (1996) remarked upon the difference between social policy and sociology, stating that social policy was the 'specific focus upon the development and implementation of policy measures in order to influence the social circumstances of individuals, rather than the more general study of those social circumstances themselves'.

Political ideology is also influenced by sociological thought. Ideology, according to Walsh *et al.* (2000), is 'a relatively coherent package of ideas and values that affect how people define social welfare issues and formulate social policy'.

The above journey through sociological theory gives us insight into the political thinking of various groups of people in society and how this might influence the way in which they tackle some of the problems we meet. When we look at the history of the development of the welfare system we become aware of just how complex and diverse the society in which we live is. But the most important revelation is that it is the concept of 'need' that has created the welfare system as we know it. Consider for a moment what we mean by this.

Think about some of the things that make life worth living. You might answer that your family and your home life are the things you most value. Perhaps your job or your health come a close second. Whatever it is, think now about what you would do if these disappeared. Who would you turn to for help? Perhaps the benefits system might help you if you lost your job – but what if those systems were not in place?

As a health and social care student you will be sensitive to the needs of others and similar concerns by politicians led to the development of what we understand as the welfare system in the 1940s. But it takes time and changes constantly. Some recent changes to welfare policy have meant that health and social care are now managed in a devolved way: that is, England, Scotland, Wales and Northern Ireland have created their own responses to welfare needs.

Social policy, then, is about how we can help those in need informally at a local and voluntary level, and formally at government level through the development and application of welfare policy. Social policy has a practical value that will impact on the lives of everybody around us.

But how is social policy made? Let's look specifically at an example from health. The aims of any policy are to improve something or to ensure that something happens. Look at any policy in your organisation and you will see it provides a set of guidelines to which you as a care worker will adhere in order to achieve something. A policy, then, is an 'authoritative decision made within government that is intended to direct or influence the actions, behaviours or decisions of others ... These decisions can take the form of laws, rules and operational decisions' (Longest, 1998).

In terms of health care policy, we would expect it to be a statement of intent adopted by the government on behalf of our society with the aim of improving the health and welfare of the population.

A number of different models for policy development are in evidence. These are:

Institutional politics This refers to the interaction between parliament, local government, pressure groups and the media.

Pressure group politics You may be familiar with this type of model in which interest groups use their power and influence by means of campaigns to lobby and mobilise public support.

Policy knowledge and policy learning This uses a rational approach, including use of evidence from research and science experts. Ideas and empirical research and knowledge then lead to policy development. Examples are the Black report (1980) and the Acheson report (1998).

The Acheson report

Worsening social conditions and inequalities for both sexes persisted despite the aims of the NHS to reduce these.

The Acheson report (1998) was commissioned to address this.

Examples of the areas recommended for policy development included:

- Promote the well-being of older people.
- Improve the quality of their homes.
- Improve health and social care services.
- Improve mobility and independence within social contracts.

The making of policy and political ideology are inextricably linked and a knowledge of these is therefore a useful tool for change and for addressing the social ills we experience.

Welfare through history, from Poor Laws, charity organisations and through Beveridge to today

By looking at the history of the development of the welfare system in the UK, we place ourselves in a better position to understand some of the reasons for the policy decisions we see today. As we change as a society, our needs in terms of welfare also change. This is well demonstrated by looking at how the changes through history have influenced our care systems.

The Industrial Revolution transformed people's lives in the 18th century. Work, which had previously been of an agricultural nature and centred in and around the home, changed with the growth of industry and the invention of machines. This meant that work gradually moved from home working to factory-based production, together with the movement of people away from rural areas to what were to become city areas. This was to have a major impact on the way in

Figure 5.8 Image symbolising industrial revolution

which people lived. The move to towns inevitably brought with it housing shortages and overcrowding, leading to sanitation problems. People experienced impoverished conditions and these brought disease associated with poor living standards.

The government and political system of the time had little to do with welfare but it was becoming apparent that the Poor Laws of 1598 and 1601 were in need of reform. These laws had ensured help for the poor in the local parishes by the levy of a local tax and were an example of an early form of benefit. Those people who could work were classed as the 'able-bodied poor' and sent to work in the local workhouses. The elderly and disabled were given funds or put into the early hospital system or 'almshouses'.

In 1832 a Royal Commission to investigate the effects of the Poor Laws was set up and the subsequent report published in 1834 recommended a number of changes. Some of the changes reflected the thinking of the time and a blame culture existed. Addressing the causes of the problem, politicians of the time asked who was to blame for the poverty. Were the people at fault and therefore poor because of their own doing or were they poor as a result of circumstances? Unfortunately, this question remains with us today and we continually see government ministers posing similar questions.

In the 18th century, much harsher ways of dealing with those who found themselves in poverty were recommended. There was a general view prevailing that people should be made to work rather than rely on 'poor relief' or the benefits of the time.

If poor relief was really needed, then the workhouse would be the only option. These places were about to become more punitive in their approach in order to deter those 'choosing' this option. A much harsher regime could be expected and families would be split. Those people who were sick and therefore could not work were to go to separate institutions.

The view of the time placed the onus firmly on the individual but failed to address the societal issues. There were also major issues with health, and reforms such as the passing of the Public Health Act in 1848 were just the start of improving the lot of people in this century.

Major issues surrounded the difficulty society seemed to have with the poor in the parishes. Those who worked hard would be able to live normal lives and could be relied upon to help themselves. Unfortunately, the changes in society had led to a rise in unemployment and a lack of jobs for individuals due to the way in which work was now organised. Even if people wanted to work, it did not follow that there would be a job for them to do in the new industrial workplace.

Foundation Degree Health and Social Care

Activity 5.5

Think about this in terms of the changes you have seen in the last ten years. How might a situation develop in our time similar to that described above? Discuss with members of your group.

Figure 5.9 Impoverished conditions in the 18th century

Things today are changing at an exponential rate. Ten years ago mobile phones were becoming commonplace and our lives were revolutionised. Today we have smartphones on which we can access the internet, book flights, access weather reports and even read books. We can record our favourite television programme using our phone. Next year who knows what will be available to us?

This, of course, has had an impact on the sorts of lives we lead and inevitably the jobs we do – and the jobs for which education is training us. Unfortunately, as has become apparent through recent government reports, the change to our education system has not happened quickly enough and as a result we are falling behind our European neighbours in terms of the skills we possess to do the jobs of the future. Might not this have an impact on employment rates just as it did in the 18th century? (See Tomlinson Report, 2004 and Delores, 2003.)

The situation in the 18th century rather split the country and the politicians of the time. There were members of society who held the view that the poor were not

entitled to help by the state since they were the cause of their own poverty. On the other hand, the early socialists of the time felt that the state should take more responsibility for welfare. These differences in opinions led to reform being undertaken with charitable influence as well as state intervention.

One of the ways in which relief was offered was through the work of so-called 'friendly societies'. These led to self-help schemes and philanthropic action becoming major influences in the 19th century. The Victorians held strong beliefs that individuals should have responsibility for their own welfare and should make lifestyle choices that were of benefit to them.

Families with religious leanings offered social welfare as long as conformity to the religious views of the group were evident. The Frys, Cadburys and Rowntrees were some of the families who at the time were foremost in their provision of social welfare.

Figure 5.10 Problems still remain today

Activity 5.6

Research Rowntree and the Fabian Society and make notes on how they made an impact upon poverty. Sociology and social welfare texts will be good starting points.

96

Benjamin Seebohm Rowntree, born 7 July 1871, believed in helping the poor, and in order to obtain first-hand knowledge of their problems took to visiting their homes. In the 1860s his father Joseph carried out two major surveys into poverty in Britain. These studies were influential in making a distinction between what was to become known as primary and secondary poverty.

'Primary poverty' described those families whose earnings were not enough to enable them to buy minimum necessities.

Families suffering from secondary poverty had sufficient income but were spending some of that money on other things.

Seebohm Rowntree carried on his father's work and spent two years researching *Poverty, A Study of Town Life,* which was published in 1901

Rowntree's study and the statistical data on wages, working hours, nutrition, food, health and housing gave impetus to the welfare system as we now know it and supplied much-needed empirical evidence to support the need for change.

Reforms influenced by Rowntree included the Old Age Pensions Act (1908) and the National Insurance Act (1911). Together with his father, he implemented a series of reforms at his own company that led to the first minimum wage for workers.

The reforms he led reduced poverty and showed that the main cause of poverty in the 1930s was unemployment, whereas in the 1890s it had been low wages.

For more on Seebohm Rowntree, see www.spartacus.schoolnet.co.uk/ RErowntreeS.htm.

Alongside Rowntree, other social reformers believed that government needed to adopt a more visible role in dealing with social issues. The Charity Organisation Society looked for a range of ways in which to administer poverty relief and developed the role of 'social caseworker', perhaps a forerunner of today's social worker.

The Fabian Society, founded in 1884, was very much an intellectual movement concerned with the research, discussion and publication of socialist ideas. Reform was to be achieved by means of a new political movement in which the society's ideas would be brought to the attention of those with power through education and debate.

In 1895, founder members of the Fabians, Sidney and Beatrice Webb, Graham Wallas and George Bernard Shaw founded the London School of Economics (LSE) with funding provided by private philanthropy. It was believed that advancing socialist causes had to be accomplished through reform rather than revolution and the LSE was established to further the Fabian aim of bettering society. The Fabians and the LSE were soon to become two of the main influences on the British Labour Party and thus shaped the future of government in this country. Some 125 years later the Fabian Society is still influencing social policy debate and discussion (see www. fabians.org.uk).

The influence of the Fabians was to try to reform the rather liberal attitude of the people of the 19th century and bring about more socialist political views in order to encourage change. However, it was not until the 20th century that socialism became apparent. The government started to take a more active role in welfare and William Beveridge began to be known as a strong advocate for welfare reform. In 1919, Beveridge became director of the LSE, where he remained until 1937. The Fabians' thinking may well have influenced his views on poverty and reform, and in 1940 the government commissioned him to compile a report into the ways that Britain should be rebuilt after the Second World War.

His report of 1942 recommended that the government find ways of fighting the five 'Giant Evils' of 'Want, Disease, Ignorance, Squalor and Idleness'.

Beveridge believed that the basic causes of poverty were to be found in unemployment, ill health and old age and he sought to eradicate poverty by putting into place the kind of help people would require. The reforms he suggested were:

- The creation of a National Health Service to rid us all of **disease** (National Health Service Act 1946).

- Secondary education for all children, to address **ignorance**. The 1944 Education Act was passed.

- Better housing would deal with the **squalor** so evident in many areas around the country at the time: the Housing Act 1949.

- Jobs for everybody, to deliver us from **idleness** or unemployment. Unemployment benefit was introduced for the first time.

- National Insurance Act 1946 helped with maternity, widows' and sickness benefits. This and the other reforms below were to deal with **want**.

- The National Assistance Act 1948 was thought to be the way of eradicating poverty by introducing a social security system of benefits. This new system was a successor to the national insurance scheme set up by Lloyd George in 1911.

- The Family Allowance Act 1945 and the Children Act 1948 ensured that poverty was addressed in a more meaningful way for those on low incomes, and powers were given to child care officers to take children into care.

In 1945 the change of government led to the founding of the 'Welfare state' and Beveridge's reforms were put into place.

In the post-war years there appeared to be political support across the parties for the new system of health care, but all was not well and flaws were identified in the system. Between its inception in 1948 and 1979 some major structural changes were to be undertaken.

Although the National Health Service was upheld as a 'unique service', attempts to nationalise it met with opposition from the British Medical Association, who were in favour of private enterprise and private insurance schemes. A deal had to be made to enable the medical profession to be substantially rewarded for supporting the NHS in order for the government to be able to run such a system. The medical profession then exerted enormous power and were at liberty to run this health care system with government funding and backing.

Another difficulty emerged with what was known as a tripartite system. Three major services, the hospital, GP and community services, tended to run separately and there were issues with their coordination. For 25 or so years this lack of communication

between the three systems meant quality of patient care suffered. A further area of concern was the recruitment to many jobs in health care of migrant workers and the further development of a racist system and discrimination, leading to lack of opportunity for these people.

In the 1960s, social care was being looked at in some depth and care in the community was addressed. Large-scale institutions and the old legacies of asylums and workhouses – a legacy of the Poor Laws – were all beginning to come under the spotlight.

From the birth of the NHS in 1948 to the change of government in 1979, the NHS had been a wholly nationalised service. Care was free of charge and funded by the tax system. However, increasing concern over spending became a major government agenda and change was about to happen.

The period from 1979 to 1990 came to be known as the Thatcher years and the New Right was born. The rising demand for health services and the economic problems of the time led Margaret Thatcher, prime minister of the Conservative government elected in 1979, to look again at Beveridge's socialist ideals for health care.

According to the New Right, the welfare state had:

- taken away responsibility and incentive for people to look after their own health

- allowed lack of competition in the provision of services, leading to complacency with respect to quality of service

- taken away choice: people were supposed to be grateful for what they were given

- created a public demand for services, with costs burgeoning costs because people used the service simply because it was free.

Activity 5.7

Think about the above. Do you agree that we are dependent upon the care services and should be more responsible for our own health?

Discuss your thoughts with the group.

Your views in Activity 5.7 may well differ from those of others but whatever stance you take will have a great deal to do with your beliefs, values and norms. It is also likely that your own political leanings colour your views and we will revisit this later in the chapter when we look at how social policy is formed.

As far as the NHS was concerned major reform to its management was to be suggested.

At the time of the New Right, the development of internal markets, purchasers and providers came about as a result of the Griffiths Report, published in 1983. General managers became members of hospital staff with a remit to improve performance and efficiency in the service. Services such as catering, cleaning and portering were open to tender from outside companies. This caused major upset among medical professionals, who fiercely supported the view that general managers could not run a health service. (Griffiths himself had been a senior director of Sainsbury's; at the time the media put out headlines such as 'Patients are people, not tins of beans'.)

Griffiths was then asked to report on social care and in 1988 his report 'Community care: agenda for action' clearly identified the market system for care. The recommendations were to separate the purchasing and provision of care in local authorities. Local authorities would commission services but not be providers. They would be able to use voluntary and privately owned companies to provide services.

Figure 5.11 Intensive care in the community (www.CartoonStock.com)

The government White Paper 'Caring for people: community care in the next decade and beyond' (DoH, 1989) and the 'Working for patients' (1989) White Paper were forerunners to the NHS and Community Care Act (1990).

The 1991 challenges from the government at the time brought about the purchaser–provider split and this has been retained to the present time. Purchasers were given budgets to buy health care from providers such as hospital services and clinics or mental health organisations – basically whatever the patient needed. Some changes to the NHS structure were implemented through the 1990s but the way the services were funded remained the same. For example, in 1991–8 the purchasers were the 192 district health authorities (DHAs) and GP fundholders. The providers were the NHS trusts, who were independent of the DHAs. The choice of the provider lay with the DHAs.

In 2002, primary care trusts (PCTs) became the purchasers, with the NHS trusts being the providers. Today there are 152 PCTs who purchase services from NHS and Foundation Trusts as well as the independent sector.

In 1997 a new Labour government was elected and inevitably changes to the health care system were on the agenda. A decision was made at this time to remove the internal market and, although the purchaser–provider split was kept, fundholding was abolished. Primary care groups were established and became the purchasers of health care. The aims of these groups were to improve the health of the local population and to develop primary and community services.

A lot was happening at this time. Research showed a trend in the increase in elderly people in the population. This increase would inevitably lead to more health services being needed to ensure the care of an ageing population.

In addition, the government was also concerned with the health inequalities previously highlighted in the Black report of 1980 and largely ignored at the time by the Conservative government. The 'Health of the nation' White Paper published in 1992 by the Conservatives was later reviewed by the Labour government and became the 'Saving lives: our healthier nation' document of 1999.

In the years since the report by Black showed how poverty was a major link to poor health, little seems to have been effective in addressing the problem. In fact, our society has become more unequal in terms of wealth and income. Subsequent governments have worked to improve this state of affairs and the battle for reduced tax and changes to welfare policy still rage today.

In 1997 the Labour government commissioned Sir Donald Acheson to look at health inequalities in the UK. His 'Independent inquiry into inequalities in health' (1998) found that the gap between the social classes had widened further and despite death rates falling there still existed a link to poverty as being one of the major killers (see Chapter 3 for more on health inequality).

Another far-reaching White Paper that led to new legislation was 'The new NHS: modern, dependable', published in 1997. This recommended the following changes:

- GP fundholding to be abolished and replaced by primary care groups (PCGs) and primary care trusts (PCTS).

- The implementation of health improvement programmes within local health care to identify aims and objectives of care, and set targets and priorities for care at a local level. A later change of title to 'health improvement and modernisation plans' or HImPs highlighted the planning function that had become a major part of the process.

- A change to the funding system to enable more efficient working partnerships between the NHS and social services and local government.

- A statutory body, the Commission for Health Improvement, would monitor quality in the health service.

- The price of drugs was to be monitored.

- NHS tribunals to be set up to address fraud.

These recommendations became law in the Health Act of 1999.

Other changes brought about during the Labour government's years in office were the development of policies that sought to 'centralise' or standardise the services on offer. As a means of regulating the standards of care there was a drive to overcome the effects of the 'postcode lottery' and to try to reduce the inequalities that existed within the system. 'Postcode lottery' refers to the differences in the geographical location of the patient in terms of where they live and the services that are available. These variations in services across the country reveal huge gaps between what is on offer: where you live defines the standard of services you can expect. It is possible that you may get a poorer service than a neighbour simply because you live on the 'wrong' side of a road.

Postcode lottery in GP services

The service provided by Britain's GPs is highly variable across the country and could get worse if recruitment problems intensify, a report says.

Inner-city areas are more likely to have fewer GPs and poorer facilities, the study by the Audit Commission found.

Oxfordshire, for instance, has twice as many GPs per head of population as Gateshead – and twice the level of funding.

The report says that GP numbers are increasing, but not fast enough to meet targets set out in the NHS Plan.

The study also found:

- Nearly one in ten premises do not meet basic minimum standards such as having a sink in treatment rooms. Most of these are in deprived urban areas.

- One in five Londoners wait three or more days to see their GP, compared to one in eight patients elsewhere in the country.

Latest figures from the Department of Health show GP numbers increased by 170 between September 2001 and March

Continued...

2002 to a total of 30,860. The NHS Plan, published in July 2000, promised 2,000 extra GPs by 2004. In April 2002, this was updated to 15,000 extra doctors by 2008, although ministers did not specify how many of these would be GPs. The report says that plans to modernise the service, which include a new employment contract for GPs and greater devolution of NHS funds down to GP-led groups, should improve matters.

The report also found that the number of GPs working in practices with six or more partners has grown from one in five in 1988 to one in three in 2001. Larger practices may offer more patient choice and higher-quality services, the report says, but a higher concentration of services in fewer centres may mean that patients have to travel further to be seen.

(BBC News, 9 July 2002)

In order to address this rather unfair state of affairs, a number of policies all endeavouring to drive up the quality of care in the service were introduced. The government White Paper of 1998, 'A first class service: quality in the new NHS' (DoH, 1998), outlined the principles of clinical governance and announced the government's intention to put 'quality' at the heart of the NHS. Kenworthy *et al.* make the point that this strategy was not an easy one to understand and many hours had to be spent teaching the principles to the staff. The whole premise of clinical governance was the reporting of development and practice in the trusts to provide evidence in an annual report that staff and clinical development as well as financial management was being undertaken in accordance with specified targets. In essence, clinical governance ensures that:

- There is quality improvement in service.

- Risk management is undertaken.

- Evidence-based practice is used effectively.

- Complaints are dealt with.

- Continuing professional development for all staff is undertaken and monitored.

- Performance is monitored and negligence identified.

Although many of these practices were already being undertaken, one of the major changes brought about by this policy was to bring all these things together. It also had a further consequence. The medical profession had to start to work closely together with other services within the NHS trusts and in many cases the medical director worked closely with the director of nursing. This changed the dynamics within the medical and nursing professions substantially and brought all the allied medical professions together to work towards a common aim, that of quality assurance.

The whole process of ensuring the improvement programme was in place was to take ten years and the government made it clear it was no quick fix.

Other policies that came about as a result of this venture included:

National service frameworks (NSFs) These are sets of guidelines that lay down the best treatments and procedures to be used for various services. They standardise the treatments patients should expect across the country.

National Institute for Health and Clinical Excellence (NICE) This addresses the drugs in the system and regulates their use. It advises on the effectiveness of drugs and treatments and makes decisions as to the whether the costs are justified for use.

Commission for Social Care Inspection (CSCI) This body regulates and inspects social care provision and assesses performance against minimum standards and performance indicators.

The Commission for Health Improvement (1999) later became the Healthcare Commission. This body ceased to exist on 31 March 2009, its function being taken over by the **Care Quality Commission**. This body is the new health and social care regulator for England and compiles league tables of primary care trusts and hospitals, and monitors the quality of care in hospitals.

Clinical governance

In 2000 the government published its NHS Plan together with an increase in funding to address the issues above. It wanted a patient-focused service, giving more choice. It invoked a competitive system in order to give incentive to trusts and GPs to develop quality services. PCTs were to be in place by 2002 ('Shifting the balance of power', DoH, 2002) and 28 new strategic health authorities were to be established. This number became 10 in 2006.

With increases in funding in 2002, the PCTs became the major purchasers for health and were empowered to purchase from appropriate providers whether private, voluntary or public. In 2005 the government introduced practice-based commissioning whereby budgets were given to GPs on behalf of their patients.

Lord Darzi (2008) introduced a report calling for improvements in quality with patient-recorded outcome measures as a tool for measuring such initiatives.

So where are we now? So much work and funding have gone into developing a health care system that delivers a first class service. Is it doing so?

Clearly there has been improvement. However, the cost of the system is becoming ever larger and is forcing government to consider the cost effectiveness of services. The most recent reform is to extend the practice-based commissioning and give GPs back the budgets to purchase the best services for their own patients.

The Department of Health published their thoughts on this in 2009 (DoH website, 2009):

> Practice-based commissioning will lead to high-quality services for patients in local and convenient settings. GPs, nurses and other primary care professionals are in the prime position to translate patient needs into redesigned services that best deliver what local people want.

Time will tell!

Activity 5.8

This chapter has provided a lot of history to take in. Construct a timeline to try to identify the major changes to the system and health policy over the years. Use the following headings to help you:

Industrial era: 18th and 19th centuries

Beveridge era: 1920s to 1950s

Post-war or consensus era: 1950–70

Market era: 1970–90

Modernisation era: 1990s onwards

Perhaps your timeline resembles the following or even adds to it:

Industrial era: 18th and 19th centuries

- Rapid house-building programme
- 1830 Poor Laws
- 1848 Public Health Act

Beveridge era: 1920s to 1950s

- NHS
- Social Security
- Employment
- Education
- 1949 Mental Health Act

Post-war or consensus era: 1950–70

- 1960–74 Managerial growth – tripartite system in place
- 1962 Hospital Plan – Hospital building programme
- 1974 Reorganisation of NHS
- 1979 Royal Commission on NHS

Market era: 1970–90 (the Thatcher years)

- Roles of state and individual re-evaluated
- 1980 Black report
- 1982 Reorganisation of the NHS – structure streamlined
- 1983 Griffiths report and Mental Health Act

Activity 5.8 Cont'd

– 1985 WHO health targets for Europe

– 1989 White Papers: 'Caring for people' and 'Working for patients'

– 1990 NHS and Community Care Act; internal market; GP fundholding and non-fundholding

– 1991 Patient Charter

– 1992 'Health of the nation'

Modernisation era: 1990s onwards

– Clinical governance

– JNSFs

– NICE

– Health Care Commission now the Care Quality Commission

– 1997 The New NHS

– 1998 The Acheson report: 'Independent Inquiry into Inequalities'

– 1999 'Saving lives: our healthier nation'

– 1999 Royal Commission report on long-term care of the elderly

– 2001 The NHS Plan

– 2002 Development of PCTs

– 2005 Practice-based commissioning

– 2010 GP commissioning

Law in health and social care and how clients are empowered in this process

As a nation and a society we have been empowered to a certain extent by the government and the democratic process in our country to have a say in our own health service and welfare system.

Empowerment (more on this in Chapter 3) refers to the ability of the individual using a care or health service to choose and to take control of their own life. This has come about through changes in policy and law over the years. This control can only be exercised when the person has adequate information about what is available to them. We have looked at how social policy has helped to meet the needs of individuals in our society; this links well into how they can now feel empowered to take control of their own destinies to a certain extent. Our final activity will help to make that link for you. Social policy requires us to consider how government legislation has enabled society to help and support its citizens. The following list outlines some of the key social policy reforms and laws that have been developed to ensure that individuals can have their needs met and can therefore have choices in terms of their own lives:

1906 The Education Act (provisions school meals)

1907 The Children Act and the Old Age Pensions Act

1911 The National Insurance Act

1918 The Education Act – raised school leaving age to 14

1919 Subsidised Housing Acts

1920 The Unemployment Insurance Act

1925 Widows and Old and Orphans' pensions

1926 Hadow report recommending state education for all

1935 The Milk Act and the Unemployment Assistance Board for those who were long-term unemployed was set up (Walsh *et al.*, 2000).

All of the above Acts have been instrumental in meeting the needs of society and ensuring that all individuals can live with a reasonable quality of life. Of course, you have covered many more in the sections above. Let's now address some of the Acts that might be important in ensuring that individuals are further empowered in their daily lives. You will need to address some of these in the summary activity.

The Children Act 1989 and 2004

The first Act made local authority social services responsible for providing children with services and support to protect them. The key feature included what was known as the paramountcy principle, this being that the needs of the child were the most important issue to be considered in any case involving a young person under 18. Children therefore had the right to be heard, to have their wishes considered and be kept with their own family where possible.

The main purpose of the 1989 Act was to keep the child safe and secure and to protect them from harm. Any reported instance of child abuse could be brought to a child protection conference and an entry in the child protection register would then ensure the child was supported by a social worker. As a result of this Act, emergency protection orders, care orders and education supervision orders came into being and the child could be made a ward of court if they were in vulnerable circumstances.

The death of Victoria Climbie in 2000 sparked an enquiry by Lord Laming, leading to 'The Victoria Climbie report' (2003), which in turn led to the Green Paper 'Every child matters' (2003).

The 1989 Act had failed to protect a child due to a lack of communication between care services and social services, so the new 2004 Act was born. A new role of director of children's services, together with inspections and performance ratings within departments, was installed as part of this new Act. Accountability for actions and shared information via a database were to be established and local authorities were instructed to set up plans for children that would account for their specific needs.

The Mental Health Act 1983

Much controversy has surrounded this Act since it enables a person with a mental disorder to be treated without their consent and seemingly therefore contravenes the Human Rights Act. By law, social workers, relatives and doctors all have rights to detain individuals to ensure their or others' safety.

Through various hearings and tribunals, mentally disordered people can be detained for treatment if their illness is severe enough to warrant it.

Unfortunately, this law led to stigmatisation of groups of people and human rights activists started to question the treatment of people in this way, so the Mental Capacity Act was brought in.

The Mental Capacity Act 2007

A person's capacity to make a decision can change at any time in the course of their life and this Act protects people who cannot make decisions for themselves due to a learning disability, a mental health condition or any other reason.

It also enables carers and professionals to take decisions on behalf of an incapacitated individual and provides guidelines about who can take decisions in which situations.

Figure 5.12 Every child matters

The Human Rights Act 1998

The way in which we behave towards each other reflects our values and beliefs. The Human Rights Act reflects those values. For example, we all have certain rights as human beings, such as the right to marry, the right to a fair trial, the right to be free from slavery and to have freedom to speak.

Under this Act, failure to protect the human rights of another individual could lead to court proceedings.

Originating from the European Convention on Human Rights set up after the Second World War, all professional care settings now have to consider this law when planning and implementing services. The strength of this Act has seen a marked improvement in dealing with discrimination, and the promotion of quality practice in care services.

The NHS and Community Care Act 1990

The new framework for health and social care was established through this Act in 1990. It enabled the change to a 'mixed economy of care' in which voluntary, private and statutory services would all work together to produce a better-quality health and social care service.

The Sex Discrimination Act 1975

This deals with direct and indirect discrimination and makes it illegal to treat men and women differently in the workplace. Marital discrimination is also dealt with and

Figure 5.13

equality and victimisation are highlighted. The Equal Opportunities Commission was set up as a result of this Act.

The Disability Discrimination Act 1976, 1995, 1998

Covering the areas of housing, employment, education and services, this Act is concerned with preventing discrimination on grounds of disability. Regularly updated, it has improved the lot of the disabled community in this country.

Figure 5.14

The Race Relations Act 1976 and Amendment 2003

Any treatment of a person less favourably than another just because of race, colour, ethnicity or national group is illegal under this Act. This has gone a long way to promoting equality and good relationships between racial groups.

Summary

The work of sociological theorists such as the functionalist and social action schools of thought has led to the development of the social welfare system we are familiar with today. Social policy is made and driven by the legal process and politics. This particular discipline has been developed by drawing from a range of other disciplines.

By looking at historical developments, we are reminded how the economics of the NHS, politics and sociology shape social policy that has real practical value impacting directly on our lives. It is invaluable in shaping our understanding of health and social care.

The development of the welfare and care systems in the last century or so shows how changes in government and reactions to the impoverished society of the time led to the changes we see today in the NHS. Society continually evolves; it is not the same as it was 50 years ago. This evolution dictates the type of welfare that we need; and for it to be effective it needs to be reshaped to be meaningful.

Legislation and codes of practice provide frameworks or models to enable the care worker to standardise tasks and procedures. Policies are intended to promote the best interests of the individual using the service (the service user) and the carer providing the care.

Summary assignment

Analyse the following Case study by identifying all the relevant legislation that applies. Undertake research on the actions and policies and comment on the relevance of policies and legislation to the individuals in the Case study.

How would you advise Joan to access help and what help will she need?

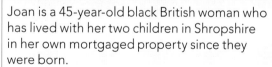

Case study

Joan is a 45-year-old black British woman who has lived with her two children in Shropshire in her own mortgaged property since they were born.

Joan married her husband Fabio while on holiday in the Caribbean 16 years ago. He is of Caribbean descent and moved with Joan to England 15 years ago. They settled in their three-bedroom house and had Laura, now 13 years old, and James, now 15.

Fabio trained as a surveyor in this country and Joan worked as a care assistant on a part-time basis in order to look after the children.

Two years ago, Fabio lost his job due to a scandal at work involving a case of negligence and a subsequent court case that left the company with huge debts. The company is currently suing Fabio over this.

Joan and Fabio's relationship was severely upset by this and Fabio moved out of the family home a year ago. Joan has no forwarding address for him.

While Joan is still in the family home, her money does not cover the mortgage and she is in arrears. Fabio has not made any financial contribution to her for eight months. She is having problems with her care job as one of the residents refuses to allow her to care for her because of her ethnicity. This has caused Joan to become very wary of attending to the lady's needs and she is causing the other staff to be quite angry with her for 'not doing what she is paid for'.

James has done fairly well at school and is described as very capable by his teachers. Lately he has missed school and last week he was caught by the police and found to be drinking. He was cautioned but the drinking continued and when he was caught doing so at school he was excluded.

Joan has contacted social services for help, since James has taken to spending nights out of the house and she is worried. They are looking at private tuition for him or residential schooling.

Laura is constantly on a diet, despite being of slim build. Her weight has dropped recently and Joan is beginning to worry. Her GP has said that he will consider admitting her to hospital if her weight continues to fall and he intends to invoke the Mental Health Act and compulsorily detain her if necessary.

Laura is attending a self-help group and her schoolwork is now suffering, since she tends to keep herself isolated and often stays at home from school, particularly when she knows that Joan is out at work.

There are no right or wrong answers to this assignment but it is likely you may have come up with the following care policies and laws to which the family could be directed.

The Children Act 2004 is likely to help with both children here and Joan should be able to access help through social services with respect to what might be done in terms of education and health care.

We have mentioned the Mental Health Act but you need to make sure that it can be applied to Laura.

In terms of help with finance, Joan should be directed to the Citizens Advice Bureau, who should be able to help her to determine what benefits she might be able to access. Her absent husband is liable to help with the maintenance of the two children and through the social service system she may be able to trace him, particularly if he is receiving benefits.

Teachers at James's school may be able to provide support in terms of his education and may also be able to arrange sessions with a counsellor to address his drinking and to find out if there is anything else he wants help with.

An eating disorder support group may well help Laura address her issues.

By approaching the bank regarding her mortgage, Joan may be able to gain some help with her payments and arrears.

With respect to Joan's problems in her care work, she should be advised to talk to her supervisor about the discrimination she is experiencing. The Race Relations Act is relevant here.

References

Acheson, D. (1998) 'Independent Inquiry into Inequalities in Health', HMSO, London.

Alcock, P. (1996) *Social Policy in Britain*, Macmillan Press, Basingstoke.

Delors, J. (2003) *Education for the Twenty-first Century: Issues and prospects*, UNESCO.

Department of Health (1989) 'Caring for people: community care in the next decade and beyond', HMSO, London.

Department of Health (1989) 'Working for patients', HMSO, London.

Department of Health (1992) 'The health of the nation', Department of Health, London.

Department of Health (1997) 'The new NHS: modern, dependable', HMSO, London.

Department of Health (1998) 'A first class service: quality in the new NHS', HMSO, London.

Department of Health (1999) 'Saving lives: our healthier nation', HMSO, London.

Department of Health (2000) 'NHS Plan: a plan for investment, a plan for reform', HMSO, London.

Department of Health (2002) 'Shifting the balance of power; the next steps', HMSO, London.

DfES (2004) 'The working group for 14–19 reform', HMSO London.

Graham, H. (1993) *Hardship and Health in Women's Lives*, Wheatsheaf, New York and London.

Griffiths, R. (1983) *NHS Management Enquiry Report*, HMSO, London.

Griffiths, R. (1988) *Community Care: Agenda For Action*, HMSO, London.

Lawson, T., Jones, N. and Moores, R. (2000) Advanced sociology through diagrams. UK Oxford University Press.

Kenworthy N., Snowley, G. and Gilling. C (1996) Common Foundation studies in Nursing UK/US. Churchill livingstone.

Longest, (1998) *Contemporary Health Policy: A Book of Readings*, Foundations of the Amer College.

Parsons, Talcott, (1967) Sociological theory & Modern Society. NY. Free Press.

Townsend, P., Davidson, N. and Whitehead, M. (1982) *Inequalities in Health: the Black Report; the Health Divide*, Penguin Books, London.

Walsh, M., Stephens, P. and Moore, S. (2000) *Social Policy and Welfare*, Stanley Thornes, Banbury.

Bibliography

Beveridge, W. H. B. (1942) *Social Insurance and Allied Services*, Macmillan, Basingstoke.

Blakemore, K. (1998) *Social Policy: An introduction*, Open University Press, Buckingham.

Blakemore, K. and Griggs, E. (eds) (2007) *Social Policy: An Introduction*, 3rd edn, McGraw-Hill, Maidenhead.

Hartley Dean (2008) *Social Policy. Short Introduction*, Polity Press, Cambridge.

Jorgensen, N., Bird, J., Heyhoe, A., Russell, B. and Savvas, M. (1999) *Sociology: An Interactive Approach*, Harper Collins, London.

6 Psychological and social models for understanding health

In this chapter we will look at the influences on our development and address the models of health together with the writings of key theorists on social and psychological models. Through such an exploration of the various models and theories applied to health, you will be better informed to understand the health and illness behaviour of clients.

Knowledge of the social, psychological and biological influences on health will mean you are in a position to meet the needs of clients in a more effective way.

Learning outcomes

By the end of the chapter you will be able to:

- discuss the factors that affect our development

- show how the psychodynamic, behaviourist, humanist and cognitive perspectives explain behaviour and development

- explore lay perspectives and social models of health, and describe their application to health and social care.

Factors that affect our development

Researchers in social science have extensively studied human behaviour, and the generation of various theories to explain it testifies to this. As a result we have a greater insight into the nature of human behaviour and are able to make a more informed decision about why it is that people are sometimes very different or very similar in their responses to situations. By studying the relationships of people with each other and their own social contexts we can, to a limited extent, start to interpret the meanings behind such behaviour. The various models developed by theorists can help us to more fully understand the individual and be able to meet their health needs more readily.

Human behaviour can be described as a catalogue of behaviours that we as humans exhibit and which have been affected by a number of things we come into contact with. For example, in other chapters we looked at how our attitudes, beliefs and values are developed through the process of socialisation and how this impacts on our emotions and the way we act in given situations. But we are all unique individuals and experience the world in a range of ways. Individuals who have been taught the values and views of a cultural and social world different from our own occasionally behave in ways that we may find unacceptable or at the very least unusual. There are clearly other factors at play that have an effect on the way we have developed. Let's explore some of these.

Nature versus nurture

This long-standing debate concerns the effects of internally determined characteristics on our behaviour, such as those ascribed to us by genetics, and those we learn from our upbringing or from the effects of the environment. The roles of heredity and environment in shaping our behaviour have been much contested over the years, with scientists making claims for either one as being the more important influence.

Activity 6.1

What do you think?

Do you believe you are born with traits that determine your level of intelligence and your personality? In other words, are you 'genetically determined'? Or do you subscribe to the view that you have been 'made' into the person you are by society and your environment – meaning that you are 'culturally determined'?

As scientists become more and more interested in unravelling the human genome, the search for 'behavioural' genes is constant. We know, for example, that eye and hair colour are determined by specific genes but more abstract traits such as intelligence, aggression and sexual orientation have fuelled the imaginations of researchers – for example, with some claiming that a 'gay' gene has been discovered. Recently the *Los Angeles Times* (16 November 2010) reported the discovery of a gene that predisposes children to hyperactivity, known as attention deficit hyperactivity disorder (ADHD):

> In the February 2010 edition of the journal *Molecular Psychiatry*, the National Human Genome Research Institute of the National Institute of Health in Bethesda, Maryland, made an amazing announcement. They reported that they had discovered a gene that not only predicted individuals who would be susceptible to ADHD but that also forecasted the ADHD patients that would have a positive response to stimulant medication … The studies that have come out of the genome project are moving us closer to a lab test that will not only provide 'proof' that a diagnosis of ADHD is real but more importantly it will allow for the appropriate treatment of thousands of people affected by the symptoms of ADHD. (LA Times, 2010)

Another discovery in 2007 was that of the 'obesity gene'. A UK team carrying out a study on 2,000 diabetics to try to determine a genetic link to susceptibility to type 2 diabetes discovered a gene known as FTO, and found strong links between the FTO variant and body mass index (BMI). The research reported (Frayling *et al.*, 2007):

> Obesity is a serious international health problem that increases the risk of several common diseases. The genetic factors predisposing to obesity are poorly understood. A genome-wide search for type 2 diabetes-susceptibility genes identified a common variant in the FTO (fat mass and obesity associated) gene that predisposes to diabetes through an effect on … BMI. An additive association of the variant with BMI was replicated in 13 cohorts with 38,759 participants. The 16% of adults who are homozygous for the risk allele weighed about 3 kilograms more and had 1.67-fold increased odds of obesity when compared with those not inheriting a risk allele. This association was observed from age 7 years upward and reflects a specific increase in fat mass.

The reaction to their studies was mixed. It was thought that overweight people may adopt a fatalistic attitude to their weight and fail to even try to reduce their weight, believing that there would be little they could do to change things. There is some logic in this. Surely, if we are slaves to our genetic disposition, any attempts to change our behaviour will end in failure. We can have little control over something we have been born with, and some individuals would adopt the view that it is pointless to try.

This very notion drove the work of the nurture theorists, who firmly believed that human behaviour can be learned and moulded or changed by the experiences we are afforded and the upbringing we have. This view tended to sit well with supporters of fairness and equality in society. It meant that rather than being bound by what our genetics dictated for us and having a somewhat fixed destiny, we are at liberty to choose our own courses of action in life and can change outcomes by learning and experience. This new thinking about behaviour suggested that human nature is capable of being moulded by culture, and the concept of the 'blank slate' was born. St Ignatius Loyola made the famous claim 'Give me the child until he is 7, and I will show you the man' (in Henderson, 2009), demonstrating the belief that upbringing was a major influence if not *the* major influence on behaviour.

But it's not that simple, is it? The nature–nurture debate continues to rage because we cannot simply discard one view for the other. Research for both views has lent support for the notion that in fact neither view is dominant but can and should coexist with the other. Genetics do have an effect on many aspects of behaviour. But behaviour is also influenced by the environment and is therefore reflective of both influences. As Henderson wrote in *The Times* ('Nature v nurture? Please don't ask', 28 March 2009):

> Nature works through nurture, and nurture through nature, to shape our personalities, aptitudes, health and behaviour. The question should not be which is the dominant influence, but how they fit together.

This view would seem to give a more positive outlook for us in that change is possible and that we do have some control over our personal growth and development.

What are the factors that affect our general behaviour and development? See Figure 6.1.

Genetics and family influences

Figure 6.1 gives us some indication as to the influences we need to recognise as having an input into our well-being. We recognise that the genetic material passed to us by our parents may predetermine us to certain conditions or traits. For example, genes influence the differences in individuals and some carry less than desirable conditions that may affect us physically. We have already seen that some of us may have a predisposition to being overweight. There are also claims for aggression running in families as well as a tendency to overuse alcohol or drugs. But in an environment where there is a lack of food, how influential will that obesity gene be? Also, in a teetotal family or in a country or culture where alcohol is not used, it is possible that any tendency to alcoholism may not manifest

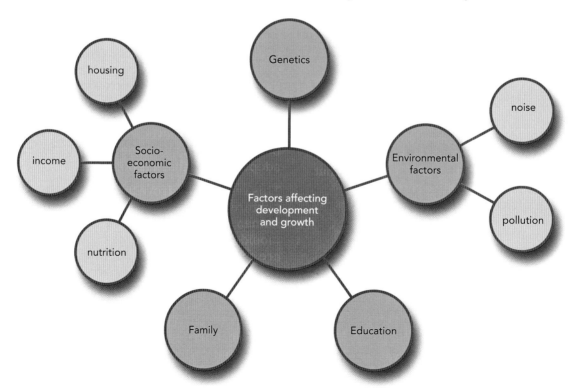

Figure 6.1

itself. We therefore have to consider the environmental influences alongside genetic predisposition.

Without doubt the genes we inherit from our parents do guide our development but this is not the whole story and the environment in which we grow up also has a strong influence.

Studies of identical twins raised in different environments have been carried out to try to determine just how much impact genes and the environment have on development. We are strongly influenced by our families and we learn the social norms of our culture through the process of socialisation (see Chapter 3). Some twin studies support this. Where twins have been brought up in different environments, characteristics such as height, hair and eye colour are, of course, strongly influenced by genetics, and were seen to be similar, but other factors such as levels of intelligence were seen to be affected by environmental factors. A child born into or brought up in an environment where education is valued may well exhibit a higher level of intelligence than his genetic parents due to the encouragement he or she is given.

We are strongly influenced, then, by our family environment. Our family network cares for us in physical as well as emotional ways. As babies, we are physically cared for and the attachment bond developed with our parents is the start of a close and important relationship. As we grow, we learn the social rules and norms to help us to live in society. The relationships we forge with close and wider family members give us a sense of belonging and can be a source of encouragement and comfort. All this happens in a close-knit community. We can begin to appreciate that a negative experience in this early family life will have a detrimental effect upon our development.

Socio-economic factors: income and its effect on housing, education and nutrition

As we noted in Chapters 3 and 5, society is not equal, and one of the areas of concern is income. In 2009 this became even more pressing when the UK went into recession

and the level of redundancy started to rise. A study carried out for the Joseph Rowntree Foundation showed how the 'economic position of families' was a 'strong influence on the present and future welfare of children' (Gregg et al., 1999). Although written ten years before the monetary crisis, this provides insightful reading into the plight of children from poor families. It pointed out that:

> economic disadvantages can lead to both economic and social difficulties in adulthood, and feed through to the next generation. So today's high level of child poverty is likely to have continuing negative effects as the present generation grows up.

Children being brought up in poverty are likely to suffer in terms of health as well as educationally and were seen to have limited choices for future employment.

Activity 6.2

Think about the effects of not having a regular or sufficient income and draw a spider diagram with 'Poverty can cause ...' as your central hub and list what poverty can cause as the arms.

In Activity 6.2, you may have referred to the following:

- stress on family members due to having no money to pay bills
- poor housing leading to more illness
- less privacy in a crowded house – therefore unable to do homework
- poor diet
- no access to extra resources needed for education or recreation
- no access to luxuries or holidays
- poorer employment prospects
- low self-worth.

The effect of poverty on housing has been demonstrated well in a National Housing Federation study carried out in 2010. The findings show the 'impact of poor-quality, overcrowded and temporary accommodation … on individuals' health and well-being, likelihood of criminality and educational attainment' (Friedman, 2010).

Highlighting the financial cost to the country of substandard housing in terms of criminal behaviour and health care, it also provides evidence for the lack of educational achievement resulting in billions of pounds in lost earnings for these young people. Children from better homes in better areas gain more GCSEs and A levels and therefore start their careers from a position of advantage.

Education is provided in this country as a 'right' for everybody. Unfortunately, children from poorer areas are disadvantaged and as a result fail to achieve as highly as their more affluent peers.

The Acheson inquiry in 1998 found links between health and educational achievement and also noted: 'Schools in disadvantaged areas are likely to be restricted in space and have the environment degraded by litter, graffiti and acts of vandalism … Children coming to school hungry … will be unable to take full advantage of learning opportunities' (Acheson, 1998).

The Acheson report further demonstrated the link between poor nutrition and low income, showing higher levels of obesity in lower socio-economic groups and poorer health due to the higher incidence of eating processed foods with higher salt content. Babies born to women from these groups were also more likely to have lower birth weights, leading to problems later in life and were less likely to be breast fed, further disadvantaging them in terms of lack of protection from infection in the first weeks of life.

Environmental factors: noise and air pollution

Living in cities and urban areas exposes us to all sorts of pollutants from industrial

Figure 6.2 Air pollution

sites and car fumes. Although the air quality in this country has undergone improvement in the last 20 years or so, we are still exposed on a daily basis to amounts of particulate matter that can and do affect our health. Living in a city environment with its attendant noise from traffic, as well as the poorer air quality, can also cause a great deal of stress and all this will ultimately affect our health.

As individuals we are the sum of our genetic make-up, the influences from our socio-economic circumstances and the environments in which we grow. As a result of all this we develop our concept of self, the learned idea about who we are and how we value ourselves. With positive influences affecting a person, such as a loving family, good housing in a nice environment, enough to eat and educational opportunity, it is not hard to see the positive influence this all has on self-concept and self-esteem. But what of the child living in poverty, with all poverty's attendant problems? Is there really no hope for that child? Self-esteem may be low and they may believe that there is little point in trying to change their position. But we all have choice and can to an extent make changes to our lives that could have an impact later in life. The choices are limited for some people but help is available and may change their outlook on life for the better.

The Child Poverty Act 2010 highlighted four targets for 2020. These are shown in the box.

Child Poverty Act 2010: targets for 2020

1. Relative poverty: to reduce to less than 10 per cent the proportion of children who live in families with income below 60 per cent of the median.

2. Combined low income and material deprivation: to reduce to less than 5 per cent the proportion of children who live in material deprivation and have a low income.

3. Persistent poverty: to reduce the proportion of children that experience long periods of relative poverty, with the specific target to be set at a later date.

4. Absolute poverty: to reduce to less than 5 per cent the proportion of children who live below an income threshold fixed in real terms.

With help to eradicate poverty, there is at least some recognition as to the disadvantage some children currently find themselves in and this can only help to widen the choices they have.

Psychological perspectives to explain behaviour and development

(See chapter 2 Table 2.4)

We have seen the effects of genetics and the environment on how we develop, and can now start to consider the subjective nature of human experience.

In seeking to explain human psychology, we will focus on four theories that have been developed and all have important implications for care work. Although we may be aware of limitations with respect to these models, as care workers the ability to take aspects from each one that are relevant to our client can result in a more informed way of working with people.

The psychodynamic perspective

Sigmund Freud

Freud (1856–1939) originated the psychodynamic perspective that he called psychoanalysis and which emphasises the role of the unconscious mind and the effects of early childhood experiences and interpersonal relationships on adult life. Freud's early training as a medical doctor later gave way to an interest in the mental suffering of individuals and he developed therapeutic ways in which to access the unconscious mind in order to interpret behaviour.

Freud's studies have been criticised as his sample was very small and limited to only middle-class Jewish women, hardly representative of the general population. However, his techniques of hypnosis, free association and dream interpretation are still used today and have been further developed by psychotherapists.

Freud's major study revolved around the workings of the unconscious mind. His belief was that most of our memories, thoughts and feelings are locked away in the unconscious and reveal themselves in our behaviour later on in life. He proposed a theory of the 'three-part self', in which the mind is distinctly split into the id, ego and superego.

The id is the part of the mind that is governed by basic drives and the need to satisfy these. These include the needs for food, drink and sex.

If the body is unable to meet these desires, then frustration and aggression may occur.

The ego refers to the conscious self or the part of the mind that tries to keep balance between the parts.

The superego is the moral part of the mind and its need is to behave in the way in which we have been brought up – that is, according to values and norms instilled into us by our parents. Guilt and anxiety result if we fail to do so.

Freud believed that neuroses occur in the conscious part of the brain, the ego, as a result of conflict experienced in the other two parts. He suggested that early childhood experiences may have been stored in the unconscious part of the mind, with the feelings about the events having been repressed.

Freud later developed his theories to include sexual explanations for behaviour

Table 6.1 Freud's theory of psychosexual development (adapted)

Stage	Drive and behaviours to gratify this stage	Characteristics of unmet drives (according to Freud)
Oral	To feed, suck and bite – involves the lips and mouth	Passive personality and dependent upon others. Immature; attracted to eating and oral pleasures
Anal	Control of muscles, particularly anal. Toileting is learned in this stage	Mean, stubborn, obsessed with cleanliness. Obstinate (anally fixated)
Phallic	The stage in which children supposedly have sexual feeling towards their parents. Giving up this sexual feeling can have repercussions in later life	Vain, self-loving, reckless and sexually obsessed. Flirtatious and promiscuous
Latency	Sexuality is latent at about 5–6	No common trait noted here
Genital	Sexuality is the main focus	Adult and mature phase

and attributed some adult behaviour to repressed desire for one's owns parents. His theory of psychosexual development highlighted stages through which humans develop, resulting in unconscious drives that need to be met for the person to develop into a mature adult.

These stages are:

- the oral stage
- the anal stage
- the phallic stage
- latency
- the genital stage.

See Table 6.1 above.

Freud suggested that difficulties experienced during any of these stages might result in 'fixation', together with behaviour that is regressive in nature. The exhibition in adulthood of stress and uncharacteristic behaviour could be attributed to fixation at a particular stage and an unconscious link to childlike behaviour. For example, Freud's explanation for a temper tantrum in an adult might be a need to regress to an earlier and safer life stage. Continual behaviour in this manner might show fixation at a certain stage.

The strong influence of childhood behaviour on a person's adult life has resulted in theories of defence mechanisms as a means of protecting us. Examples include:

- denial: removing difficult thoughts from one's mind ('It hasn't happened')
- repression: removing unpleasant memories to the unconscious mind
- rationalisation: reinterpreting memories to make them fit us in a better way ('She's not a very nice person anyway, so I didn't expect her to call')
- sublimation: changing the way in which we direct our energy, such as aggressive behaviour being channelled into sport
- displacement: shifting one's emotions to a safer situation, such as kicking a football instead of the boss
- projection: transferring the blame for one's own shortcomings to somebody else; in other words, criticising others' behaviour to avoid admitting that behaviour in ourselves.

Undoubtedly you will be aware of the use of some of these terms and may even have used them yourself. Freud's work, despite criticisms of its overly sexual links to behaviour, has influenced many other psychologists, including Jung and Erikson, and their work has retained many of Freud's concepts.

Carl Jung

Jung (1875–1961) was a contemporary of Freud and worked closely with him for a while. Jung developed his own theory of analytical psychology and, significantly, criticised the importance of sexuality in Freud's work. One of Jung's major developments was what we now recognise as the 'eight basic psychological types', which we still use today. He also developed theories on dreams and the psyche, in which he identified archetypes as part of the conscious and unconscious mind.

The personality types were the means by which Jung defined the attitudes of individuals as being either extrovert or introvert. He believed that if one trait was dominant the other would become unconscious and act in a compensatory manner within the person. Alongside these two traits Jung also identified four functional modes.

Jung's eight personality types

introversion: thinking

extroversion: thinking

introversion: feeling

extroversion: feeling

introversion: sensation

extroversion: sensation

introversion: intuition

extroversion: intuition

You will have come across the terms 'introvert' and 'extrovert' and the implications on personality of being one or the other. Jung's 'introversion' type typifies a person who is more aware of their subjective consciousness and is more inward looking. The extroverted type is said to place more importance on objectivity rather than on inner cognitive processes.

The four functions that Jung described – feeling, thinking, sensation and intuition – describe methods by which we understand the value of conscious activity and whether or not it is good or how we understand the meanings of things. Sensation refers to the means by which we know something exists and intuition the means by which we know about something without a conscious understanding of how we know it (Hyde and McGuinness, 1992; Morison, 2001).

Jung was aware of the fact that some individuals were a mixture of several types and that we might change types as we progress through life. One of the merits of this theory has been the impact it has had on our understanding of people and how they view the world. It has become a major part of some psychological testing systems, particularly the Myers–Briggs personality test.

Erik Erikson

Erikson (1902–94) was influenced by Freud, and while he believed that the ego exists from birth, he was of the opinion that our development continues well beyond the childhood stages of life and that events in adolescence and adulthood also shape our behaviour. Erikson believed that our development is determined by the interaction of the body and mind with cultural influences and that as we progress through life we encounter various crises through which we pass and either succeed or fail to adapt to.

He identified eight developmental stages:

Infancy: birth to 18 months; ego development outcome: trust versus mistrust

In this stage we learn to trust. If as a child our needs are not met we grow up to mistrust. The most significant relationship is with the maternal parent, or whoever is our most significant and constant caregiver. This view is later taken into the work of John Bowlby and his attachment theory.

Early childhood: 18 months to 3 years; ego development outcome: self-control versus shame and doubt

When a child learns to walk and talk, they are also building self-esteem and control over their bodies. Toilet training becomes an issue at this stage. In Erikson's theory, if this is problematic the child may be left feeling ashamed and doubtful of their capability.

Play age: 3 to 5 years; ego development outcome: initiative versus guilt

In play situations the child is experimenting with life and what it means to be an adult. Erikson believed that in this stage the child was likely to experience conflict with the parents; failure to resolve the conflict could result in guilt.

School age: 6 to 12 years; ego development outcome: competence versus inferiority

At this age a child is learning and developing numerous new skills and knowledge. Serious issues arise here if the child experiences feelings of inadequacy in terms of competence and self-esteem.

Adolescence: 12 to 18 years; ego development outcome: identity versus role confusion

At this stage the young person is struggling with the development of their own identity and can become very confused. Life becomes more complex and social interactions and moral issues become prominent.

Young adulthood: 18 to 35 years; ego development outcome: intimacy versus isolation

As young adults find satisfying relationships and begin to start a family, they can experience intimacy. Failure to do so leads to isolation.

Middle adulthood: 35 to 55 or 65 years; ego development outcome: generativity versus stagnation

During middle age we seek to be creative and find meaningful work. Major life changes in this stage such as being made redundant or children leaving home can lead to the mid-life crisis and to the struggle to find new purposes. Stagnation can occur if we fail to handle this stage successfully.

Late adulthood: 55 or 65 to death; ego development outcome: integrity versus despair

Older adults who can look back on life with happiness and fulfilment are blessed with a feeling described by Erikson as integrity. If, however, we feel we have failed at some point we may reach this stage of life with a feeling of despair.

Activity 6.3

Psychodynamic theory gives us an interesting way of interpreting past experiences. How far can you explain your own development, using some of the theory identified above?

Criticisms of the psychodynamic perspective

A major criticism of the psychodynamic approach is that it is impossible to test scientifically – it is 'unfalsifiable'. Testing the unconscious mind is just not possible. Further, Freud's work is based on studying very small samples of people, namely middle-aged women in Vienna, who are hardly representative of the general population.

Finally, the humanist school of thought believes that the psychodynamic perspective is too deterministic or reliant upon external influences that cannot be changed and does not take into account free will.

The behaviourist perspective

This approach views our development and subsequent behaviour as being the result of learning from experience. This approach arose as a reaction against the psychodynamic way of thinking. The criticism that the latter was unfalsifiable and could not be tested or disproved led to a more positivistic stance being taken. In this approach, the use of experiments to explain human behaviour meant that it was based upon rigorous observation leading to the existence of empirical data.

Psychologists such as Watson, Skinner, Thorndike and Pavlov were instrumental in developing the behaviourist school of thought.

Classical conditioning (Pavlov) and operant conditioning (Skinner) are two major components of the behaviourist school of thought and have been influential in describing how we learn. Classical conditioning can best be described by looking at the work of Pavlov, who demonstrated how we learn through association.

While carrying out experiments on dogs, Pavlov noticed that when the dogs were fed the sound of a buzzer led them to salivate. Later experiments confirmed that dogs would salivate just at the sound, without the presence of food.

When this finding is applied to humans, we can explain to a certain extent how phobias develop. Our fear of animals may have come about as a result of a frightening experience as a child and now association with animals brings back the fear.

Operant conditioning explains how the consequences of behaviours that act as reinforcers shape further behaviour.

In Skinner's most famous study into operant conditioning in 1935, rats and pigeons were placed in a box (see Figure 6.3) with a lever that dispensed food when pressed. Accidental activation of the lever soon led to the animals learning to press the lever deliberately. Skinner took this a step further and was able to teach the animals to perform other actions to release food – for example, pressing a circle. Skinner was able to show that the reward meant that the behaviour was more readily undertaken. If no reward was forthcoming, then the behaviour was less likely to occur.

Thorndike also studied animal behaviour and set up experiments of trial and error, believing that any action that produced a good effect is more likely to be repeated. This came to be known as the 'law of effect' and described the theory that action is governed by consequence.

Skinner took this a step further with his work on reinforcement. By positively or negatively reinforcing certain behaviour, it is possible to strengthen the response. This concept has had major implications on education.

These experiments all looked at reward and its effect on behaviour. We can see how this might influence the behaviour of animals and small children, and teachers often comment that the merit system in schools tends to work with younger children but tends to diminish in its effect as the child gets older. Conditioning and reinforcement theory are useful for understanding influences on human behaviour but they cannot explain all aspects of human development and this fact has led to theorists further developing the behaviourist perspective.

Social learning theory can be seen as an extension of behaviourism and was developed by theorists such as Albert Bandura. Bandura's early work was influenced by the behaviourist perspective in the way that it focused on learning and observable behaviour, but he did recognise the need to understand cognitive processes.

A major study by Bandura demonstrated how aggression is learned and shaped by role models. In the study, 72 boys and girls from a nursery school individually watched an adult behaving aggressively towards a doll. The results showed that children who saw the display were more likely to copy this

Figure 6.3 Skinner's rats

behaviour. The experiment confirmed for Bandura that imitation and copying were also a major factor in shaping behaviour, rather than it being influenced only by reinforcement or conditioning. In particular, further characteristics were evident. If the person showing the behaviour was respected, then the behaviour was more likely to be copied. This would be further reinforced if there was a reward available.

Activity 6.4

Compare the studies by Bandura and Skinner, showing their similarities and differences.

In Activity 6.4, you may have written some of the following:

> Bandura used human participants whereas Skinner used animals.

> Bandura's study showed learning that did not have any reward attached to it whereas Skinner's study did reward the animals.

> Bandura's study of aggression showed that no reward was needed to initiate the children's imitation of the adults. Skinner's animals could only be made to act if they were rewarded.

Both studies were carried out in highly controlled situations. Skinner invented a box that meant the conditions were the same for all animals; Bandura carried out controlled experiments with the only variable (the factor that differed) being the behaviour or sex of the role models.

The behaviourist perspective has useful applications in the field of care and education. To change behaviour we can adopt reward systems; this is certainly used with young children and babies. If we want a child to change a response that we feel is dangerous for them, we would use a negative reinforcer. To reward a behaviour we would like to see repeated, a smile or praise or treat can often work well. The criticism of the

psychodynamic approach, that it was difficult to test empirically, is not the case with this theory. Scientific ways of studying behaviour have been used – although it is difficult to generalise findings from laboratory studies on animals to humans.

In terms of application to therapy, we see that the behavioural perspective is alive and well in the cognitive behavioural approach, which takes on a behaviourist approach while also recognising the role of cognition.

One criticism of this approach is the fact that any changes in behaviour may be short-lived. Aversion therapy and token economy or merit systems used as a way of changing behaviour do so for a limited time only. Another criticism is the reductionist nature of the approach, which seemingly fails to recognise the complex nature of human experience (Kenworthy *et al.*).

The cognitive perspective

Similarly to the behaviourist perspective, this theory takes the view that although behaviour is shaped by environment, there are thought processes at play in responding to these external influences. It therefore assumes that due to previous experiences and different ways of thinking, the experience by two people of the same event may well be reported differently. For example, my experience of the care given by my GP to me may well differ from that experienced by you. The central difference here is that our interactions with the GP may be interpreted in different ways by all parties involved.

Jean Piaget (1896–1980) was the major contributor to this school of thought. His theory of cognitive development is well known for children and the linking of mental process and behaviour.

In Piaget's theory, schemas are mental representations of situations that are made up of ideas and concepts. They are developed through experiences and can be changed as a result of learning. They are important in communication and when we share schemas with others we are able to understand their world view. Piaget determined four processes in the development of schemas: accommodation, assimilation, equilibrium and adaptation.

Accommodation refers to making changes to an existing schema that take account of new learning and therefore change our view of the world. In this process the child is learning to fit new knowledge into existing knowledge or schemas.

Assimilation is the changing of a schema when new knowledge is acquired.

Equilibrium is making sense of the new knowledge by trying to balance it with the existing knowledge. An example can be acknowledging that not all cats are the same colour. A child may own a black cat. But as she grows she notices other cats of different colours. This new knowledge may come as a surprise. So she learns that cats come in different colours and this new knowledge needs to be built into her existing schema.

If we find that new information cannot be comfortably assimilated, then we accommodate this by trying to generate a new schema. This stage in development is known as disequilibrium and may be quite uncomfortable. Change for some individuals is quite distressing and this stage might cause stress.

Piaget also developed the theory that children pass through various stages in their development. The first stage, from birth to 2 years, is the sensorimotor stage. In this the child is learning to use their muscles and senses to physically experience the environment. At this stage, the child imitates what they see but has no understanding of what they are doing. So the child builds up pictures of behaviour and then repeats them. The end of the stage occurs when the child begins to understand that objects have a permanence. The child realises that when Mum leaves the room she still exists and it wants her to come back. So the child has a 'picture' of Mum in its head and knows that she must have gone somewhere.

The pre-operational stage, between the ages of 2 and 7, is when the child starts to think but cannot understand logic, so we can also refer to it as the pre-logical stage. Words and images are useful to the child and the child is starting to speak. Piaget's experiments at this time were interesting and have been reconstructed countless times in nurseries all over the country. The child cannot at this stage understand mass and conservation of number. Give the child two pieces of plasticine of the same size and weight. Roll one into a long sausage shape and ask them to comment on which is the bigger of the two. At this stage the child will say that the sausage shape is now the bigger one.

The concrete operational stage occurs between the ages of 7 and 11. The child develops logical thinking and is making sense of the wider environment. In this stage the child can think in a logical manner only if they have pictures to help them. If you asked, for example, 'John weighs more than Clare but John weighs less than Harry. Who weighs the most?' the child would have trouble thinking this problem through. But if they saw pictures that clearly showed the weight difference they would be able to answer this immediately. It is the mental imagination that is the problem here.

The formal operational stage is from about 11 years. This is the final stage and is when abstract notions and adult thought processes are being developed. Formal logical thinking enables us to understand complicated ideas without having to resort to pictures to help us work things out.

Piaget believed that intelligence, rather than being a fixed entity from birth, is one in which the environment plays a part. A child learns by interacting with the environment and understanding the world they inhabit. As they take in the information and process it, the child's behaviour will change accordingly. The child is constantly adapting to new information, and in learning theory it is thought that the best type of learning is that which comes out of experience – thus the teacher who creates a learning experience to stimulate the child to think will have more success than the teacher who merely talks at the child or teaches in a didactic manner.

This perspective has undergone rigorous testing and has been applied in care settings with the development of social cognition models to explain information processing and predicting health-related behaviour. Strong links with education have led to a curriculum that focuses on learning by doing and problem solving.

The humanist perspective

It is fitting to end this section with a look at humanism. Psychologists recognised limitations in the behaviourist and psychodynamic psychology view, namely that these approaches were 'dehumanising'. So the main emphasis in the humanist theory is on the subjective reality of the person themselves. As people experience life in vastly different ways, this approach holds that they are the experts on what is good for them. Carl Rogers, the psychologist who developed this theory, stated that it emphasised the study of the whole person. Human behaviour is connected to the person's inner feelings and self-image, and a major factor is to facilitate personal development. The focus in this approach is on the self. The person is free to choose their own behaviour and need not slavishly react to environmental stimuli.

In emphasising the personal worth of the individual and their drive to be creative and active, we recognise that each person is capable of building their self-regard or self-concept. If you have studied counselling you will have come across the terms 'unconditional positive regard' and 'conditional positive regard'. Unconditional positive regard occurs when individuals, especially parents, demonstrate unconditional love. Conditional positive regard is when that love comes at a price or when certain conditions need to be met.

Rogers's theory states that we all have the capacity to develop to our full potential and therefore have an inbuilt tendency to value ourselves. This is damaged in a society where the influences upon us act to destroy our feeling of self-worth in some way. We saw this earlier when we discussed the effect of the environment on a person's development.

A child is influenced by family and friends, and their idea of who they are is changing constantly. If they are in loving families who reinforce the child's self-worth, they will grow into well-adjusted individuals. However, those who are subject to distorted beliefs about themselves may find that their self-esteem is low and they may develop negative and destructive behaviours as a result. For example, the child who is neglected in some way or constantly told they are stupid or not wanted will develop behaviours to reflect this and start to believe what they are being told.

This theory has given us a better understanding of human nature and the human condition. It has also broadened the range of effective methods in the professional practice of psychotherapy.

Maslow's work was similar to Rogers's. In his study, Maslow developed the theory of self-actualisation (see Chapter 2). When our four deficit needs are met – physiological, safety, the need to belong and the need to be respected – we are free to concentrate on the higher needs: the need to 'become'. According to Maslow, if we are no longer worrying about meeting the four deficit needs, we are in a position to explore our creativity and potential.

Self-actualisation, then, is about psychological growth, fulfilment and satisfaction in life.

Applying the theories to care settings

In any care work we will be coming into contact with people from all walks of life and with all sorts of behaviour, some of which may be challenging for us. By applying theories of development, we can better understand what is happening in certain situations, and can suggest how to deal with distressed or vulnerable people.

Let's think about this in terms of somebody who is displaying aggressive behaviour.

Activity 6.5

You are on duty in the emergency department and have been asked to come and help with a young woman who is displaying anger due to being kept waiting for an hour. She is threatening staff in the reception area and is verbally abusive. She is now threatening to throw a chair through the reception window if she is not seen at once.

How might you explain the behaviour by applying the theories we have looked at: psychodynamic, behavioural, cognitive and humanistic?

Psychodynamic. The young woman may be projecting her past tensions and anger onto the current situation. She may have struggled in the past with a family member who made her angry and the current situation has served as a reminder of previous tension. This could be a transference, then, to the care workers of an emotion she felt as a child. We might suggest she is projecting her unconscious feeling onto the situation now and could suggest that psychotherapy might enable her to deal with these feelings in a more constructive manner in the future.

Behavioural. As a result of an upbringing where she has learned that the only way to get anything done is to behave in an aggressive manner, she has found that aggression in the past has been rewarded in some way and she is therefore using it in this situation to force the outcome she seeks. As a health professional in this sort of situation, you might be able to manage her behaviour by reinforcing any positive behaviour she displays and by not reinforcing her aggression. Shouting at her is likely to make the situation escalate as it is important not to reinforce the aggression by showing an emotional reaction. The best option would be to deal very calmly with the young woman and to defuse the situation.

Cognitive. The young woman's aggression may be the result of distorted thinking and perhaps the belief that it is not her fault that she feels angry but somebody else's.

She ascribes blame to others for her anger. She may well believe that she is feeling angry because of the way in which she is being treated.

Humanistic. The young woman may have a very negative view of herself, so a caring and nurturing approach may be needed. If you can find some way to show her that she is valued and understood, you may get through to her and enable her to change the current display of anger. Rather than trying to take control in this sort of situation, the humanistic practitioner will attempt to understand how the young woman is feeling and will support her emotions in a way that builds her self-esteem.

Lay perspectives and social models of health, and their application to health and social care

Clearly, our upbringing and social circumstances, and all external influences, have an effect on our lives and health. Psychologists have tried to explain our behaviour by developing theories that attempt to show the impact of our life experiences and how these affect our unconscious minds. From these theories a number of therapies have emerged, and in this section we shall look at some of these. We shall also revisit the models of health we started to look at in Chapter 4.

Of major interest to health professionals is the way in which people view their own health. Why do some people continue to smoke despite the fact that there is overwhelming evidence to suggest they shouldn't? Is it simply too difficult to give up despite there being so much help to do so? Why is it that we are aware of the need to eat healthily to ward off cancers and heart disease yet continually fail to eat foods that are good for us and choose the processed options?

One of the things researchers have long been interested in is referred to as the 'health locus of control', which is the degree of control individuals believe they possess over their personal health. See Figure 6.4.

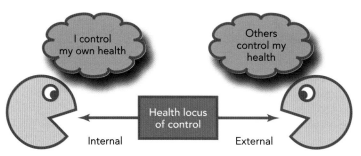

Figure 6.4 Health and well-being

The two dimensions are internal and external. An internal locus of control is shown by individuals who believe that they can control their environment to bring about change that will be good for them. It is linked to a person's sense of empowerment and ability to manage their own lives in an efficient manner. In terms of health outcomes, they believe that these can be controlled to some extent by their own choices and behaviours. They are more likely to take responsibility for their own health and make changes if they feel it will be of benefit to them. For example, a person who has a responsible attitude towards their own health will take dietary advice in order to lose extra pounds if need be.

Individuals with an external locus of control believe that it is more likely to be luck that controls their fate or at the very least that somebody else should be responsible for their health. In terms of health outcomes, these individuals consider that these are beyond their own control and are likely to be due to much greater external forces. They have a somewhat fatalistic view of their own health. They tend to attribute the responsibility of health to others and rely upon health professionals to help them when they are in need, without any sense of working in partnership to achieve goals. The person who is obese in this situation is likely to accept their size as being the result of 'glands' or 'bad luck'. They will not be amenable to change and are likely to dismiss suggestions of exercise and healthier eating.

This passive acceptance of their fate with respect to health behaviours means they are unlikely to be able to see change as being part of their responsibility. This is of interest to health professionals who need to be aware of the behaviours exhibited by individuals in the health care setting when trying to promote healthy lifestyles.

Activity 6.6

Previously we looked at the medical model and behavioural changes models of health. Remind yourself of these now and make notes on what each entails.

Perhaps in Activity 6.6 you had notes along the following lines. The medical model ascribes to the medical practitioner the role of expert. The knowledge the practitioner possesses is viewed as professional, scientific and far superior to lay beliefs, which are generally devalued and believed to be ill informed. The focus is on objective, measurable signs and symptoms that enable the professional to make diagnoses.

The behavioural change model makes it clear that individuals should be responsible for choosing healthy lifestyles. People are encouraged to change lifestyle habits such as smoking, drinking, risky sexual practice and poor eating leading to obesity and malnutrition. The emergence in health promotion practice of the behavioural change model was a move towards a more client-focused or a social model, the clear message being to adopt healthy lifestyles and be responsible for your own health.

The behavioural change model was   health, which gave a more holistic view of health. This model subscribed to the view that biological and psychological (thoughts and emotions) as well as social factors all play a role in human functioning and health. In this view the origins of ill health were being addressed and it became a popular concept because it started to look more closely at the health differences of some groups and the complex interaction of environment, material and structural factors as well as culture. It linked well with the lay perspectives in health addressing the vast definitions of health that people hold. As we mentioned in Chapter 4, defining the actual term health is complex and we all have various views on this. For most people, being healthy is simply a case of not being ill and this somewhat negative view prevails even today. But our view of being healthy has been shown to have some bearing on how we take responsibility for it.

Lay perspectives (or, as they are sometimes referred to, 'folk' concepts) are models used by individuals or cultures to explain health and illness. Moonie (2005, after Stainton Rogers, 1991) provides a useful account of the various views:

Body as a machine Similarly to the medical model, illness is a medical fact and science has the answer.

Inequality of access Also similar to the above; the person relies on medical expertise but is aware of inequality in the health system.

Health promotion account The person take responsibility for their own health and changes lifestyle to address ill-health issues.

God's power This spiritual view of health determines the way in which the person will live their life in order to maintain health. For example, they might abstain from alcohol in order to live righteously.

Body under siege 'The world is out to get me in terms of all the germs it throws at me.'

Cultural critique of medicine This view sees the medical model as taking away the rights of the individual to use their own free will. Oppressive practice is highlighted.

Robust individualism 'I will choose to do what I like with respect to my health'.

Will power We are responsible for our own health and must demonstrate will power to do things the right way.

As we can see, these ideas about health and illness include references to the way the body functions, as in the body as a machine that needs to be kept in good running order lest it break down. But we note also cultural and religious differences in the views, which might lead to delayed diagnosis of potentially serious conditions. For example, a person who subscribes to the robust individualism view may well ignore a persistent cough and continue to smoke since that's what they really want to do.

It is also interesting to note how we sometimes view illness as being caused by the person themselves and the way in which they live their lives. We tend to blame people for their poor diets or lack of exercise and almost blame them for their illness.

Clearly, there are models in abundance that attempt to make sense of how we view health and illness and how our development is likely to affect our behaviour. We could categorise health models into three distinct areas:

1. Models that focus on the individual to explain health behaviour. In this type of model the onus is on the individual and how they perceive the threat of a health problem. They are therefore more active in dealing with the threat and will seek ways to change their own behaviour to prevent and manage health problems.

2. Models that look to communities and their plans to change health. In this type of model the community in which we live is actively participating in solutions to health and social problems.

3. Models that explain changes at a more global or organisational level by creating supportive organisational practices. This model describes how large organisations adopt healthy policies and programmes in order to ensure the health of the workforce and society in general.

For further discussion about models of health, refer to Chapter 4.

We now turn our attention to how we might adapt this knowledge of models and developmental theory to practice.

Links to practice

One of the major things we have learned from reviewing the way in which we develop as individuals has been that although we are similar in some ways, the differences we possess require recognition by those in the field of care. Our definitions of what constitutes health and ill health are subject to various interpretations by both lay people and health professionals, and can lead to misunderstandings and failure to embrace health promotion activity.

Effective care requires an understanding of what the individual presents with, together with their own values and schemas. Assessment of the individual is vital in determining the best way to approach the care the patient requires. A knowledge of the person's health locus of control will also help us to choose the most apt approach to treatment.

Whichever model we subscribe to or favour, it is the application to practice that is important.

One of the major areas of concern for the health service is the management of mental health issues and the need to prescribe different ways to deal with conditions such as depression and anxiety. The effectiveness of psychological therapy in the NHS has been considered by the National Institute for Health and Clinical Excellence (NICE) and as a result the Improving Access to Psychological Therapies (IAPT) programme was launched in May 2007.

One of the recommended treatments, and one favoured by many health care professionals, is cognitive behavioural therapy (CBT). This treatment helps to change how an individual thinks (cognitive) and subsequently what they do (behaviour) in an effort to make them feel better. We can see a direct link here with the cognitive and behavioural perspectives shown earlier.

Unlike counselling and regression-type therapies proposed by humanist and psychodynamic perspectives, this treatment focuses on the 'here and now' and looks to improve the situation that the individual currently finds themselves in. It is a popular therapy at present. However, it can be limited in some conditions, particularly those where repressed feelings and memories may be causing problems.

Psychodynamic psychotherapy would be a treatment of choice in conditions where experiences from early childhood need to be analysed to try to change destructive behaviours or emotional problems.

Psychoanalysis is one method by which the patient's unconscious is accessed in order to resolve early-life issues that may be impacting on current feelings. A longer-term therapy is yet to be established within the treatments offered by the health service since this can be costly and take time. This type of therapy also includes family and couples therapy, group and play therapy

Behavioural therapy, which has developed as a result of the behavioural perspective, encourages the learning of new principles and skills to change behaviours. By learning specific skills, the individual obtains rewards and satisfaction. We see this type of approach in schools where teachers give praise and attention for behaviour that is good. In therapeutic settings, behavioural therapy can be used successfully in stress management and relaxation training.

Rehabilitation services and community support programmes

In addition to individual therapies offered, there has been a community response to addressing mental health issues. For the growing number of individuals with severe mental illness, community support programmes and rehabilitation services have been developed and offered by mental health teams in the UK. In order to help these types of clients to live and work independently and productively, these agencies have set up a variety of activities to enable such individuals to learn new skills.

A major area of concern in 2001 was the plight of people with learning disabilities. The White Paper 'Valuing people: a new strategy for learning disability for the 21st century' proposed improvements to the life chances of such clients by the development of a person-centred health service. Personal health action plans, together with the offer of extra help or facilitation to ensure that good health was attainable, were a key initiative.

Health advocacy then came on to the government agenda to ensure that this programme and other health policies were effectively delivered. Advocates work to support patients in the health care system by focusing on available, safe and quality care and enabling the patient to access to direct service and activities that promote health. In the past, vulnerable groups were unable to access care services in this way, and the development of a system of patient representatives and health advisers as advocates has strongly influenced the way in which these patients' needs are now being met.

By collaborating with health care providers, advocates are able to provide mediation when conflict arises and facilitate positive change for clients who formerly had no voice in their own care.

The improved access to quality care, protection and enhancement of vulnerable patients' rights has meant that partnership approaches to care have been established and as a result such groups have been empowered.

Summary

In this chapter we have looked at psychological perspectives that attempt to explain how we develop our personalities, together with the impact of environment, upbringing, social class and poverty. The medical model of health and the biopsychosocial model have also been described and evaluated. Such an exploration of the various models and theories applied to health means that we can be better informed in understanding the health and illness behaviour of our clients. By treating clients as individuals and with a sound knowledge of how they view their own health and illness issues, we can be assured of providing effective care.

Summary assignment

Compare the biomedical model with any psychological and any social model with which you are familiar and show how they can be applied to practice. Give reasons for their use and purpose in understanding the concept of health.

Prepare an essay plan outlining how you might approach this particular essay.

References

Acheson, D. (1998) 'Independent inquiry into inequalities in health', HMSO, London.

Bandura. A. (1973) Aggression: A Social Learning Analysis. New Jersey, Prentice Hall.

Frayling, T. M. *et al.* (2007), A common variant in the FTO gene is associated with body mass index and predisposes to childhood and adult obesity', published online 12 April 2007, available at: http://www.sciencemag.org/content/316/5826/889.abstract-fn-1.

Friedman, D. (2010) 'Social impact of poor housing', ECOTEC National Housing Federation.

Gregg, P., Harkness, S. and Machin, S. (1999) 'Child development and family income', Joseph Rowntree Foundation.

Henderson, M. (2009) 'Nature v nurture? Please don't ask', *The Times*, 28 March.

Hyde, M. and McGuinness, M. (1992) Jung for Beginners. UK Icon books.

Kennedy, S. (2009) 'Child Poverty Act 2010: a short guide', HMSO, London.

Moonie, N. (2006) *A2 Level for OCR Health and Social Care,* Heinemann, Oxford.

Morison, J. (2001) *Analytical Hypnotherapy; Volume 1: Theoretical Principles*, Crown House Publishing, UK and USA.

Bibliography

Barry, A.-M. and Yuill, C. (2002) *Understanding Health. A Sociological Introduction*, Sage Publications, London.

Blaxter, M. (2004) *Health: Key Concepts*, Polity Press, London.

Busfield, J. (2000) *Health and Health Care in Modern Britain*, Oxford University Press, Oxford.

Costello, J. and Haggart, M. (2003) *Public Health and Society*, Palgrave, London.

Department of Health (1999) 'Saving lives: our healthier nation', HMSO, London.

Department of Health (2004) 'Choosing health: making healthy choices easier', available at: www.doh.gov.uk

Kenworthy, N., Snowley, G. and Gilling, C. *Common Foundations Studies in Nursing*, Churchill Livingstone, Edinburgh.

Llewellyn-Nash, I. and Tilmouth, T. (2011) *Social Policy for Health and Social Care Students*, Reflect Press, Exeter.

Naidoo, J. and Wills, J. (eds) (2001) *Health Studies. An Introduction*, Palgrave, Basingstoke.

7

The safe working environment: health, safety and managing health conditions and disease

It has become increasingly important that all care workers know the fundamentals of health and safety in order to deal with clients and patients in a safe manner. In this chapter you will start to learn safety with respect to handling medical emergencies and health conditions. By developing an awareness of potential clinical problems, the common hazards encountered in clinical practice will be dealt with in an efficient manner. Common conditions, infection control and how to deliver first aid will be demonstrated in this chapter and the support services to which you may turn will be shown. You will first learn about how health and safety legislation affects you in your work placement and the responsibilities you have with respect to yourself, your environment and your clients.

Learning outcomes

By the end of the chapter you will be able to:

- show how to avoid danger to self and others
- demonstrate an understanding of your role in infection control and its prevention
- discuss and show what actions to take in the case of common emergency conditions
- understand the role of support services in emergency situations and disease management
- understand the need for careful record keeping.

How to avoid danger to self and others

Every time you set foot in your workplace you are subject to a number of hazards with respect to the environment and the people with whom you work. This may sound dramatic but think about it for a moment. How safe are you from infection, hazardous substances, fire, visitors, intruders, faulty equipment? The list is seemingly endless when we consider the dangers with which we come into contact on a daily basis. So how do we keep ourselves, and others, safe in a potentially hostile environment, and who is ultimately responsible for the safety of all who come into contact with the setting?

Workplace safety

This is a shared responsibility between yourself and your employer and you are responsible for the safety of the people who use your setting and those who visit it,

whether they are tradespeople or family of clients. Let's take a look at the responsibility we all have.

Together employer and employee must ensure that the people who use the setting are safe, and this means a lot more than simply being aware of the potential hazards. You have a duty of care (UNISON, 2003) to those with whom you interact on a daily basis and must be vigilant about checking and dealing with any risks. Your employer may have ultimate responsibility for the health and safety of individuals in the setting but you also have individual responsibility to deal with anything untoward that you may come across.

Activity 7.1

Think about the hazards in your own workplace with respect to the environment, people and equipment. Reflect on how you might deal with these hazards.

Figure 7.1

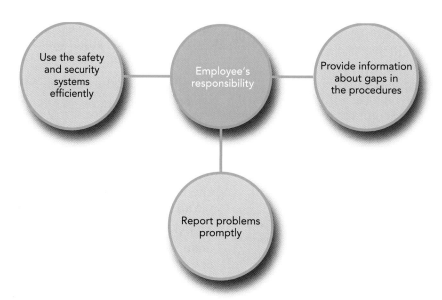

Figure 7.2

In Activity 7.1 you may have come up with the areas of concern described in the following sections.

Hazards connected to the environment

These depend very much on the setting in which you work. Wet floors, worn carpets, trailing flexes and electrical appliances or furniture are in all settings and can be problematic. But some of you will work in more specialised settings and these will have specific guidelines to which you need to work in order to ensure your own and

others' safety. For example, if you work in an operating theatre or an X-ray department, you have additional environmental hazards. If you are working in a community setting and visiting individuals in their own homes, the environmental hazards will pose different threats. The bottom line is to be aware of these hazards and deal with them as they occur. We cover risk assessment later in the chapter and although you are wise to carry out such a procedure in a client's home you cannot insist they then make changes to the environment if risks are evident. You can only make suggestions as to safety.

Figure 7.3 Hazard

Hazards connected to equipment

Faulty appliances in the kitchen of a care home, or damaged hoists, furniture or beds can all cause issues to our safety and need to be dealt with. In hospital settings and depending upon the type of work being carried out in that setting, the hazards may well be more pressing and specific guidance will be needed.

Hazards connected to people

In this group of hazards we are looking in particular at how we handle people. This again may well pose more problems in some areas. We are aware of the threats to colleagues who work in settings such as emergency departments and who come across individuals who may be violent and aggressive towards them. But even in care home settings we may potentially have visitors who are unhappy about an aspect of care and can pose a threat should they become agitated. These sorts of hazards need to be dealt with in a specific manner, and we shall spend more time on this later.

In a situation where the solution is simple, you need to take the initiative. If you see a wet floor, put up a sign or mop the floor. If you realise the fire exit has been blocked with a box, then move it. It is, after all, your responsibility to do so. If there is a visitor in the building whom you do not recognise, then ask them to identify themselves.

If, however, you are unable to deal with the hazard presented you must ensure that correct reporting procedures are followed, and the manager of the setting needs to be informed of the problem.

Intruder alert

In many settings there is general open access for all and sundry to enter premises, and this can have major implications with respect to our own and our client's safety. In larger organisations where there is a use of identity badges, it is fairly easy to identify the staff but smaller premises may not have this luxury and rely on staff to be vigilant about who is entering the premises.

A visitors' signing-in system is a fairly good idea and then at least you have some idea who is on the premises. In fact, you will need this sort of information if there is a fire and you are asked to account for people in the building. However, an intruder is unlikely to stop and sign the book!

In work settings where independence is encouraged, this can prove very difficult to manage. Vulnerable individuals may be confined to their own homes or in schools and nurseries or even leisure settings where young children work and play and in such settings a policy needs to be in place to provide protection.

Figure 7.4 Intruder

Activity 7.2

Define what you consider is good practice in your own setting with respect to protecting against unwanted visitors and intruders.

You probably have a policy in place that gives guidelines as to how you are to proceed if such a situation arises. Read this policy now to familiarise yourself again with the protocols.

Some of the golden rules are:

- Challenge unknown individuals with a polite enquiry: 'How can I help you?'

- If they are a visitor, escort the person to where they want to go. Don't just give directions.

- Make sure you are aware of new faces in the building.

- Do not tackle an intruder – raise the alarm.

Challenging behaviour

Some of you may work in settings where tensions run high and there is a danger of situations escalating and of abusive behaviour posing a safety risk. Even the most pleasant of settings can be a potential trigger for verbal and physical abuse if individuals become upset and the situation is dealt with poorly.

Activity 7.3

Think about the 'flash points' in your own setting. What might cause somebody, either visitor or client, to become upset and start to behave unreasonably?

Write these situations down and then consider how you dealt with them. How did it make you feel and do you think you handled it well?

Discuss them with somebody in the group and compare your findings.

Some of the things we can experience include:

- teenagers losing their temper and behaving unreasonably

- visitors unhappy with aspects of care that a loved one is receiving starting to shout

- being blamed by a colleague for something you did not do

- a patient or client shouting and behaving in an aggressive manner.

Whatever your situation is, it is the way in which you deal with it that will make the biggest difference to all concerned. There are many factors that can lead to the escalation of violence and abuse in a setting but your interpretation of the event and the person's feelings may also contribute to the situation becoming worse or better.

Let's look at the following Case study. Read it and then discuss.

Case study

The case of the pain in the neck

Mrs Phillips, a 76-year-old lady with advanced Alzheimer's disease, assaulted Jennifer, a care worker in a residential care home. During a routine morning span of duty when Jennifer was assisting with Mrs Phillips's washing and dressing, Mrs Phillips' behaviour became aggressive and she pushed Jennifer to the ground and kicked her. Jennifer sustained bruises to her upper thigh and banged her head on the chair as she fell.

At the next staff meeting, staff were adamant that 'something needed to be done' about the elderly client's behaviour, which had become increasingly challenging over the last few days.

Think about this scenario and say why you think the behaviour may have started to become worse and what you would have done about it. Now ask somebody else to read the Case study and get their perspective on it.

Chances are that you may both have had different ideas as to why Mrs Phillips became so aggressive. If you then go on to ask others you may add to those reasons. For example, some may say Mrs Phillips is seeking attention, or that she is severely depressed. Others will say it's all part of her condition or that you approached her in a negative way and are therefore to blame.

These differences in perspective lead to different ways in which you will deal with the behaviour. If we favour the depression explanation, then Mrs Phillips may well be given medication to solve this issue. Perhaps counselling will be the answer – or assigning her a carer who is more sympathetic.

Perhaps Mrs Phillips is seeking attention and we have missed something. Perhaps she is in pain and the clue to her behaviour was in the title of the case study.

Bissell *et al.* (2005) report the case of a man with learning difficulties whose behaviour became less violent following dental problems being sorted. Mrs Phillips may well be suffering with a neck pain and therefore merely require some analgesia.

The point here is that challenging behaviour may be the only way a person can communicate at that time and it is important for us as care workers to find out what the 'function' of that particular behaviour is. For example, the man shouting at staff in the emergency department may well be feeling pain, frustration, anxiety and even be very frightened. His behaviour is potentially dangerous to us but, by trying to understand what that behaviour is doing for that individual, we can help to change the situation. It is easy to shout back or to manhandle somebody out of the department but by standing back and trying to determine what led to the behaviour and what is actually being communicated by that behaviour we can go a long way to defusing the situation. Mrs Phillips could not communicate her pain verbally but vigilance on the part of the staff caring for her may have given several clues as to how she was feeling.

Consider this for a moment. If we describe behaviour in a negative manner we are likely to deal with it as such.

The term 'attention seeking' carries negative connotations of being manipulative and just plain spoilt. But if we view it as a way of drawing attention to a problem we might have a different reaction to it. The child who fails to understand the lesson being taught may behave badly and in a disruptive manner and be unable to ask the question they most need to ask. The teacher who recognises that behaviour will seek to help that individual in a different way and not just remove them altogether from the lesson.

By working out what the 'function' of the challenging behaviour is and what it helps the person to achieve in a given situation, we can then start to help the individual to deal with the situation they find difficult in more constructive ways. For further on this, see Lowe and Felce (1995).

So we have identified several areas of potential hazard within our work settings to which we need to turn our attention. At the start of the chapter we highlighted the responsibility for health and safety from both the employer's and the employee's point of view and we now return to that topic to see how that has arisen and more specifically what it means for us as care workers.

The Health and Safety at Work Act 1974 (HASAWA)

You may be familiar with this act but it is well to return to it from time to time to allow ourselves to reflect on what it means to us as care workers. The updates and amendments that have occurred to this act over the years have led to the term 'umbrella act', describing the various facets which make up the whole. These are:

Manual Handling Regulations 1992

Control of Substances Hazardous to Health Regulations 2002 (COSHH)

Reporting on Injuries, Diseases and Dangerous Occurrences Regulations 1995 (RIDDOR)

Health and Safety First Aid Regulations 1981

Management of Health and Safety at Work Regulations 1999.

While it is not imperative that you know what these guidelines consist of in detail, you do need to know how to act in response to the legal requirements.

Each workplace where there are more than five employees is required to have a written health and safety policy in place. The National Minimum Standards for Care number 11.2 (DoH, 2000) states that:

> The agency delivering the care has a comprehensive health and safety policy and written procedures for health and safety management defining:

- individual and organisational responsibility for health and safety

- responsibilities and arrangements or risk assessments under the requirements of the Health and Safety at Work Regulations (1999).

Take a look at that policy in your work setting now and see whether it details the following points:

- a commitment to ensuring the safety of all employees, patients, clients and visitors to the organisation

- a statement of intent to that purpose

- an implementation plan that shows how this will be achieved

- a list of procedures with respect to action to be taken in the event of accidents or need to evacuate premises.

You are also likely to have a health and safety poster displayed which details the staff who are designated safety officers and first aiders.

Failing this, staff need to be given leaflets and directions on how health and safety law affects them in their daily work.

As an employee, your responsibility in the workplace is to take care of your own safety and that of others and to cooperate with your employer on all aspects of health and safety.

The Health and Safety Executive (HSE) is part of the government Health and Safety Commission (HSC) and these bodies are responsible for the control and monitoring of the risks within the workplace to ensure that workers remain safe. The belief that prevention is better than cure informs their

Figure 7.5 Health and safety

mission statement (www.hse.gov.uk): 'to protect people's health and safety by ensuring that risks in the … workplace are properly controlled'.

One of the duties of an employer is to carry out risk assessments for the premises and then to put into place risk control measures. To comply with the Safety Representative and Safety Committee Regulations (1977) and the Health and Safety Consultations with Employees Regulations (1996) (www. hse.gov.uk), the employer must talk to staff to identify the common hazards within the workplace and carry out risk assessments.

We may view risk assessment as a somewhat onerous task but we need to carry out such assessment prior to any activity being undertaken. The key stages within the process seek to address the following areas:

> **Step one**: looking for hazards. An investigation of the premises, activity or procedure needs to be undertaken. As we mentioned earlier in the chapter, the hazards identified will depend very much on the type of work being carried out. The risk assessment

in a school is unlikely to be the same as that in a restaurant or a sawmill.

Step two: identifying who could be harmed and how.
This seeks to show special arrangements for the types of hazards that people may come into contact with either through their daily work in an area or as clients. We are all familiar with hard hats being worn by anybody entering a building site. But you might be at risk of infection during a span of duty (more about this later).

Step three: evaluation of the risk.
In this part of the assessment you are making a judgement as to the arrangements already in place for dealing with a potential problem area. An example might be simply changing storage arrangements to free up the fire exit or identifying safer ways to transport clients to outpatient appointments.

Step four: record the findings.
A record needs to include checklists identifying the hazards, the people likely to be at risk and arrangements to reduce the hazard.

Step five: assess the effectiveness of the precautions in place.
Following any dangerous occurrence, staff are expected to complete accident forms and sometimes to inform the HSE. If this occurrence shows up several times, then clearly the risk assessment needs to be revisited and safer actions put into place.

Let's consider a simple example. Needle stick injuries have become less of a problem since the development of user-friendly syringes and needles. As a student nurse, following the administration of an injection, I was required to re-sheath the needle and then break it at the point of contact with the syringe prior to disposal in the sharps bin. Inevitably a number of us managed to prick ourselves with the needle during part of this procedure. Changes to the procedure now do not require us to re-sheath the needle but merely to dispose of it immediately, as it is, into plastic sharps bins. Much safer, and the

result of evaluating a risk (Tilmouth and Tilmouth, 2009).

COSHH and RIDDOR

A reminder about these two pieces of legislation as they affect those who work in care. The Control of Substances Hazardous to Health Regulations (2002) require all settings to do the following:

- identify the substances specific to the setting and the risk posed by these to health
- decide on precautions to take when working with these substances
- control any exposure to substances where this is unavoidable
- ensure safe procedure is followed at all times
- monitor exposure if unavoidable
- carry out health assessment
- prepare a plan of action should an accident occur
- ensure all staff are trained and supervised and that a COSHH file is available in the workplace detailing where the substances are stored, how they are to be labelled, what their effects might be, safe exposure times and how to deal with an emergency if one arises.

Activity 7.4

Access your COSHH file and re-familiarise yourself with the details.

You will notice that any substance that is toxic is always labelled with a yellow triangle indicating that the substance is dangerous. Be sure to check that these symbols are in place in your work area.

The Reporting of Injuries, Diseases and Dangerous Occurrences Regulations (RIDDOR) is a legal requirement and all major injuries, accidents and outbreaks of disease need to be reported to the incident contact centre, which was set up in 2001. These occurrences are then logged and

Figure 7.6 Hazard signs

passed on to either local environmental agencies or the HSE. Anything which may have occurred and has the potential to be dangerous must also be reported. See Table 7.1.

Table 7.1 Reportable occurrences and injuries

Injury	Disease
Fractures, amputations and dislocations	Poisonings
Loss of sight or penetrating eye injuries	Skin disease such as occupational dermatitis
Burns, electric shocks causing unconsciousness	Lung disease due to occupational influences: for example, asthma or asbestosis
Any injury resulting in unconsciousness	Legionnaires' disease and other infections such as TB or hepatitis
Any illness resulting from exposure to toxins or infected material	

As you will no doubt be aware, the first thing you will be required to do following such an incident is to administer first aid, and we will cover this aspect later on in the chapter. Your responsibility, however, does not end with the person being taken to hospital or returning to work but has to be reported and documented. Any accident book or forms used need to comply with the Data Protection Act 1998 and personal details and details of the accident must be kept

confidentially. We will look in more detail at this later on in the record-keeping section of the chapter but in the meantime you need to be aware of reporting the following:

- date, time and place of accident
- people involved – ensure confidentiality
- details of what you saw, what you heard and what was said (caution must be exercised here: you must take care not to write down your own opinion of what happened)
- what the individual presented with in terms of signs and symptoms
- time help was summoned, what help it was and what time it arrived
- witness names
- equipment involved.

Activity 7.5

Access a copy of your accident book and evaluate the contents. Does it provide the correct information? Does it comply with the Data Protection Act 1998?

Infection control and its prevention

Health-care-associated infections or HCAIs have proved to be problematic in care settings for a number of years, and high on the agenda of health care professionals is the need to control infection. The battle over the last ten years or so has been the rise of so called' superbugs' which do not respond to common antibiotics and this has caused no end of media alarm. You will be aware of the rise of MRSA (methicillin-resistant *staphylococcus aureus*) but also on the increase are VRE (vancomycin-resistant *enterococci*), E. coli (*escherichia coli*), ESBL (extended-spectrum β lactamases) and the C. diff infections (*clostridium difficile*).

The effects on patients' and clients' lives as well as the cost to the health system are huge and have led to government initiatives to address the problem.

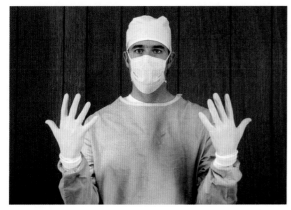

Figure 7.7 Infection control

There is a wealth of information about how infection is spread and controlled in various books and you are encouraged to look at the detailed texts if you require more

---

Government initiatives on superbugs

1998 Report of the House of Lords Select Committee – 'Resistance to antibiotics and other antimicrobial agents'

1999 'Resistance to antibiotics and other antimicrobial agents': action for the NHS

2000 DoH: 'The management and control of hospital acquired infection': action for the NHS

2001 The EPIC Project: 'Developing national evidence-based guidelines for preventing health-care-associated infections. Phase 1: Guidelines for preventing hospital-acquired infections'

2001 The mandatory surveillance system for serious infections caused by *staphylococcus aureus* (MRSA) was started.

2002 DoH: 'Getting ahead of the curve: a strategy for combating infectious disease (including other aspects of health protection)'

2003 NICE produced guidelines on the prevention of health-care-associated infections in primary and community settings

2004 'Winning ways: working together to reduce health-care-associated infections in England'

2007 Gordon Brown pledged to rid the Health Service of superbugs ('A brave pledge!': *Observer*, 23 September) when he introduced the Deep Clean campaign

---

information. A good website to access, which also gives up-to-date data, is that of the Health Protection Agency at http://www.hpa.org.uk/.

Our daily exposure in health care settings to blood and bodily fluids places us at high risk of contamination and therefore we need to be vigilant in protecting ourselves. We are also duty bound to ensure that the patients and clients we come into contact with are not at risk from poor practice on our part.

The core principles related to infection control can be summarised as follows (Tilmouth and Tilmouth, 2009):

- effective hand washing
- protective clothing
- isolation nursing
- laundry and waste management
- cleanliness of the environment
- decontamination of equipment.

Effective hand washing

Our hands are among the foremost ways in which infection can be transmitted from patient to patient, and despite knowing this for years, the wealth of information and research about this simple procedure is testament to the fact that we still fall short in our compliance.

Think of it this way. Our hands are heavily populated with micro-organisms which we acquire through various activities we undertake in the case setting. These micro-organisms survive on the hands and can then be transmitted to others when we carry out procedures in our daily activity. We can also collect disease-causing organisms, so we are at risk of becoming ill ourselves. With good hand-washing techniques we can remove large numbers of these microbes.

Correct technique

Ayliffe *et al.* (1978) devised a useful six-step technique to ensure that all parts of the hand were washed efficiently. See Figure 7.8.

Step one: using soap and running water, start with the palms

Step two: right palm over back of hand and left palm over right back of hand

Step three: palm to palm and interlace fingers

Step four: backs of fingers to palms with fingers interlocked

Step five: rotational rubbing of each thumb

Step six: rotational rubbing with clasped fingers of right hand in left palm and vice versa.

You will have noticed that hand rubs and alcohol have also been introduced into care settings and other establishments to try to reduce the risk of infection.

In 2003 Sir Liam Donaldson questioned the accessibility of hand-washing facilities and it became apparent that one of the reasons why hand washing was not being carried out was simply due to lack of facilities. The use of alcohol gels and hand rubs then began to be introduced and, although not a substitute for soap and water, do have a part to play in infection control.

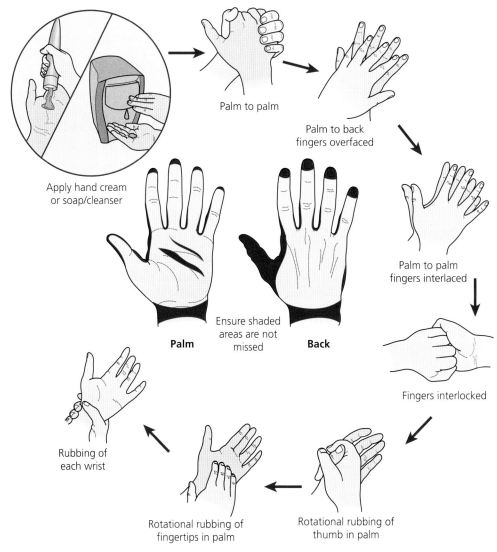

Figure 7.8 Correct hand-washing technique

Protective clothing

Another area for our own and others' protection is the use of personal protective equipment (PPE). PPE is mentioned in the Health and Safety at Work Act 1974 and all employers must supply clothing, aprons gloves and gowns where there is a risk of infection.

In any procedure where blood or bodily fluids are likely to be touched, the employees must wear gloves and aprons. After contact these need to be disposed of safely in correct waste areas.

Gloves must be used only once and must be discarded after contact with each patient/client. You need then to wash your hands.

There are various types of gloves that you may come across depending upon your setting. In surgery the gloves used will be sterile but for other use a non-sterile glove may be used. In any procedure where asepsis is required, a sterile glove must be used. So if you are changing dressings or inserting catheters or cannulae, then a sterile glove must be employed. If, however, you are washing a client or emptying a bedpan, then a non-sterile glove may be used.

Uniforms need to be clean as they are a potential source of contamination from micro-organisms. Staff need to be encouraged to change out of their uniforms prior to leaving work.

Activity 7.6

Go to www.rcn.org.uk/search?qeuries_sear_query=wipe+it+out to read the guidelines produced with respect to uniforms.

Isolation nursing

We need to mention this particular type of care here since the safety of staff and other patients/clients may be at risk from infection if we do not adhere to policy. Your care organisation will have in place a policy for dealing with infective disorders where they pose a risk to others. Make sure you are aware of that policy.

Where a contagious patient/client is identified, all attempts to isolate the infection need to be undertaken and if possible a separate room should be available for use. All staff entering the room need to be aware of the standards required, and the need to wear gloves, gowns and aprons should be clearly identified. Separate equipment which stays in the room must be cleaned and sterilised according to strict guidelines. Any bedding or clothing must be sent for special cleaning and therefore may need to bagged in special bags to show contamination. The Environmental Protection Act of 1990 gives guidelines as to the disposal of contaminated waste (you can view this at www.opsi.gov.uk/acts/acts1990/Ukpga_19900043_en_1.htm).

Laundry and waste management

Since July 2005, new regulations exist with respect to how we classify the waste we generate in care settings.

Hazardous and non-hazardous labelling now applies and the former refers to waste that is potentially disease causing. This waste needs to be incinerated and must be placed in yellow bags. Any other waste can be placed in black bags.

Sharp objects must be put into the yellow sharps bins with wording on the side in black and red.

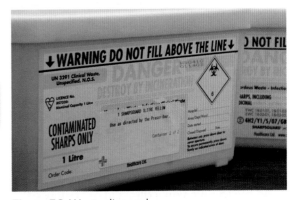

Figure 7.9 Waste disposal

Cleanliness of the environment

In 2001 a new role in the NHS emerged, one that was to help with infection control within health organisations. The role of matron was reinstated in order to ensure higher standards of care and to address cleanliness and generally drive a quality initiative for patients. The 'Modern matron' report published by the DoH in 2003 showed that since the new role had been introduced, £60 million had been spent on improving cleanliness in hospitals and standards had improved from 23 per cent to 60 per cent.

While this role clearly has had an impact on general cleanliness it seems unfortunate that the government had to resort to such measures to try to drive the need for cleaner hospitals. With our increased knowledge of infection transmission and our superior technologies it is shameful that we have to remind ourselves of the need for basic cleanliness when it comes to disinfecting and cleaning equipment, beds and bedding.

Decontamination of equipment

The use of chemicals to decontaminate various pieces of equipment carries a risk to care workers as well as to clients and patients. The COSHH regulations 2002 are in place to ensure that all substances used to disinfect areas are clearly labelled and safely stored.

Substances you may be familiar include methylated spirits, hand rubs, chlorhexidine, gluteraldehyde, hycolin and Jeyes fluid.

Activity 7.7

Identify in your own organisation some of the substances that may be subject to COSHH regulations.

Common emergency conditions and what actions you need to take

Within the remit of this text it is only possible to give you a general overview of the sorts of situations that may arise in your care setting and which you may need to deal with as the first person on the scene.

We will refer to clients and patients here as casualties since we cannot assume that anyone you give first aid to will come into the former categories.

Being faced with a potential emergency situation is a frightening experience and feelings and emotions can often escalate, causing us to act in irrational ways. You will, of course, have been required to undertake some first aid training and while these courses are generally very good they give us only hypothetical scenarios. Faced with the real thing, we can often forget everything we have been taught. So first things first. Have a look at Activity 7.8.

Activity 7.8

The case of the sleeping man: part one

On entering Mr Brown's bay you see that he is still asleep. You need to get him ready for his physiotherapy session. It is 8.45 a.m. and you are somewhat surprised he has lain in for so long. You approach the bed and try to wake him but he fails to respond to your voice.

What will you do?

Did you say 'Panic'? 'Shout for help'? 'Press the call button'?

Possibly you said all of those things – but you then need to set into motion the first aid procedures.

What you need to do first of all is to ensure that you are not in any danger. In this instance it is unlikely but suppose you come across a casualty in a car accident. You might be in danger of injuring yourself in the process of helping them – we would then have two casualties. You might realise that a building is on fire and somebody is shouting for help. Is it wise for you to go into the burning area or do you need to wait until help arrives? That's your call, but remember two casualties are worse than one.

So if there is no danger to yourself, you can proceed by gently shaking Mr Brown and asking him if he is all right. If you still fail to get a response, then you need to summon help. Our initial panic may mean we shout for help before we ascertain that the patient is actually only in a deep sleep and when help arrives, the patient is sitting up in bed and yawning and wondering what all the fuss is about.

Figure 7.10 Look, listen and feel for breathing and pulse

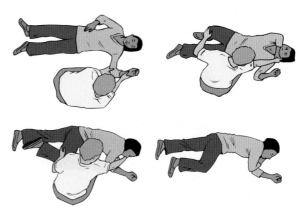

Figure 7.11 Recovery position

After you have called for help, you need to ascertain that Mr Brown is breathing. This is your first priority.

To check that he is breathing normally, you listen and watch for ten seconds, checking whether you can hear breathing and watching to see if the chest rises and falls. If Mr Brown is still breathing, then you can be fairly certain his heart is still beating. So if you are happy with the fact that there is still circulation, you then need to determine another cause for his failure to wake. A check around the rest of Mr Brown's body may reveal a bleed somewhere or another injury. As Mr Brown has been in bed all night, it is unlikely that there are any broken bones we need to take care of but we will carry out a general survey of the patient before we move him.

If nothing is found and while we wait for the paramedics to arrive, we need to put Mr Brown into a position which will ensure he can continue to breathe without any problems. This is the recovery position. What you do not have to do is to diagnose the reason for Mr Brown's failure to wake up. That is for the medical staff to do. What you have to remember is that as the first person on the scene your aims are to do the following (Barraclough, 2008):

- preserve life
- prevent the situation from getting worse
- promote recovery.

Now let's look in detail at the recovery position to remind ourselves how we can achieve this.

The recovery position

When a person lies on their back, there is a potential for their airway to become blocked because the tongue tends to touch the back of the throat. (Disregard the fallacy that an individual can swallow their tongue; this is not possible since it is attached.) If a person vomits in this position, then the airway can also become blocked. Best to reduce both these risks by turning the person on their side.

Straighten both legs and bend the arm nearest to you outwards and at right angles, palm uppermost.

Bring the casualty's other hand up to their face and lay the back of the hand across the cheek. This will act as a support and cushions the head. Remember you will have to hold the hand in place since a person who is unconscious will have no muscle control to do so.

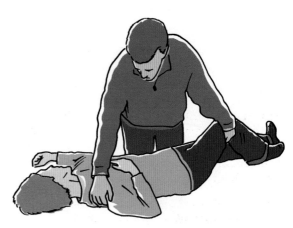

Figure 7.12 Step one recovery – arm nearest to you at right angles, lift knee and hand on shoulder

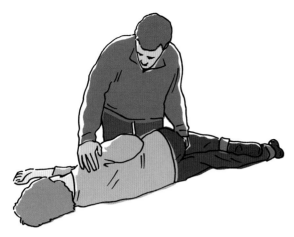

Figure 7.13 Step two – turn towards you

Now with your other hand bring the far knee up, foot firmly placed on the floor, and, using the knee as a lever, pull the casualty towards you, placing the knee onto the floor. The casualty will now be on their side.

Practise this on a colleague. You will soon see just how easy it is to do.

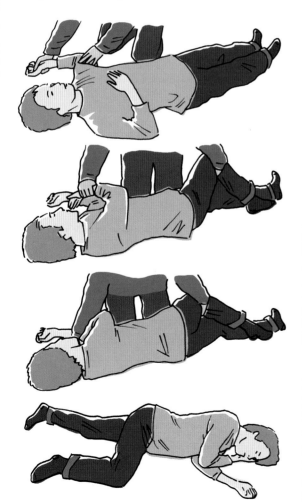

Figure 7.14 Procedure

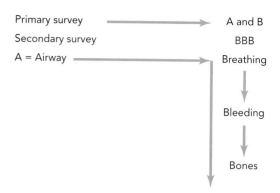

Figure 7.15 A primary and secondary survey

Danger → Response → Airway → Breathing

Figure 7.16 DRAB

In the space of a few seconds, what you have done is to carry out what is known as a primary and secondary survey. You can remember this by the mnemonic 'A and three Bs'. See Figure 7.15.

Let's put this together in another way. The acronym DRAB will help you to remember. See Figure 7.16.

Let's take our scenario a step further in Activity 7.9.

Activity 7.9

The case of the sleeping man: part two

This is a bad day for you. As soon as you have put Mr Brown into the recovery position, you notice that Mr Green in the bed opposite is looking a little agitated and starting to complain about a pain in his chest. Happy that Mr Brown is safe for the time being, you approach Mr Green's bed just as he collapses.

What will you do?

Hopefully you carried out the same procedure as for Mr Brown – only this time you realise that the collapse is due to Mr Green's breathing having stopped. This means that no oxygen will now be coming into his body and his heart is likely to stop soon and his brain cells will start to die off in minutes. So you need to act fast. Let's go through the protocols for action now.

You checked there would be no danger to yourself. You got no response from Mr Green. Although his airway was clear, it was apparent that his breathing had stopped. So what to do?

You now need to get help and ask somebody to dial 999 and say that the casualty has stopped breathing. It is then up to you to start cardio-pulmonary resuscitation (CPR). The ratio of compression to breaths is 30 compressions to 2 breaths.

First you need to breathe for Mr Green. You do this by tilting Mr Green's head back gently and lifting his chin, thereby opening the airway. This action means the tongue is brought forward and the air passages are then clearly opened. See Figures 7.17 and 7.18.

This is hard work and you need help with it, otherwise you will become a casualty yourself.

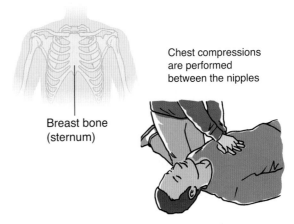

Chest compressions are performed between the nipples

Breast bone (sternum)

Figure 7.19 Chest compressions are performed between the nipples

To see how it is done, see Figure 7.19.

Place the heel of your hand onto the middle of the chest, then interlock the fingers of your other hand over that. Keep your arms straight (not like they do in movies!) and press down on to the breast bone (sternum) to about 5 cm, then release and do that 30 times. What you are doing is pushing the ribcage down to squeeze the heart, allowing it to pump blood around the body.

When you have finished that cycle you need to tilt the head back, nip the patient's nose and then breathe two breaths into them. This gives them some oxygen for the heart to pump around to feed the tissues and brain cells. Watch the chest rise as you breath in – if it doesn't do so, then check you have cleared the airway sufficiently.

Every now and then you will need to check that the patient has not started breathing again or that the airway remains open and some oxygen is getting in.

CPR for children

For children, the rate can be the same as the adult rate (30:2), but initially 5 breaths are given before continuing with 30 compressions.

Modifications need to be made to the pressure. A good rule is: for children over one year, use one hand; for babies, use two fingers in the compressions.

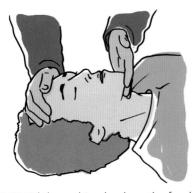

Figure 7.17 While pushing back on the forehead, use your other hand to lift the chin forward

Figure 7.18 Place your mouth over the victim's mouth and exhale

Hygiene during CPR

People are concerned about the potential of coming into contact with an infectious disorder through mouth-to-mouth resuscitation and it is not uncommon for a patient to vomit. Some first aiders carry face shields and airways with them and if you are in a care setting it is possible you may have access to such items – in which case, use them. If you can clean the face prior to starting the CPR, then do so; but if there is no shield handy, then by all means use a tissue over the mouth. If you are still not happy to give mouth-to-mouth, then just carry out compressions until help arrives.

Activity 7.10

You are leaving work and you see a lady who has collapsed in the street. You offer your assistance since nobody in attendance seems to know what to do.

Draw a flow diagram to show how you would proceed with dealing with the casualty.

Did you have anything like Figure 7.20?

Common causes of collapse

A really good way of remembering the causes of unconsciousness was coined by Barraclough in *First Aid Made Easy* (2008). The mnemonic FISH SHAPED identifies the causes as:

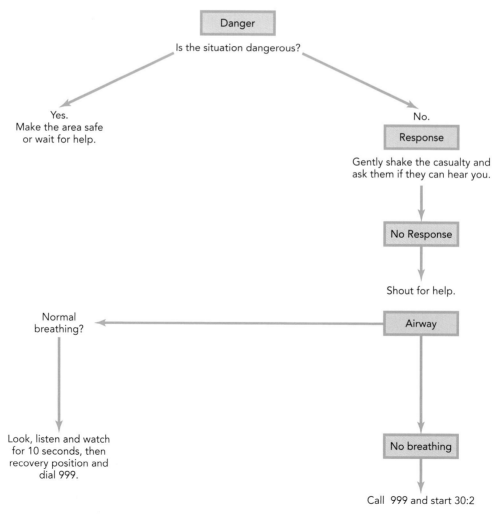

Figure 7.20

F: fainting

I: imbalance of heat

S: shock

H: head injury

S: stroke

H: heart attack

A: asphyxia

P: poisoning

E: epilepsy

D: diabetes.

We will look at the first aid treatment for a few of these causes.

Unconsciousness is a sleep-like state which disables the normal bodily reflexes and places the casualty in danger of airway obstruction and consequent lack of oxygen. Any unconscious casualty should be treated with the primary survey you carried out above. You need to make sure they are breathing, call for professional assistance and then try to ascertain what may be causing the unconsciousness.

You can do this by carrying out what is known as the secondary survey and we mentioned this very briefly above. Here it is in more detail

The secondary survey involves a check for other injuries and must be carried out quickly and methodically. See Figure 7.21.

If you happy the casualty is breathing, you can do the following:

Check for bleeding Check all the way down the body to see if you can find any bleed.

Check under the back If you do find a bleed then follow the correct procedure for controlling haemorrhage. (See below.)

Head and neck Has the casualty had an accident that may have resulted in injury to neck or head? Check for swelling, deformity or bleeding. (Other clues may be the surroundings and the environment; for example, there might be a ladder nearby, an object that may have fallen onto them, an overturned chair or, in the case of a car accident, perhaps the casualty sustained a severe whiplash.)

Shoulders and chest Carefully run your fingers along the collar bone (clavicle). Look at both sides to see if they are symmetrical or whether there a distinct difference to indicate a possible break.

Check the ribs Do they look normal?

Abdomen and pelvis Check for breaks in bones or even swelling in the area.

Legs and arms Is there a medic-alert bracelet which might indicate a reason for the collapse? Do the legs and arms look as though they may have sustained a fracture?

Pockets Any objects or tablets in the pockets? Make sure nothing can injure the casualty as you turn them into the recovery position.

Anything untoward found during this survey will now need to be treated to prevent the condition from worsening.

We shall now look at some of the likely conditions you may come across in the course of your work. Of course, a risk assessment of your own setting will reveal any conditions that may be more likely to occur and you will need further training at work. For example, if you work in the occupational health department of a factory which deals with welding or electrical maintenance, it is likely that you will come across different types of first aid treatments that might be needed. You may need to ensure you are familiar with the types of injuries or accidents that could occur in these specialist areas.

Figure 7.21 Secondary survey

Fainting

A simple faint can occur for a number of reasons and is sometimes heralded by the person complaining of feeling 'woozy' or looking as if they are swaying. This may look like a case of shock. You may notice the person has a cold clammy skin. The pulse will be slow.

Action If the person is about to faint, lay them down on the floor. Often this will enable the blood to return to the vital organs, in particular the brain and heart, and the person will start to feel better.

In the case of actual loss of consciousness, you need to carry out the DRAB procedure and then place the person in the recovery position.

Make sure the airway is maintained by tilting the head back and check for breathing.

Then carry out a secondary survey to try to ascertain the cause of the faint.

Do not give anything by mouth (you may compromise the airway).

Do not leave the person alone (unless you have to go and get help).

Haemorrhage

Any bleed from any injury requires prompt treatment to prevent severe shock occurring.

The severity of the haemorrhage depends largely upon the type of injury and the vessels involved. We have three types of blood vessel and each type delivers blood to tissues in different ways.

Arteries are larger vessels which pump blood under pressure. A wound to an artery can cause the blood to spurt out of the body at high speed and occasionally for some distance. This means that the casualty will soon lose a lot of blood volume, which can be fatal. The blood is bright red in colour due to being highly oxygenated.

Veins, while carrying the same amount of blood as the arteries, are not under so much pressure and a bleed from a vein tends to come out much more slowly. The bleed from a varicose vein may be slow but is potentially very dangerous since a lot of blood can be leaked at one time.

Capillaries are tiny vessels; blood flow from a cut to them may at first be quite profuse but generally eases to a trickle after slight pressure is applied. (You may recall cutting your finger and wondering if it would ever stop.)

The effect of any blood loss therefore depends upon the size of the wound, the injury and the vessels involved, but loss of blood over a prolonged time can cause severe shock and can be fatal.

You need to stop the bleed if you can see it and you can do this by applying direct pressure to the wound. Sometimes the bleed may be due to an internal haemorrhage and the only indication you will have of this being the case will be the casualty's shocked appearance and the symptoms that go with internal haemorrhage (which we will cover later).

If you can elevate the part affected, this will have the effect of reducing the flow of blood to the area and will slow the bleed.

You need to cover the wound to reduce the infection risk and to keep the pressure constant.

Ensure you maintain your own safety by checking for glass and embedded objects in the wound that might cut you. If gloves are available, wear them and then wash your hands thoroughly after treating. Any cuts on your own hands should always be covered when you are at work, in order to provide a barrier from blood-to-blood contact.

Call 999 if the wound is severe.

Do not apply a tourniquet that could cause long-term tissue damage.

Do not secure the dressing too tightly.

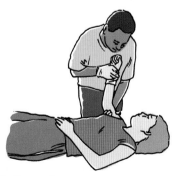

Figure 7.22 Cover the wound to reduce the infection risk and to keep the pressure constant

Shock

If blood pressure falls low enough and there is inadequate blood getting to the tissues, a condition known as shock is said to exist.

There are three types of shock:

> hypovolaemic

> cardiogenic

> anaphylactic.

Hypovolaemic shock occurs when there is a low (hypo) volume (vol) of blood (aemic) circulating and may be caused by internal or external haemorrhage.

Cardiogenic shock refers to the fall in blood pressure caused by heart and respiratory problems such as heart attack or 'myocardial infarction', heart valve disease or lung problems. We deal with this type of shock later.

Anaphylactic shock is an allergic reaction in which histamine is released in large quantities, causing the blood pressure to drop and the heart to contract more slowly. We will also deal with this type of shock later.

Recognising the casualty in shock

Initial stages of shock In any shock condition the body responds by releasing adrenaline. You will remember the 'fight or flight' analogy in which, faced with a dramatic event or stress, we make the decision either to run away or to stay and deal with the situation. Whatever we decide to do, our body responds by releasing adrenaline, which has the effect of raising the pulse rate. Our skin will start to become pale and clammy.

Second stage shock As the condition gets worse, our breathing becomes faster and more shallow and the pulse starts to weaken. This has the effect of less oxygen getting to the tissues and will therefore cause a slight blueness around lips and nose (cyanosis), subsequent dizziness and perhaps vomiting.

Critical stage This is a condition known as 'air hunger', characterised by deep sighing breaths, leading to confusion and perhaps aggressive behaviour and finally unconsciousness.

Action Lay the casualty down and raise the legs (if there are fractures in the lower limb, raise one leg). This will aid blood return to the brain and heart.

> Dial 999.

> Keep the casualty warm.

> Keep a close eye on breathing and respiration and be prepared to resuscitate.

> **Do not** allow the casualty anything to eat or drink, or to smoke.

Seizures

A person who has been diagnosed with epilepsy may have regular seizures and will know exactly what to do in the event of one occurring. In this case your treatment is to ensure the safety of that individual during the actual seizure.

The types of seizure can vary from a moment's loss of consciousness or the appearance of daydreaming, as in 'absence seizures' (formerly known as *petit mal*) or major seizures, which, when experienced for the first time, can be very frightening to watch.

Action Help the casualty to the floor. Prevent injury by moving anything that may be in the way. Cushion the casualty's head. Ask bystanders to leave the scene. Check airway and breathing, if possible to do so.

Dial 999 if seizure continues for longer than three minutes, or if another seizure follows recovery, or if this is the casualty's first seizure.

Do not restrict the casualty's movements in any way.

Do not put anything into their mouth during the fit stage.

Following the seizure, check airway and breathing. Keep casualty in recovery position until fully awake.

Febrile convulsions

This sort of seizure can occur in children and babies who have a high temperature, and may be the only time they suffer from a seizure. It is clearly very distressing and can also lead to a cessation in breathing.

Figure 7.23

The action here is to reduce the temperature by removing clothing and cooling the body. If a fit does occur, then you need to deal with it as before.

Choking

When a person inhales food or a sweet they will be unable to tell you what they have done. The signs to look out for are:

- distressed look
- clutching at and pointing to throat
- inability to speak or cough
- pale skin, leading to cyanosis
- breathing becomes compromised.

Action Encourage the casualty to cough. If this is not successful, shout for help and then bend the casualty forward and give five firm back slaps between the shoulder blades.

If breathing is still obstructed, stand behind the casualty and grasp them around the waist. Make a fist and place it above the navel. With your other hand, pull the fist sharply upwards five times (known as abdominal thrusts).

If the casualty becomes unconscious, you need to carry out CPR.

Anaphylaxis

This is a serious condition in which there is a sudden swelling of the face, tongue and lips. It is usually due to the ingestion by the patient of something to which they are allergic – such as peanuts, medication or other foodstuff. It may also be brought on in some people by wasp or bee stings. Whatever the cause, a rapid deterioration

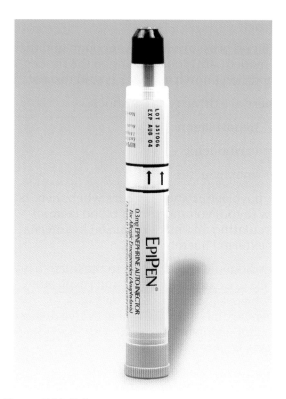

Figure 7.24 Epi pen

of the situation can lead to the airway being constricted and the breathing becoming compromised.

The casualty may have a rash on the skin, complain of itchiness and have a rapid, weak pulse. Fast action is required.

Action Call 999. If the casualty has their own treatment with them due to previous knowledge of allergy, you may assist them with the treatment. These treatments usually come in the form of adrenaline in an auto injector, which is a little like a pen – hence the term 'Epi-pen'.

Otherwise, treat airway and breathing as for an emergency and, if the casualty is faint, lay them down.

Diabetes and the problems that may occur

It is becoming more common to deal with clients and patients (casualties) who suffer with diabetes – a disorder caused by a reduced production of the hormone insulin, which is used by the body to break down sugar we digest. Without insulin the body cannot use the sugar taken in and this has major health effects.

There are three types of diabetes:

Diet controlled Casualties with this type of diabetes can control their symptoms by reducing and monitoring the amount of sugar they ingest. Their bodies are producing some insulin.

Tablet controlled These casualties need to control their diets and take medications that reduce the level of sugar in the body. Their supply of insulin is limited.

Insulin dependent With this type of diabetes, the casualty has no insulin in their body – or only a minimal amount – and needs to inject insulin several times a day in order to keep their sugar levels under control.

A mismatch of sugar and insulin is known as hyperglycaemia.

Hyperglycaemia

High (hyper) sugar (glyc) levels in the blood (aem) become quite toxic to the body. Acid builds up and sets off a chain of events that makes the person ill. As the body tries to get rid of the acid build-up, the person is likely to present with the following signs and symptoms.

After a long period of time, 12 to 48 hours, the patient will become increasingly drowsy and may even become unconscious.

They will have a rapid pulse and are likely to breathe slowly and deeply. They pass a lot of urine and are constantly thirsty and hungry. Occasionally the breath smells of pear drops.

As you will appreciate, it is possible to put these symptoms down to other causes, so we need to be very aware of what is happening over time.

Action The treatment for this condition is always to contact the emergency services and to treat airway and breathing as in the protocols above.

Hypoglycaemia

You are more likely to come across this condition in which there is a low (hypo) level of sugar (glyc) in the blood (aem). In fact, you may have experienced this at some point yourself. It does not mean you are diabetic; it just means that you may have expended the insulin in your body and not taken in enough sugar, giving you a slight lowering of the blood sugar level. This sometimes happens if we do not eat enough and have taken lots of exercise and then we feel a little dizzy and weak. We can sort this out usually with a drink and something to eat. For the diabetic casualty the same treatment generally applies, although they are more likely to experience this type of episode more regularly.

The signs and symptoms are likely to be as follows.

The onset is rapid and within minutes the patient may exhibit weakness, lack of coordination, confusion and slurring of speech. The casualty may also start to behave in a way that is aggressive and may become quite belligerent. The behaviour may be quite uncharacteristic and the patient may seem to be a little drunk.

If you feel their skin, it will be cold and sweaty, and their breathing is likely to be rapid, as will also be the pulse.

Action It is quite possible that the casualty may have had their insulin and then either forgotten to have breakfast or left it a little too late. As this condition occurs quickly, you will notice that when you start to treat the casualty they will quickly return to their normal self.

Sit the casualty down and give them a sugary drink or some chocolate or a biscuit. If the casualty is becoming unconscious, you can still help them by rubbing something sweet onto their gums. This will have a slower effect but can be useful to make the casualty alert enough to then take a drink.

If there is no response after ten minutes, you need to contact 999.

Cardiovascular accident or stroke

You may have seen the television adverts that have introduced us all to the FAST test. This mnemonic refers to:

F: facial weakness

A: arm weakness

S: speech difficulty and problems

T: time (which is of the essence for full recovery).

A cardiovascular or cerebrovascular accident (CVA), or stroke, is an emergency situation and the sooner the casualty is sent to hospital the sooner treatment can be given. First aid is limited in this instance.

A CVA occurs when there is a reduction of blood flow to the vessels in the brain. This may be due to a narrowing of the cerebral arteries or a blood clot blocking the flow altogether. This is easier to understand if you think about the following. It is a little like the flow of water in a blocked hosepipe. The water is unable to get to where it is needed, your garden perhaps, and the consequence is that the garden dies. The blockage of a flow of blood to parts of the brain is similar. The blood will be unable to deliver nutrients that are needed to a part of the brain and the tissue will therefore cease to function. That part of the brain will not work sufficiently well, if at all. Hence the variety of different effects on the casualty a stroke can have. See Figure 7.25.

For example, paralysis to one or other side of the body, speech problems or memory problems all indicate specific areas of the brain that have been affected and these will only be identified once the casualty has further tests at the hospital. However, your quick action as a first aider in recognising what might be happening is crucial to recovery.

The signs and symptoms may vary but usually the casualty will complain of a headache and then may become confused and perhaps have sight and speech difficulties. You may notice they are unable to balance well and it is possible that if you get to look at their pupils you may see that they are of different sizes.

If unconsciousness occurs, then you need to follow the DRAB protocols and call 999 at once.

Heart attack/myocardial infarction and angina

We used the analogy above of the blocked hosepipe and its failure to keep your garden alive. The same analogy can be applied when we look at angina and heart attack.

Angina pectoris is a condition of the heart in which the flow of blood through the coronary arteries is reduced due to a narrowing of those arteries. See Figure 7.25. The narrowing is due to a build-up of fatty acids and cholesterol (in the hosepipe it might be clogging from soil). This reduces the lumen of the artery and the casualty will notice this when the heart needs to work hard. The casualty with angina will therefore complain of pain when they exercise or in times of stress, when the heart has to pump a little harder to get the tissues oxygenated. The lack of blood getting to the area means there is a smaller amount of oxygen getting through and it is this that causes the pain.

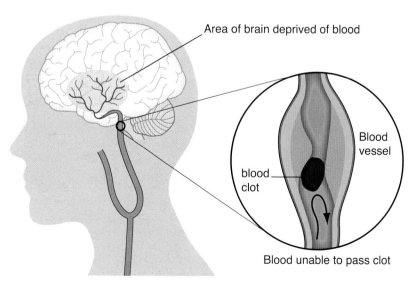

Area of brain deprived of blood

Blood vessel

blood clot

Blood unable to pass clot

Figure 7.25

Action for Angina Get the casualty to rest. This should result in a lowering of the heart rate and the pain will subside. If the casualty knows they suffer from angina, then they are likely to have medication to relieve the symptoms. If this is the first time they have had an attack, then it is wise to get medical assistance.

While the signs and symptoms of angina are similar to those of a heart attack but subside with drugs or rest, the casualty who is suffering from a heart attack will not get relief from rest and this is because the actual artery involved is totally blocked by a blood clot and therefore no oxygen is being delivered to part of the heart muscle – thus causing severe pain. This is an emergency situation and could result in the casualty's death if not treated efficiently.

The onset is sudden and although the pain may be mistaken for indigestion it can also be so severe that the casualty complains of a crushing sensation in the chest. The left arm and shoulders may also be painful and the casualty will be very pale and sweating, and the pulse may be fast and irregular. They will be short of breath and very anxious. They may feel sick and may even feel that they are going to die.

Action for MI The casualty should sit down while you call 999 immediately. The casualty who has angina should be encouraged to take their medication, which may give some relief.

Although you are unable to prescribe medication, it has been shown that aspirin chewed slowly has an anticoagulant effect and can help the casualty. You need to inform the casualty of this potential treatment and allow them the choice of whether they will take it. You should, however, check that they are not already taking anticoagulants such as warfarin or heparin.

If the casualty becomes unconscious, then the DRAB protocols need to be applied.

We are aware that we have omitted the first aid treatment of a number of injuries and conditions, which you may come across in the course of your day-to-day work. However, it is not for this text to give you a first aid course and, as we mentioned before, a risk assessment of the common conditions you are likely to come across in your own work setting must be carried out so that you can be prepared for any eventuality. We have covered common conditions here and for your assessment in this unit we include at the end a sample assignment which you may like to try. The practical aspects of that assessment will go a long way to helping you understand the emergency protocols that can be used to save lives.

The role of support services in emergency situations and disease management

In the course of your day-to-day work you will come into contact with other health professionals. In the last section we dealt with 999 calls and therefore paramedics are likely to arrive on the scene when you have an emergency. Your role in helping them to do their job is one of supplying accurate information, together with times, treatment and protocols you have carried out. This will be documented later in an accident report for your own organisation.

With respect to health and safety in the workplace, infection control and emergency situations, there will be a different group of people involved. It is useful to know what their responsibilities are, particularly with respect to how you deal with outbreaks of infection and who you need to inform.

If you work within the NHS, you will have come across the infection control teams who are responsible within primary care trusts for the control and prevention of infection.

Comprising nursing, medical staff and an infection control committee, their remit is to endorse and make policy, and to monitor the effectiveness of infection control within the trust. So too health and safety teams are also present in large organisations and are required to report on and maintain safe environments for staff working in the organisation and for visitors and users of the services.

But what of those of us who work in community and residential care settings? Who has responsibility for infection control and health and safety here?

With respect to infection control, guidelines published by NICE in 2003 show the measures for preventing and maintaining safe levels of infection control in community settings. Additionally the Department of Health published 'Infection control guidance for care homes' in 2006 and clearly identified the roles of personnel in such settings (DoH, 2006a).

According to these guidelines, the home owner or care manager is required to ensure that policies which identify procedure with respect to how infection is controlled are available and followed. In fact, the Health Act of 2006 (DoH, 2006b) clearly states that employers must 'ensure … that health care workers are free of and are protected from exposure to communicable infections during the course of their work and that all staff are suitably educated in the prevention and control of HCAIs'.

In order to be able to deliver this care, the care manager must have links with the primary care group in the area, who can advise and help with information about infections and disease.

The GP is therefore the first port of call. With responsibility for the care of residents and clients in care homes in their locality, the GP not only provides treatments but can also respond when there is an outbreak of infection. For instance, an outbreak of a notifiable disease in a local care establishment requires the GP to inform the consultant in communicable disease control (CCDC) whom the Health Protection Agency (HPA) employs (a list of these conditions is supplied at www.hpa.org.uk/topics).

The HPA has responsibility for controlling infection in the community and employs a number of staff. The health protection nurse and the community infection control nurse provide education and guidance on infection control and may be contacted by staff in community settings. Environmental health practitioners also have a remit to advise on food safety, waste and pest control and disposal in the community and can be contacted through the environmental health team at the local authority.

Other professionals you may come into contact with are those who work for the Commission for Social Care Inspection (CSCI). Their role is to inspect care homes to ensure that national minimum standards are met and this will also include health and safety and infection control measures.

In recent years the World Health Organization and local departments of health have been preparing for a major outbreak of influenza. Preparations have been such that at-risk staff and patients are being offered vaccinations against this infection. Over 12,000 people die each year in the UK from influenza and your role as a care worker will be to ensure that your clients and patients are conversant with the preventions that are available to them – and this includes staying healthy and promoting healthy eating and lifestyles in our care settings. The primary care group and health promotion staff will be able to give guidance to clients and staff in your setting about how to help individuals stay healthy and so prevent infections.

But suppose we are particularly unlucky and an outbreak of infection occurs. Let's look more closely at the chain of events with respect to such an outbreak.

Activity 7.11

Mr White has developed stomach cramps and when you see him at 7 a.m. to give him his breakfast he says he is not hungry and has been up several times in the night with bouts of diarrhoea. He looks pale and sweaty so you decide to take his temperature. This is raised, at 37.6 °C, and you notice that he has sweated profusely during the night and is now generally feeling very poorly. You change his sheets and put him back to bed. He complains of nausea and then starts to vomit. You ask him what he has eaten and suspect food poisoning.

What do you do now?

In Activity 7.11, your initial response is very important since this is a case of an infectious condition and you need to ensure that it is isolated so that others do not contract it.

Your first action should be to contact the person in charge and report the overnight changes in Mr White's condition. You must then inform the GP. The GP is required under the Public Health (Control of Disease) Act 1984 and new regulations which came into force on 6 April 2010 to notify the incidence of any condition which presents a public health risk. The notification is made to the HPA.

You will want to isolate Mr White and put into place measures of infection control to reduce the traffic into and out of his room and also ensure that the waste disposal and laundry procedures for infective waste are followed. A sign must be put on his door to inform staff and visitors of the procedures that must be followed.

Reasonable steps must be taken to reduce infection and therefore maintain a safe living environment for our patients and clients. It is the responsibility of all staff to ensure that safety with respect to how we go about maintaining a clean and infection-free environment for our clients is observed.

The need for careful record keeping

All of the situations we have covered in this chapter will require documenting in some form, and issues arising here are where the information is to be stored and whether it is required to be confidentially maintained.

Any records maintained need to be:

- accurate
- ordered
- up to date
- safe.

The last point is one of the most important to remember since it is a legal requirement to protect any data we may have on our clients or staff and maintain the data in a confidential way. Any use of such information in an unsuitable way or any breach of confidentiality needs to be dealt with promptly and must be reported to the person in charge. The security of information is a safeguard for vulnerable clients and any breach of that security can be detrimental to clients.

Compliance with the Data Protection Act 1998 is imperative. This Act gives individuals the right to access their records whether they are stored as paper files or on computers.

It is worth revisiting the eight principles concerning data the act refers to:

- Data must be secure.
- Data must be not be kept for longer than necessary – you will need to check the requirements in your own organisation for the length of time (for example, antenatal records are kept for 25 years).
- Data must be accurate.
- Data must be fairly processed.
- Data must not be transferred without protection.
- Data must protect individuals' rights.
- Data must be processed for limited purposes only.
- Data must be adequate, relevant and not excessive.

In 1987 the government appointed a committee to recommend how the information collected for patients' records should be processed. The Caldicott principles produced by the committee recommended the appointment of a person in every organisation to be responsible for the maintenance of confidentiality. In care homes this would be a senior staff member who would be legally required to ensure that a policy was in place to protect the individual in the home.

The most important of the principles outlined were (Houghton and Tilmouth, 2003):

- The purpose of the information and the transfer of such has to be clearly justified.
- Client-identifiable information should be limited if possible.
- Reduction of client-identifiable information should be worked towards.
- Accessibility: staff should be permitted to access information on a need-to-know basis only.
- Staff should be made aware of their responsibilities with respect to confidentiality.
- All information kept on clients must conform to law.

So with respect to confidentiality of data, we need to ensure that all care staff are cognisant of their responsibilities with respect to data handling. There needs to be a confidentiality policy in place to which staff can refer should they have any doubts about handling of information.

Now let's look at the reasons we need to maintain records about our patients/clients. The National Minimum Standards for Care require that all organisation records relating to health and safety matters are accurate and kept up to date. Earlier on the chapter we looked at how accident records need to be completed, and it is worth quoting Hershey and Lawrence (1986): 'If it is not recorded then you did not do it'.

Documenting accurately what happened provides an account of what was actually done at the time and what actually took place. We rely on these records, and if years later the case becomes part of a legal process we need to be able to return to the records to remind us of the details.

Records, then, do the following:

- provide an account of the care given (although it does in no way show what the quality of that care was)
- give a record of continuous care (in the case of nursing and medical records)
- provide a source of reference for care
- provides an audit and quality assurance trail
- conform to legal requirements.

Unfortunately, we live in a highly litigious society and in order to protect ourselves when we are being held accountable for the care we give, we need to be aware of the role played by records. If a complaint is made against us, we would find it hard to answer if we had inadequately prepared records. If negligence is suspected in any care setting, any records and statements pertaining to the case will be taken and scrutinised. Think again about Hershey and Lawrence's words: 'If it is not recorded then you did not do it'.

But remember, this is not just about recording the incident; the way in which the record is detailed is also important.

Dimond (1997) highlighted the major areas of concern in such care reports. She revealed that in many records there were major omissions including:

- no dates
- illegibility
- use of abbreviations
- callers' and visitors' names not included
- no signatures
- inaccuracy with respect to dates and times
- delays in record writing
- inaccuracies about clients
- unprofessional language being used.

Activity 7.12

In light of what you have learned, write a checklist of the sorts of things you will bear in mind when you next need to record information on a client.

In Activity 7.12, hopefully you had written the following:

- Have I written legibly?
- Have I put information in time order – in other words, as it happened?
- Have I got dates and times in the record?
- Have I put in signs and symptoms? I might even have written how the patient/client is feeling.
- Did I carry out a risk assessment?
- Have I included names of other people involved?
- Have I written in a professional manner?
- Have I signed the forms/records?

Our responsibility with respect to record keeping is clear. We need to make records on clients and patients but the way in which we use and store that information is paramount.

We must handle all information effectively and be aware of the need to maintain confidentiality of that information.

Summary

The chapter has dealt with all aspects of safety of ourselves and of those who use our particular service. Potential hazards include equipment, the environment and even people coming into the setting; and therefore all these need our attention. Responsibility for health and safety from both the employer's and the employee's points of view has been highlighted and the use of risk assessment in the workplace was identified as being a legal requirement. Challenging behaviour is also an area of concern and the measures by which to deal with such situations have been shown.

Health-care-associated infections, or HCAIs, while problematic in care settings, are high on the agenda of health care professionals and the chapter has given guidance as to how we can ensure our environments remain infection free as far as possible.

With respect to handling medical emergencies and health conditions, an awareness of potential problems you might encounter, together with possible actions to be taken, have been dealt with. Common conditions and first aid protocols have been shown.

The health professionals you are likely to meet in the course of your work, together with a brief outline of their roles, will help you to understand what you need to do in order to deal efficiently with enquiries from these people. The importance of record keeping and law surrounding confidentiality and the main principles in the Data Protection Act have also been covered in this chapter.

There now follows a sample assignment you might like to undertake in order to prepare yourself for the final assessment you are likely to be given in this unit.

Summary assignment

Demonstrate competence in following the correct protocol for the collapsed casualty who is *not* breathing (CPR).

Demonstrate competence in following the correct protocol for the collapsed casualty who *is* breathing (recovery position).

Answer questions on the signs and symptoms, causes and first aid treatment for a range of conditions.

Research and test yourself on hand-washing protocols. Students also need to demonstrate their awareness of the need for cleanliness in the work areas.

Prepare an outline for the following essay: 'Demonstrate your knowledge of the role of support services in the case of communicable disease management and emergency situations, showing how you would document and report on the outbreak of a communicable disease in your own care setting. You may use the policies from your own care setting to support your work.'

References

Ayliffe, G. A. J., Babb, J. R. and Qouraishi, A. H. (1978) 'A test for "hygienic" hand disinfection', *Journal of Clinical Pathology*, **31**:923–8.

Barraclough, N. (2008) *First Aid Made Easy*, Qualsafe.

Bissell, L., Phillips, N. and Stenfert Kroese, B. (2005) 'The experience of a man with severe challenging behaviour following a resettlement from hospital: a single case study design', *British Journal of Learning Disabilities*, **33** (4): 166–73.

Department of Health (2000) 'Domiciliary care – national minimum standards', HMSO, London.

Department of Health (2006a) 'Infection control guidance for care homes', HMSO, London.

Department of Health (2006b) 'The Health Act', HMSO, London.

Dimond, B. (1997) *Legal Aspects of Care in the Community*, Macmillan, Basingstoke.

Hershey, N. and Lawrence, R. (1986) 'The influence of charting upon liability determination', *Journal of Advanced Nursing Administration*, **35/37**, March/April.

Houghton, T. and Tilmouth, T. (2003) *Providing Information to Support Decision Making*, Network Training Publishing.

Tilmouth, T. and Tilmouth, S. (2009) *Safe and Clean Care. Infection Prevention and Control for Health and Social Care Students*, Reflect Press.

UNISON (2003) *Duty of Care: A Handbook to Assist Health Care Staff Carrying out their Duty of Care to Patients, Colleagues and themselves*, UNISON, London.

Further reading

Lowe, K. and Felce, D. (1995) 'The definition of challenging behaviours in practice', *British Journal of Learning Disabilities*, **23** (3): 118–23.

8

Research for practice

Evidence-based practice is now a common expectation for all health and social care practitioners

Students need to acquire knowledge and the skills to meet these expectations and to participate in research initiatives as part of their every-day practice.

This chapter will help you to understand wider organisational, ethical and service user-led considerations of evidence-based practice.

Learning outcomes

By the end of the chapter you will be able to:

■ understand how the wider organisational and ethical context of evidence-based practice impacts upon the service user

■ demonstrate knowledge of the different research methodologies, methods and analytical techniques

■ show how to carry out a critical review of relevant literature

■ start to demonstrate the skills required to carry out an empirical study in practice.

The wider organisational and ethical context of evidence-based practice and how it impacts upon the service user

Our starting point for this chapter has to be to provide a definition of evidence–based practice. What exactly is it and why do we as practitioners need to know about it?

The reforms we have seen in the NHS over the last thirty or so years and the subsequent devolvement to health authorities of the responsibility for assessing the health needs of clients, has changed the performance of the health service enormously. The purchaser–provider split and reviews into the public health of the nation led by Acheson (1988) pointed to the need to monitor the services offered and to appraise the options available in order to contract with providers who would deliver high quality care. Research thus became a major agenda item for all health authorities and professionals and led to the development of the Research and Development or R and D initiative (1993).

Further initiatives in 1998 saw 'Clinical Governance' being introduced into the NHS, and this was described as a framework for accountability. Its implementation heralded the development of quality services which were to 'safeguard' high standards of care and create excellence in clinical care environments (DoH, 1998).

As practitioners we are duty bound to perform care in a safe way and one in which we are enabled to question practice. Alternatively, we may be asked to account for why we undertake a particular practice, and therefore the skills and knowledge for doing so need to be up to date. To 'do no harm', then, is the essential premise of evidence-based practice and the need to be able to demonstrate that the care we provide is safe and effective is a reasonable expectation.

Carnwell (2000: 56) defines evidence-based practice as

> the systematic search for, and appraisal of, best evidence in order to make clinical decisions that might require changes in current practice, while taking account of the individual needs of the patient.

Activity 8.1

Think about a care duty you carry out on a daily basis and write notes on how you obtained the knowledge and skills for the practice. How do you know that what you are doing is based upon the best evidence?

Figure 8.1 Planning care

Your answer probably highlights the various sources from which you gained your knowledge. You may have attended lectures or read accounts and theories for the practice. You may be acting according to policy within your care setting or an assessor or another health care professional may have shown you how to carry out the practice and talked to you about it.

The evidence you have for the practice then is:

- evidence based on theory
- evidence based on experience
- evidence passed on by role models and experts
- evidence passed on through policy.

As an effective practitioner accountable for your own safe practice you need to have access to research related to your own area and be able to critically appraise such work. The link between evidence-based practice and research then becomes important. As the above quote showed us, we need research to provide evidence which can inform our decision making in order to bring about changes in practice.

In making a decision about how and what care is to be given it is important to have an accurate picture of the research available and to take sufficient evidence from it to support our actions. One or two articles are clearly not sufficient to make a change to our practice and therefore we need to access evidence which has been evaluated critically and tested and is of sufficient depth and breadth to support our work.

Nowadays we can access several evidence-based practice journals, as well as the Cochrane Library, an international body dedicated to gathering and disseminating published research and the National Electronic Library for Health. Bandolier is a free full text journal library available online and is useful for accessing information from systematic reviews, trials and observational studies. The NHS also has an online library where you can obtain Clinical Knowledge Summaries. Check the end of this chapter for further websites and addresses you can access for information.

Evidence-based practice is about incorporating evidence, making professional judgements and applying our knowledge to formulate care decisions. We also need to involve the client in our deliberations and, together with individual client preferences, any evidence obtained from research needs to inform our practice so that the most efficient care is possible.

According to Erikson-Owens and Kennedy (2001) there are three elements to evidence-based practice:

- the needs and preferences of clients
- evidence-based health and social care research
- the best available evidence and resources together with the expertise, skills and judgement of the professional practitioner.

The use of the best available evidence and research, then, is an ethical consideration not only from an individual practitioner's view but also from the organisational view. As an individual practicing in health care using evidence to inform your decisions will contribute to your knowledge base of what you do and will also ensure that you are accountable for your practice. In this way you can be assured that you are delivering enhanced care that is safe. For the

Figure 8.2

organisation, safe practice contributes to reduced numbers of incidents surrounding patients and their care and fewer risks in the workplace, and thus also the potential for litigation. It can also raise the profile of the organisation, help to outline the best practice and constitute an important tool to provide safe and ethical care.

To summarise then, evidence-based practice advances the quality of care provided and enables the practitioner to make effective clinical judgements. As a result it increases client satisfaction and also provides evidence of your own professional development.

Research and evidence-based practice – the difference

Research involves systematic investigation to discover facts or relationships and enables us to make conclusions using scientific methods (Burns and Grove, 1987; Becker and Bryman, 2004; Bowling 2002).

Evidence–based practice is about using that research to make professional judgements and apply our informed and enhanced knowledge to make care decisions. We shall go onto the research aspect in more detail now.

Research methods and analytical techniques

There are a number of texts listed at the end of the chapter to which you may turn in order to enhance your knowledge of research methods. For the purpose of this chapter we will supply only a brief overview of the methods of research to which you may turn when conducting your own study.

Research methods can be divided into two types: primary and secondary.

Primary research focuses on original research which you yourself originate and carry out.

Secondary research, on the other hand, is the presentation of other writers 'primary' research and is something you do constantly. It is the focus on available research carried out by others and the conclusions we draw from it. When engaging in any research for a project or an essay you are accessing secondary sources. When talking about research methodology we also use the terms quantitative and qualitative.

These two terms refer to the way in which the research is carried out and the methods used. In addition the data presented at the end of the research is also different.

Originally developed to study natural phenomena, quantitative methods were the method of choice of natural scientists and have now been adopted for use by social scientists, and are widely used in education and health care. The methods include surveys, experiments, and statistical data. The quantitative approach is considered to be one which operates strict rules in terms of rigour in conducting the study, objectivity and control of variables. We shall look at these terms later.

If your research is focusing on questions such as 'How many' and 'How often' then you are likely to present your data in terms of numbers and statistics and it will therefore be quantitative in nature.

Strengths of the quantitative approach

Quantitative research is subject to rigorous controls and checks throughout the process and this is one of its strengths. A more objective approach is favoured and therefore the results are often thought to be more accurate than those of the qualitative type. Because of the large numbers of participants in this type of research, a huge amount of information can be obtained thus enabling the finding to be generalised to the wider population.

The term 'generalisation' refers to the degree to which the work can be applied to the whole population and not just the sample used. This means that if the sample is large enough and the research has covered a wide cross-section of the population as a whole then the study might be said to be generalisable. A study carried out on a group of students in one medical school in the whole country may prove to be useful to that medical school. But they may have atypical medical students and therefore it would be difficult to say that the findings are representative of all medical students across the United Kingdom. If the same study was carried out on a hundred medical students in a hundred medical schools across the UK then it might be possible to apply the findings to all medical students or at the very least suggest strong support for the findings. Because the findings from such work can be generalised to the wider population funding may be more readily available, and financing the study is always a major issue for any research.

Another strength is the ability to replicate or repeat the studies and by doing so the results obtained means the work can be more readily compared with other similar studies. It is therefore considered to be reliable. In this type of work it is also possible to reduce the personal bias simply because researchers are able to keep their 'distance' from participating subjects.

Other strengths are the fact that this type of research is well controlled and the methods and instruments used are standardised. We look at this in more detail later.

Methods for gathering quantitative data

There are a number of ways in which quantitative research is carried out.

Research which involves observation with the use of checklists, questionnaires, experiments in which variables are manipulated in some way, attitude scales and analysis of statistics are all ways in which quantitative data is collected.

If we want to know how frequently something happens or to test whether there is a cause and effect relationship occurring this type of research is useful. Pre-test post-test designs measure a variable before and after a procedure, for example heart rate before and after exercise to measure recovery rates.

Weakness of the quantitative approach

Some of the methods involve the use of laboratory conditions and this is not entirely appropriate when studying human subjects. Therefore we have to question the 'validity' of the study and we define this term later, see page 169. Also, when using questionnaires or survey methods the way in which these are written and presented may not elicit responses that are useful or real. Misunderstandings about the questions can occur. Also the relationship between what somebody says and actually does cannot be truly tested in this manner. Human beings all have their own unique experiences and this can certainly change the manner in which they behave. When gathering primary data this can result in unreliability of the data (page 169).

Qualitative research

Qualitative research methods were developed in the social sciences when it was felt that the study of social and cultural phenomenon required a different means of enquiry. This approach seeks to gain insight into people's lives. Their attitudes, behaviours and value systems are the areas of interest for the qualitative researcher who wants to seek out the 'why' of a particular topic. Rather than merely trying to describe a certain phenomenon this approach attempts to gain a greater understanding and depth about what is happening in a given circumstance.

Using the phenomenological approach (see chapter on social policy) as posited by sociologists in an attempt to study the experience of the subjects and how they interpret their world, the researcher becomes an interpreter and attempts to reveal concealed meaning.

There are four major qualitative approaches.

Ethnography

This approach comes from the field of anthropology and is mainly associated with studying culture. Although in the past such research usually concentrated upon culture in terms of ethnicity and geographical location it now accepts a wider definition and includes studies of any group or organisation. So it is as acceptable to study the culture associated with a business as it is to study the behaviour of a tribe in another part of the world.

The participant observer method from field research is the method of choice in the ethnographic approach. In this respect the researcher becomes a participant in the culture and observes and records extensive notes.

This approach is sometimes known as 'going native'.

Phenomenology

Phenomenology focuses on individual's subjective experiences and interpretations of the world and how it appears to others. (see Chapter 5). Sometimes considered a philosophical and sociological perspective it is used in social research disciplines including psychology, sociology and social work.

Field research

Field research is the means of gathering qualitative data where the researcher goes 'into the field' to make his/her observations of the phenomenon in its natural state.

Extensive field notes are generated which are coded and analysed in a variety of ways.

Grounded theory

Grounded theory is an approach that was originally developed by Glaser and Strauss in the 1960s. The purpose of grounded theory is to develop theory about phenomena of interest that is *grounded* in observation.

The research begins with the raising of questions which guide the research but do not confine it. Such questions are quite loose and flexible at this stage. As data is gathered the researcher begins to identify, core theoretical concept(s) and links between these are developed. This stage in the research can take months. It is only at a later stage that the researcher verifies and summarises the data, which is beginning to evolve toward one core category that is a central element to the study. The analysis taking place in this is as follows.

Coding – this process is method by which qualitative data is categorised and described. The first stage involves looking at the data in minute detail and developing initial categories. As themes emerge this coding becomes more selective and the researcher can start to systematically code towards a core concept.

Memoing refers to the recording of the researchers thoughts as they develop throughout the study. It's a bit like making notes and comments in the margin of piece you might be writing. Like the coding stage, memos tend to be very open in the early stages of the research while later they focus in on the core concept.

As themes start to emerge diagrams help make sense of the data and move the researcher on to an emerging theory. The diagrams can be shown in any form. They might be concept maps, graphs or cartoons that can summarise the theory.

Finally the researcher is coming to a new emerging theory which resembles the main core concept of all the data collected. This new theory leads to new links and revisions in the theory and thus more data collection. The whole process described could continue indefinitely and that is a strength of grounded theory. The project ends when the researcher decides to do so, but it could

Foundation Degree Health and Social Care

potentially evolve with each new data collection and concept being discovered and reviewed.

So, in a nutshell, grounded theory constitutes a well-considered and documented explanation for a phenomenon of interest. Explained in words and presented with much of the relevant detail collected it can be a useful study into topic which has had little previous data gathered. Glaser and Strauss's (1965) work on 'dying' has led to some major research in this particular field of study and was one of the first of its kind.

Another method is that of action research, which is a practical method used to solve problematic situations in a work setting.

Below are shown the steps involved in qualitative research and these are covered more fully in the section dealing with action research:

- Collecting qualitative data
- Analysing qualitative data/generating hypotheses
- Planning action steps
- Implementing action steps
- Collecting data to monitor change
- Analysis and evaluation.

Strengths of the qualitative approach

This sort of study produces some very in-depth work and rich data about phenomena which is impossible to collect from sets of statistics. It enables the researcher to look far more closely at the meanings within behaviour and to understand what is actually happening in settings and to question participants responses to certain issues.

By studying people in their own settings, naturally occurring events and data can be collected and this provides rich data for study.

A major strength is the ability to collect information in areas where there has been little knowledge in existence in the past and where the issues under study may be sensitive. This type of research enables the researcher to get close to the material under

study and to gain in-depth data which can later be subjected to quantitative research.

Methods for gathering qualitative data:

There are a number of techniques to gather data for qualitative studies including;

- Interviews, both open ended to semi-structured, where questions are asked by the interviewer to obtain information from the subject.
- Focus groups, which constitute a group of people being asked about their attitude towards a product, service, an idea, or even the packaging on a brand.
- Open ended questionnaires and surveys.
- Observational techniques, whereby a group or single participant are asked to perform a specific task or action which is then observed. The observations of their behaviour or actions are then subject to analysis.

We will come back to these later in the chapter.

Weakness of the qualitative approach

One weakness is the time it takes to conduct enough of this type of research to gain a valid response. Collecting and analysing the material collected, which is often unstructured in nature, can be time consuming. Finding themes in reams of notes can at the very least be a little daunting and trying to find meaning in the materials can also take time. Also the sample size is usually quite small with just a few participants taking part.

Some critics are concerned that this type of study lacks rigour since variables cannot be easily controlled and the results produced cannot be generalised to the population as a whole. This type of research lends itself to small scale study and therefore data obtained, whilst rich, is too limited to make valid conclusions.

When we embark upon any research the method you will use will depend upon what you need to know. The question we need to ask ourselves is 'what am I trying to do here?' and 'what do I want to find out?' not 'what method shall I choose?'. In taking this sort of approach it is likely that you will consider several methods and you will choose the method that best suits the job in hand. We will look at these methods in the next section.

Primary research methods

Primary research is enquiry which is new. Although you may use a similar method or repeat a study which had been carried out before, what makes it new is that it will involve different participants and will therefore show different results. Or may be a totally new area of interest and be unique in its own right.

Many types of primary research exist and for the purpose of this chapter we will focus on the following:

- interviews
- surveys
- observational research and ethnography
- case study
- action research
- experiments.

Interviews

If we are trying to gain detailed information from a single individual or a small number of individuals then interviews are the vehicle for doing so.

In addition, if you need to gain an expert's view or want more in-depth knowledge of a certain phenomenon then an interview can provide this

Several different types of interviews exist the most common being the face-to-face interviews, that is sitting down and talking to somebody. You can adapt your questioning to the answers of the person and you can record the interview. Other types involve the use of technology such as phones, emails and even messaging boards such as MSN or Facebook. The strengths of these methods are that you can interview people from around the world if you so wish, although there may need to be specialist equipment to record data. They are, however, less personal ways to collect information and may limit the amount of information you gain and prevent follow up questions.

Surveys

If your study demands a response from a lot of people then you are more likely to want to utilise the survey method. Using a more rigid form of questioning than interviews they are useful if you want to learn what a larger sample of the population thinks. The types of questions to be asked in the survey do need to be considered and can limit the responses you get. There is also the question of 'reliability' and 'validity' in terms of the data generated if the questions are biased in any way. See page 169 for definition.

We list the types of surveys you may be involved in below.

Interview surveys
These are face-to-face surveys conducted either 'in-street', as in the market researchers who occasionally stop us for just 'one minute' to answer questions or those who may knock on the door to ask questions 'on-the-doorstep', or 'in-house'. The person to interview may be randomly selected from a list or database, or specifically chosen.

Postal surveys
Postal surveys are commonly used in lifestyle research and a sample of names and addresses are drawn from a database of the population, such as the national census, and sent to those homes.

Telephone surveys
Telephone surveys are becoming increasingly popular and offer an opportunity for good coverage of the population. They can require a team of interviewers, preferably using a computer-assisted telephone interviewing (CATI) system, so resourcing this type of research is costly due to the specialist equipment needed.

Internet surveys
With the increase in the use of the internet you may find yourself answering online surveys more often these days. They can be either web-based, where individuals are invited to visit a website to complete the questionnaire to be found there, or you may be sent a link. Alternatively an email survey will have an attached questionnaire.

Observations and ethnography.

Observations involve watching people or animals interact with each other and the setting around them. As a means of gathering information, this type of primary research is excellent since observations do not need to be structured around a hypothesis (we come back to this term later). Before undertaking more structured research a researcher might choose to go into a setting and merely observe what is going on. In this way one can more readily form a research question. There are different types of observation and each will affect the results you get. First try the following activity

Activity 8.2

Think about the following. You wish to study the activity of an outpatients clinic in the local community hospital to try to determine why there have been so many complaints. You intend also to interview and carry out a survey. With respect to the observation, what questions come to mind before you embark upon this part of the study?

It is likely that you may have asked yourself what level of participation you will take in this exercise. Will you sit, watch and make a few notes about what is happening in the course of the morning or afternoon clinic? Will you talk to the clients attending the clinic? Or perhaps book yourself in to the clinic and become a client yourself?

Whichever way you choose to observe you will need to consider how you as an observer may change the event being observed. Have you ever been in a situation where you are aware of a person with a clip board jotting down notes? The chances are this event in itself will make you change what you are doing. I recall students during OFSTED inspections and the change in their behaviour as a result of having a visitor in the room.

If you choose to talk to the clients in the clinic, there may be a different outcome. However, becoming a participant in the clinic may mean you gain a lot of information but you may also miss

something. Also you would have to question the ethics of not fully stating why you are there, particularly if you are looking at how the staff interact with clients.

There are ways to address these issues in order to maintain an objective stance, but you will need to be very focused on what it is you are trying to observe and sometimes several visits to the setting will be required in order to address the effect of your presence. If you are attending that clinic once a week for four weeks it is likely that you may start to blend into the background and your presence be forgotten, thus enabling the clients and the staff in the clinic to act in a more normal manner. This is what anthropologists and ethnographers do in studies of different cultures. By becoming part of the culture or community for a period of time they can blend into the culture and observe from the stance of a participant.

We call the types of participation in observation 'Covert' and 'Overt'.

In covert observation the people being studied are unaware of the researcher's presence or the purpose of their being there. There have been a number of studies where this approach is taken and it means the researcher needs to assume a false identity and so immediately raises ethical concerns. Is it right to deceive people for the sake of research? A number of the studies have actually contributed to the greater understanding of so-called deviant behaviour but critics are concerned with the ethical issues this throws up. This presents the main drawback to covert observation, and the issues involving informed consent and privacy are critical.

In order to be able to generalise the findings from such observations several observations of a representative sample must be carried out. This is especially difficult when looking at a particular group. Many groups and individuals have unique characteristics and this in itself makes for interesting study. But it makes repeating the study difficult.

In overt observation the researcher reveals him/herself to the group and then carries out observations. This deals with the ethical constraints but, as we mentioned previously, it may also change the manner in which those under study may act and therefore may not give a true picture of what is happening.

If people know that you are watching them they react to you and are likely to change their actions. Although the behaviour may be contrived because they are being watched, it does in fact reveal something of how they feel about being watched or about showing their feelings. One point of note, however, is the fact that such behaviour is often difficult to maintain over a long time. If your study is over the long term you will be observing natural behaviour at some point.

The ethical issues with this form of observation are minimal since the participants know you are there and potentially have the ability to stop the proceedings if they feel it is necessary.

A **Case Study** usually takes a group or family and provides an in-depth study of a certain aspect of their lives or setting. The strength of this approach lies in the fact that the researcher can concentrate on one issue in depth. For example, you may be interested in finding out how a school is implementing the Safeguarding Agenda and decide to spend time in the school gathering data about how this particular institution is addressing this issue. You will be able to question, observe, listen, access documentation and then write a report on your findings. Critics of this type of research identify the lack of generalisability of the findings.

Activity 8.3

Generalisability

Remind yourself of this term. We referred to it earlier in the text.

You may have recalled that this term is used to describe how representative of the greater population the findings are. In other words, can we safely assume that the school we are conducting the case study in is similar, and contains teachers and staff who are similar, to another school in another part of the country? Probably not, and as such we cannot therefore use the findings to suggest that all schools are at the same level

of operation as the one we have studied. To apply findings in studies to the wider population we would need to conduct research which involves a bigger sample and more widespread data gathering. The case study, then, does have limitations.

Action research

As the term implies, this is research which is active in nature and is firmly grounded in practice. A form of self-reflective enquiry, it encourages the participants in a particular setting to improve their own practices by addressing their understanding of these practices and making change.

Again, the problem of generalisabilty rears its head and the findings are applicable only to the setting in which the research is carried out. However, this does in no way invalidate the results. Cohen and Manions (1980) definition of this type of research is still valid.

> an on the spot procedure designed to deal with a concrete problem located in an immediate situation … the step by step process is constantly monitored … over varying periods of time and by a variety of mechanisms… so that the … feedback may be translated into modifications, adjustments, directional changes… so as to bring about lasting benefits to the ongoing process… (Cohen and Manion, 1980: 178).

This definition implies an ongoing cycle of events. It can be described as a 'cyclical process of change' or a series of planning actions initiated within the setting to address a problem or issue which needs to be explored. The researcher takes on the role of a change agent and works together with the clients in the setting.

The steps in action research are as follows:

Step 1. Identifying a focus of interest or a problem.
An area that requires change may be clearly identifiable. You may notice that a particular ward in the hospital gets 50 per cent more complaints than that of a similar ward and you wish to find out why. Occasionally, though, this step can be the most difficult since you may be unsure as to what the actual

problem is. In that case, a reflection of what is happening is required. An observation of the event or, in our case above, a shift on the ward at various times during the week, may reveal the actual problem to you and you can then go onto the next step.

Step 2. Collecting data
The data you collect may take many forms. In our example of the ward with the complaints your first set of data may be notes from the observations you have done. It may be the actual complaints forms and minutes from ward meetings. It could be letters, or patient notes. In fact any documents which have been produced in the day-to-day running of the ward can be used. In other settings it might be files, records, memos, emails, rotas, care plans, photographs, or reflective accounts.

As you can see, in this type of research you would not rely upon just one kind of data but try to obtain as great a variety as you can.

In collecting the data, it is wise to try to maintain an open mind as to what you are seeing and to try to refine your research question(s) as you progress. If you share your interests and findings with others this will encourage a more cohesive approach and others will be brought into the work as well.

Once you have a clear research question you can then decide how to proceed. Perhaps you wish to answer a specific question; 'why does ward A get 50 per cent more complaints than ward B?'. You may simply decide to change the practices on the ward since you have already discovered the 'why'. Alternatively you may produce a case study for the management team.

Whatever you choose to do will guide you in the information you need to collect, and already you will be beginning to notice the data that is irrelevant to your particular work.

Step 3. Analysing data and generating hypotheses.
You are possibly undertaking analysis as you go along and therefore this may not be a distinct step. However, generating hypotheses will take place sometime after you have begun to carry out your study. One of the things you have to contend with in any type of research is the presence and influence of other people. In our example (the complaints on ward A) we may discover that it is simply a failure of communication that is a problem, meaning that patients are not receiving the required care. You are clear about the problem and have an understanding about the need to change practice and how it can be accomplished. In making that change you may find that some of the staff are happier with the new regime that is being implemented but you become aware of comments being passed in the staffroom and you realise that you do not have all the staff on board with the change. As a result of this your focus may change and you may wish to address the wider issues associated with the staff who are not fully embracing the change.

The data you are collecting needs to be made sense of. As you read through your notes you may begin to see certain themes and patterns emerging. This will allow you to ask further questions about the data. If you are familiar with the literature in the field under study you will notice the important themes. and your reams of notes will start to be transformed into *evidence*.

In the section dealing with analysing data we will address this further.

Step 4. Planning action steps
By the time you have collected your evidence it is possible you will be more than ready to try to make a change. The change you make largely depends upon the people and the issues that are involved. In trying to make a change on ward A it would be wise to involve all the staff on that ward in any decision making and to make the Senior Management team aware of what is going on. The staff on the ward will be affected by the change and it is therefore important to have them aware of what is going to be required.

In this process of planning the change we are also starting to build theory. In research we constantly develop and test theories in practice. We may have built up evidence to suggest that the staff on ward A fail to communicate efficiently because they appear to misunderstand the systems in place. We have evidence from what people say, and what people do in different situations.

The final step in action research is to formulate action plans.

A plan needs to include the following:

- the aims of the proposed change

- the reasons for this change

- a statement which details the new routines, activities, or materials required to aid the change

- a statement which outlines the philosophy of the change

- the means of monitoring changes

- the means by which the change will be evaluated.

Step 5. Implementing action steps There is risk with any change, but we can only achieve change if we actually go ahead and do something.

In the group situation it is useful to ensure that everybody is fully aware of what they need to do and then schedule meetings to discuss the outcomes of what they have achieved.

Step 6. Collecting data to monitor change, analysing and evaluating. This brings the action research cycle to its conclusion and also back to the beginning again. In this stage the action researcher describes the situation as it stood at the end of the first action step and is then in a position to explain the new situation. By doing this the next stage is put into action and change is set off again on a seemingly never ending cycle. New data will be generated as you go along and you will have different perspective on the situation.

Activity 8.4

Using the above steps in action research identify an area in your own work placement which might be studied to improve practice. Make some notes about how you would approach this. (This activity is linked to the final summative activity in this unit.)

Discuss the plan with your tutor and then write a reflective account.

Experiments

An experiment generally involves two or more groups: a test group and a control group to which an intervention is applied, and then the results are observed and measured. This type of study involves the control and observation of variables which are characteristics of an object or phenomenon that can be manipulated e.g. volume of temperature.

When conducting an experiment of this type the test group is subjected to an intervention whereas the control group receives no intervention. So, an example might be the administration of a drug or a treatment to a test group but nothing given to the control group. We need the control group to ensure that any changes in key variables resulting from the intervention can be measured in the test group.

Experimental research is where the researcher affects (controls) what happens to the subjects or sample and then investigates the effects of the intervention. This type of research is usually conducted to make comparisons between groups and to examine causal relationships. It is invariably associated with laboratories where there is an assumption that more control can be applied.

It is referred to as the 'Scientific Method' and you may come across this term in your further reading.

Four steps are involved.

Step One – Observation and description of a phenomenon.

Step Two – Hypothesis formulation (we cover this term later).

Step Three – Use of hypotheses to predict the existence of further phenomenon. There may be a quantitative prediction of results.

Step Four – Performance of experiments to test predictions using properly performed experiments.

One of the major drives for this type of method is the desire to minimise the influences of personal or cultural beliefs on a phenomenon. Therefore this method is concerned with eliminating bias or prejudice in testing a theory. Bias simply means any influence that may affect results or distort our view of the data and can be the downfall of many experiments and research studies. If we set out to try to prove something because we have a preference for a particular outcome then this will 'bias' our results. Alternatively failure to acknowledge certain results which would seem not to support our preference is also a common mistake in experiments and research.

In February 1998, research by Dr Andrew Wakefield identified a 'genuinely new syndrome' when he reported a link between the MMR vaccine and autism and gastrointestinal disorder. His research was carried out on 12 children only and yet his conviction led to enormous media interest. In March 1998 a panel of doctors disputed the link and other studies around the world also concluded no links were evident. Over the next ten years to 2008 Wakefield carried out further studies, determined to show a link. His determination to prove his hypothesis despite compelling evidence to the contrary led to a major enquiry into his practice and his subsequent removal from the GMC. This is an example of bias and prejudice in research affecting the outcomes of a study (BBC News – MMR Research Timeline 2010).

The scientific method appears simple and methodical in its approach but there are some things which are just not amenable to testing in this way and social interaction is one such situation. Individuals come to research with a variety of values and beliefs and as such the variables to account for are enormous. It is virtually impossible to control or even monitor all of these variables

We mentioned earlier the subject of 'sample' and at this point we need to describe what this is.

Sampling is the selection of a subgroup of a population which is representative of the whole population. In any study the people who are interviewed or observed should be as representative as possible of the group that you are studying and the results will only be seen as useful if your sample are deemed to be typical of the whole population.

Some key terms in sampling:

- Members of a group are called a 'population'.
- A 'census' is collecting information from each member of a group.
- Collecting information from only some members of a groups is called a 'sample'.
- A 'sampling frame' is the list of people from which a sample is taken, for example electoral register.

It is important to understand how samples are elected and there are two types of sampling, probability and non-probability.

Probability sampling

In this method each member of the population has an equal chance of being selected.

There are four main types of probability sample.

1. Simple random sampling
2. Systematic sampling
3. Stratified sampling
4. Multi-stage cluster sampling

Simple random sampling

We select a group of people for a study from a larger group, that is from a population.

Each person is chosen randomly by chance.

Each person has the same chance as any other of being selected.

A sampling frame is used.

Each person within the frame is allocated a unique reference number starting at one.

The size of the sample is decided and then that many numbers should be selected, from the table of random numbers.

Systematic sampling

Systematic sampling is similar to simple random sampling. Instead of selecting random numbers from tables, move through the sample frame picking every nth name, every tenth for example.

Stratified sampling

Stratified sampling is a modification of the former two types.

It is more representative and thus more accurate.

It is obtained by taking samples from each subgroup of a population, for example age or marital status.

Multi-stage cluster sampling

This is a combination of several different samples.

The entire population is divided into groups, or clusters, and a random sample of these clusters are selected.

Smaller 'clusters' are then chosen from within the selected clusters.

Stage 1: Define population – (say) children 8 years old in schools in the North East of England.

Stage 2: Select (say) 100 primary schools from the North East region at random.

Stage 3: Select a number of smaller areas (for example classes) from within each selected school.

Stage 4: Interview *all* children within the smaller areas.

Non-probability sampling

Whilst probability sampling should be our first choice in selecting a sample, because it allows a random approach to selection, non-probability sampling is used when there is either no sampling frame or the population is too wide to allow cluster sampling.

These sorts of techniques are often used in exploratory studies and there are five main non-probability sampling techniques:

1. Purposive sampling
2. Quota sampling
3. Convenience sampling
4. Snowball sampling
5. Self-selection.

Purposive sampling

A purposive sample is a group of people who have been selected by the researcher subjectively. In this instance the researcher pick a sample that he/she believes to represent the population of interest.

Quota sampling

Again this is not a random sample but most commonly seen in face-to-face interviewing. You may have been approached on the street by an interviewer who may have picked you out because you seem to fit the age, or gender specified in their 'quota controls'. These refer to quotas given to interviewers with the final sample being representative of the population. Accuracy of the sample may be a problem here due to lack of randomness.

Convenience sampling

A convenience sample is simply that. Convenient and any person who is willing to participate is chosen. The lack of randomness means the accuracy of results is questionable since the likelihood of bias is high.

Snowball sampling

Sometimes a study is directed at groups who might be hard to reach and so this type of sampling is used. In this case you simply ask the first few people contacted to direct you to others who are like minded.

Self-selection

You may have been asked to be in a survey or to complete a questionnaire. As it says, you have self-selected to undertake this.

The decision as to which sample to use or how many people will make up your sample is dependent upon the nature of the research aim, the desired level of accuracy in the sample and the availability of a good sampling frame, money and time. You also need to consider the type of research, and the population size.

When we looked at the methods above we used two terms to which we now draw your attention.

Reliability

Any tool or test used in research to measure data must be reliable and by this we are referring to how consistent a measuring device is. The quality of the research itself will be measured by these criteria.

A measurement is said to be reliable or consistent if the measurement can produce similar results if used again in similar circumstances. For example, if a speedometer gave the same readings at the same speed it would be reliable. If it didn't it would be pretty useless and unreliable.

This term also refers to accuracy.

Validity

This refers to whether a study measures or examines what it claims to measure or examine. A researcher who is trying to measure peoples attitudes to pregnant women and smoking needs to construct a tool that he/she knows is measuring that specific attitude and not something else.

Reliability and validity do however exist side by side and cannot be mutually exclusive of each other. For example a measuring tool that is not reliable cannot at the same time be valid. How so? There is no validity if the instrument being used to measure a test is doing so in an inaccurate way. How can your measures of weight be valid if the scales do not operate accurately and reliably?

On the other hand though can a measuring tool be reliable without being valid?

Consider your scales again. An accurate and reliable scale cannot be used as a valid measure of blood pressure however reliable they are!

So the high reliability of the tool does not make what it is measuring valid but a low reliability tool, your dysfunctional scales, will cause the weight data you have collected to be invalid.

Analysing the data from quantitative and qualitative research

Whatever method you use for any study the collection of data and information requires some form of explanation and analysis and quantitative methods and their analysis differ from those in qualitative approaches.

For quantitative studies we analyse the collected data by using statistical measures. Data generated in quantitative studies will be numerical in form and is therefore more amenable to testing in such ways.

Descriptive statistics are used to provide a summary of the data and to enable the researcher to use it.

There are four levels of measurement and you are more likely to be involved personally in the first two shown below. The latter two require the use of more sophisticated statistical measures and tools.

Ordinal data refers to the type of data with a small number of categories and where ranking from the lowest to the highest, for example. very small risk, moderate risk, severe risk, is required. If the values or observations can be put in order then they are said to be ordinal.

Nominal data – in this type of data the numbers are labels and codes for a given group. For example, males could be coded as 0, females as 1. The numbers here are not to be counted and do not mean that 1 is better than 2 or vice versa.

Interval measurement – this data is ranked in order and the interval between the objects also used. For example, the educational tests we have in use today are based upon this type of measure. A score of 50 in an A level test is better than 40 and 30. The interval between 30 and 40 is the same as the interval between 40 and 50 and this data then can lend itself to be averaged more meaningfully.

Ratio measurement – on these scales zero appears and can therefore provide information about the absolute magnitude of an attribute. Ratio scales which do have a rational zero do exist in some physical measurements. For example, weight comes under this sort of scale. So a person who weighs 80 kgs can be said to be twice as heavy as somebody who weighs 40 kgs etc.

Frequency distribution is one way in which some order can be imposed upon data. By ordering the numbers from your data lowest to highest and by counting the number of times the number was obtained you can display the information in terms of the shape of the distribution.

The shape can be symmetrical with even distribution (normal distribution) or skewed. It may also have only one high point or be known as unimodal or multimodal in the case of data showing more than one high point.

It is possible you will have come across the terms mean, median and mode and these are measures of **central tendency**.

The **mean** is the average value and we calculate this by adding all the observations and dividing by the number of observations.

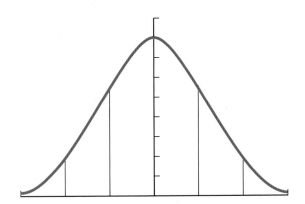

Figure 8.3 Frequency distribution curve

The **median** – refers to the middle value of a list and this type of test is used when there is an uneven distribution of numbers. If you have numbers, 31, 32, 35, 36, 37, 38 and 39, the median is 36.

You will note that the above list is easy to calculate since it has an odd number of figures in it. The median then is the middle number in the list after sorting the list into increasing order.

In a list with an even number of values in it the median is the sum of the two middle (after sorting) numbers divided by two.

The **mode** is the most common (frequent) value. So in a list of 5, 5, 5, 6, 6, 6, 6, 6, 4, 4 the most frequent or mode is 6.

You may have come across the phrase '**statistically significant**' and this is a reference to the level of significance or the 'p' value.

Standard deviation is a measure of the variation from the mean of a data set. If a data set has a large standard deviation you can conclude that the data is spread widely from the mean. If the data set has a low comparative standard deviation you know that the data is clustered around a mean value and that the data is more reliable.

Hypothesis testing

A hypothesis is a testable statement based upon observation. For example apples are shiny (observation). This is due to a layer of wax on the surface (hypothesis). If I apply wax solvent the apple will lose its shine (prediction). Whilst this is a very simple example it does illustrate the main points.

Here is another example. A teacher hypothesises that his class responds well to watching DVDs. He hypothesises that showing a DVD on study skills prior to taking SATS tests in one group will result in an improvement in their scores compared to those who do not watch the DVD.

He then compares the scores of the two groups in his class and finds that indeed the group (half of the class) who watched the DVD did in fact do better.

Foundation Degree Health and Social Care

Can he conclude that his hypothesis can be supported?

Activity 8.5

What do you think? Jot down some of your thoughts on this and discuss with a partner.

It certainly looks as though there are positive results here, but could the results be due to something other than the DVD? Are the two groups of similar ability or has his sampling put some of the lower ability children into the group who do not view the DVD? In fact how did he split the two groups and will this have an effect? Were there an even number of boys and girls in each group? Were they from similar backgrounds? Or was the difference just due to chance?

Activity 8.6

Possibility and chance

If you were to toss a coin one hundred times you might expect to get fifty heads and fifty tails or thereabouts. If you got fifty one heads and forty nine tails you would conclude that this difference is due to chance. However when do you conclude that it isn't?

Draw a vertical line on the table below where you think that the difference is due to chance.

Heads	50	55	60	65	70	75
Tails	50	45	40	35	30	25

All of the above results are possible, but there comes a point where we do not feel comfortable assigning the difference to chance alone. So what do we do? We use statistical analysis to tell us the probability of any difference/relationship being due to chance. Probability is expressed as a percentage or decimal, such as 5 per cent or 0.05. So what probability are we prepared to accept before we draw our conclusion?

One would hope that if our statistical test told us that there was fifty per cent probability that drug A had a positive effect on condition X we would be unimpressed. But what level of probability do we accept? If we were to insist on probability that our results are due to chance, we would never get anywhere. Any single piece of anomalous data would mean we would have to accept our null hypothesis. So what are we prepared to accept? The answer is 5 per cent. If our statistical test tells us the probability (p) of our results being due to chance is 5 per cent / 0.05 or more we would conclude that is it due to chance and accept our null hypothesis (the statement that tell us no relationship exists).

So the onus is on the experimenter to gather data that supports their experimental hypothesis. He/she assumes that their results are due to chance unless they can conclude the probability of it being due to chance is less than 5 per cent.

The assumption our teacher has made is that the intervention of the DVD is better for his students since it improves their scores. But there are two explanations for this.

- The intervention did improve the scores.
- The differences in the scores received were due to chance (i.e. differences in make up of the group, differences in ability etc.).

The first bullet point is referred to as the researchers **experimental hypothesis** or a statement that predicts a relationship between two or more variables.

The second bullet point is known as the **null hypothesis**, a statement which expresses that the differences in scores is due to chance.

Rejection of the null hypothesis means the teacher can support his original hypothesis. This is where the statistical testing comes into use.

Our teacher needs then to apply a test to the data to determine the probability of the differences being due to chance. If this 'p' value is 5 per cent/0.05 or more he must accept his null hypothesis. He cannot then say for certain that his conclusion will be true of the whole population since he has only tested a few children.

There is still the probability that the conclusion drawn is wrong. Using the coin analogy it is possible that if you tossed the coin 100 times you could get 100 tails – it seems very unlikely but it is possible. So there is still a chance that our teacher may come up with the wrong conclusion.

This means there is a risk of error in this type of testing. These errors are known as type I and type II errors. Type I error refers to the rejection of the null hypothesis when in fact it is true. So, in this instance our teacher may assert that the intervention was in fact useful and did result in the improved scores when in fact it was the group differences which were the major influence.

The opposite is true for a type II error. Our teacher accepts the null hypothesis and suggests that the intervention was not the reason for the improved scores, it was the sampling of the groups and therefore chance.

There are many different statistical tests that you may come across that are applied to different types of data for example t-test, chi squared test and analysis of variance or ANOVA. For a greater in-depth look at these tests your attention is drawn to the further reading at the end of the chapter.

Activity 8.7

We have come across a great deal of new terms as we have progressed through the chapter. Start a glossary of some of those you have learned as a result.

Analysis of qualitative data

Data generated from qualitative study is likely to result in huge amounts of written material, making analysis on an on-going process rather than a task undertaken at the end of the research.

As the research progresses, it becomes more focused and detailed as the material generated is coded and conceptualised. There are a number of steps the qualitative researcher is likely to take to analyse their results.

Step 1: The material from interviews and observations is read and recurring themes are identified.

Step 2: Themes are sorted into categories.

Step 3: Links between categories are identified and charts, thought maps, matrices, flow charts, or time lines may be used to group data.

Step 4: The data is validated (triangulation) using group discussions, and perhaps statistics to investigate how often themes occur. This helps to maintain accuracy.

Step 5: Thematic pieces are integrated into a whole – a theory may be posited or an integrated description of the findings made.

Figure 8.4 Qualitative analysis

Step 1. The material from interviews and observations is read and recurring themes are identified. At this stage the researcher needs a very good understanding of the subject matter.

You will have started your study by collecting data through interviews and observations and will have built up a complete and accurate record of what was said. It may be that you have collections of tape recordings of conversations, videos or copious notes. The next stage is to make a record of this information by constructing a hard copy of transcripts of tape recording / notes of video tapes and comprehensive notes of any conversations you have had. This makes it much easier to refer to them in your writing and make notes in the margins.

Step 2. Themes are sorted into categories.

This step involves the use of coding which refers to the process of identifying themes, ideas and categories in the data and then marking similar passages of text with a code label. Retrieving data at a later stage to undertake further comparison and analysis is helped enormously by this process.

Coding enables the researcher to search the data and to compare it and identify patterns that might be of interest or require further investigation.

Codes can be applied to themes, topics, phrases, concepts and keywords which are found in the data. Where the researcher sees recurring phrases or items being continually referenced they will apply the same label or code to it for easy recognition later.

So for example, if a participant uses the term 'healthy attitude' and 'health and well-being' several times this might be a recurring phrase and will be coded in some way. It might then be that other participants use similar expressions which are also coded with the same label. This process of coding involves close reading of the data collected. If a theme is identified from the data that does not quite fit the codes already existing then a new code is created. As this process is undertaken the number of codes will evolve and grow as more topics or themes become apparent.

As you go through the data you will have some questions as to what might be coded. The following provides a list and some examples of the sorts of things you will be looking for. Let's use an example.

You are interested in the management style in your place of work and want to get opinions of staff in the area. You have noticed some are reluctant to say what they actually think but are willing to be interviewed. As you start to delve into the data collected certain things start to emerge.

Behaviour – compliance. 'Keeping quiet when the boss is around'. 'Looking busy', 'speaking up in meetings to get noticed'.

Activities – staying late at work to gain approval. Doing extra shifts. Not missing meetings

Practice – 'ensuring I do everything by the book', ' following guidelines and policy to the letter'.

Relationships or interaction – 'keeping in with the boss', 'make sure I get on well with the team', 'not letting anybody down.'

Activity 8.8

What sort of impression are you getting from the above responses to the data?

Perhaps you have got the impression that there is some fear in this setting. The comments seem to show that individuals are feeling threatened in some way. Further interviews may well reveal that there have been talk of redundancy cuts and this threat has resulted in changes in the way people approach their work and their seniors.

Step 3. Links between categories are identified and charts, thought maps, matrices, flow charts, or time lines may be used to group data.

In this stage you are arranging the data so that all the pieces on one theme are together. You can achieve this in a number of ways

- Folder systems – One folder, one theme. By taking each theme and compiling copies of it you are more able to compare what each interviewee said. It is essential to mark papers with the participant's name, or initials to enable you to remember who said what.

- Card index system – Using a card for each theme you are able to cross-reference each card with each transcript and in this way you can find what everyone said about a certain topic.

- Computer analysis – There are computer packages that can be bought which analyse qualitative data. By uploading your transcripts the software allows you to mark different sections with themes. It will then sort all those sections marked with that themes and print them off together.

Step 4. The data is validated (triangulation) using group discussions, and perhaps statistics to investigate how often themes occur. This helps to maintain accuracy.

By involving the participants in checking the work you have done you can help improve the accuracy and credibility of the research. In this method the interpretation and report carried out by the researcher is given to the participants to check as to the authenticity of the work. They then comment on the viability of the interpretation.

This process can be done during the interview process, or at the end of the study, or both. By summarising information given during an interview, the researcher can question the participant to determine accuracy. If the checks are done at the end of the study then the participants can critically analyse the findings and comment on them. By agreeing that the summaries reflect their experiences, the participants affirm the accuracy and the study is said to have credibility.

Group discussions with peers can also be used to check findings and questioning can help to validate findings. This is a technique used in Masters and PhD vivas when the researcher is asked questions about the research.

Statistics can also be used. In research where themes are emerging it might be possible to count how many times something occurs and thus a very basic statistical test can be applied. A percentage value can then be applied and may enhance the data.

Step 5. Thematic pieces are integrated into a whole – a theory may be posited or an integrated description of the findings made.

In this final stage the researcher presents the findings. As we mentioned earlier in the action research section, although this may be the end of this particular part of the study and a theory may have emerged, it can also be seen as the starting point for further study.

We used a new term above and now should address the concept of 'triangulation'. This refers to the use of several methods to test the results in a data set.

In order to ensure that the work being carried out is valid the researcher is wise to use multiple methods to compare findings in the data. If the researcher relies on one method only there is no external check to test the result. By using three methods to get at the answer to one question, it is hoped that two of the methods will give similar results, thereby validating the study. If the three methods all come up with conflicting results at the very least the researcher knows that they need to refine the question and readdress the data.

The following method may be used;

■ Method sources – the use of questionnaires followed up with interviews of the same participants.

■ Investigator triangulation – the use of different individuals to analyse or interpret a single data set.

■ Peer debriefing – by offering a debriefing session the researcher is subject to questioning about the data by peers who can review the work and explore the work further.

■ Member checks – this method involves going back to the participants in the study to relay findings to date to check their reactions. In this way the data collected can be used to determine how credible the findings are.

To summarise: qualitative research is very labour intensive in terms of generating data.

There are many ways in which data can be analysed but the following constitute the most common methods.

■ Quasi-statistical style. The construction of codes, themes and even words to which statistical tests may be applied.

■ Analytic induction – in which the researcher gathers data, makes tentative hypotheses and refines them when new information emerges. Grounded theory, a favoured method of this type of work starts with coding in which data is categorised with subsequent comparisons between categories being made. Second stage coding re-categorises the previous information by connecting categories and making subcategories.

In the final stage the researcher is searching for the category that underpins all the others and represents the central one. This core category results in a theory that is 'grounded' in the data.

Let's look at an example of this.

A researcher wants to study the admission to an elderly care home as a life changing experience and aims to try to discover the basic meaning surrounding the event with the aim of generating a theory on negative self-esteem due to changed living accommodation.

She collects in-depth interviews and observational data over a year-long period from ten elderly people and their families. The interviews were conducted in groups at first so as to observe how the families worked and interacted together. She was able to gain information on how the families felt about the admission and how the elderly person was coping with the change. She then conducted individual interviews with each group member and gained more information which could be used to check that already obtained.

The analysis was carried out as an ongoing process and interviews were videotaped and audiotaped to provide peer review material as well as checks for coding. Transcripts were compiled and coding was carried out with similar data being grouped. Comparisons were made and categories emerging were regrouped. Themes emerging were reviewed by the family members.

The analysis resulted in the identification of a family process/strategy that enabled the elderly person to retain a positive position in the family circle, despite not being physically present, and thus lessen the reduction in self-esteem.

This is of course an imaginary research project but in essence describes the process of the sort of methods a qualitative researcher would employ and the process through which they might progress.

Presenting the findings of quantitative and qualitative research

The final part in any research is ensuring your findings are reviewed by others and that those using the study can access and understand the work.

All research needs to be accompanied by a report and this should include the following sections.

Abstract This provides the reader with a summary of the work including findings and conclusions.

Introduction The subject area is introduced together with aims and outline of the hypothesis.

The methods used A justification of the choice of methods is given here. The use of quantitative and/or qualitative methods, the primary and secondary sources are all mentioned, and the ethical considerations are also considered in this section. Reliability, validity and confidentiality are also mentioned here.

Data presentation Any data collected is presented in forms of tables, charts and graphs and need to be in this section clearly labelled.

Analysis of results This constitutes the main part of the report and the results are summarised and shown to either support or undermine the hypothesis.

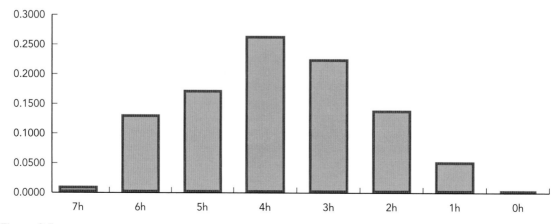

Figure 8.5

Conclusion All the information is finally drawn together and what has been found is discussed.

Evaluation of the study This is a reflection on the success of the study. Strengths and weaknesses are identified and discussed.

This section determines whether the aims and objectives were well set and achievable. It also addresses the ethical considerations taken into account and whether the methods chosen were appropriate. Further discussion should involve a comment about the project itself and the timings as well as what might have been changed.

Recommendation of future research Future research can be identified here and suggestions as to how this research may be moved forward is made in this section. A **bibliography and reference list** is included in this section.

Activity 8.9

Complete a table to show your understanding of the difference between qualitative and quantitative research methods.

Critical review of relevant literature

Secondary research, as we mentioned at the start of the chapter, is something you are doing in your degree work constantly. It is the focus on available research carried out by others and the conclusions we draw from it. In this section we will be looking at how we can get the most from the reading we do and how we can make sense of it.

When we undertake a review of literature we need to ensure that what we are reading is of good quality and that it will be useful for our practice. In order to do so, critical appraisal of what we are reading must be undertaken. This can be very hard for somebody who is new to the subject since we may feel unqualified to comment upon a seasoned researchers work. Also we may lack the skills in which to carry out such a task.

Critical appraisal of research has proved notoriously difficult for some of my students and even qualified nurses and care professionals approach this particular activity with some misgiving. So let's look at the skills necessary to carry out this vital research work.

Reviewing literature has number of purposes.

It helps you to:

- define the subject you wish to work on
- gain a historical perspective of your subject
- make a judgement about the research methods used in the studies
- enables you to suggest further research on the basis of previous knowledge in the area.

This exploratory activity enables us to get a really good idea of the subject area we are interested in and gives us a good working knowledge of the studies carried out in a field. But you need to be able to read with a critical eye in order to get the best out of the review. When we use the words critical or critique we often attach a negative connotation to it. We may feel uncomfortable 'criticising' another's work but we need to put this into some perspective. The study you read may well be a really good one – you are still undergoing a 'critique' of it but will be showing it in a positive light. Critical appraisal, then, is not always negative.

Here are some pointers to help you to read in a critical way

- Keep your purpose in mind when you read. Ask yourself why you are reading this particular study.

- Don't let any extraneous arguments in the book or article distract you from your reading

- Think first about what you are expecting from the article or chapter.

- Skim the headings and the abstract of the piece,

- Look at the first line of each paragraph and the conclusion.

- Don't read everything with equal attention.

Finding the right reading sources

At the start of your course you will have had an induction week in which you were taken to the library and shown how to access texts, journals, books and the search engines to help you find relevant research for study purposes. You may have a guide which details the various library catalogues and bibliographic databases available to you.

Searching the bibliographies and reference lists of the materials you read will widen your knowledge of the research in the area. These will show you more articles relevant to your subject area.

Having collected a list of references you then need to access the articles and this can be a little tricky. At university you have the luxury of being able to contact subject specialist librarians who can assist you in using and accessing library resources and may be able to access inter-library loans for you. Further help is available in the research school or faculty in your university and a research consultant may be a very useful contact to cultivate.

Managing the reading materials

There is nothing worse at the end of a long piece of work than having to try to access the resources you used in order to reference them correctly. Get into good habits now and start to reference correctly at the outset of your course of study (see Chapter 1)

You need to set up a referencing system and 'End note' is one with which you may be familiar. You should get into the habit of putting the publication details into your selected system as soon as you pick up an article.

Any photocopied material needs to have a note about what you copied and where you filed it.

Web-based material

We are fortunate to have an abundance of materials from the internet but we need to deal with such articles with some caution.

Journal articles and most scholarly books have undergone critical review, but subject matter appearing on the internet may not undergo such scrutiny so you need to be aware of this.

Reading these articles must be done in an objective manner.

Make sure you are looking at the work of authors with credibility. Check their qualifications if you can. Also, try to ensure that the material is correctly referenced or linked to other online information. You need to be sure of how old the material is and determine whether logical arguments are put forward. Finally is there any support for what the author is saying from other sources?

Asking questions

As you read, have some specific questions in mind to help you to concentrate on the material in an active manner. You may wish to address whether there have been any other studies in this field before. Perhaps you might ask if the results you are reading compare to others you have read?

Look at the following questions;

- What were the authors trying to do and find out?

- What is important about this piece?

- What was done in the research ?

- What information is given about the sample?

- How did the researchers collect the data?

- What were the results?
- What do the authors conclude and how have they evaluated their findings?
- How can you apply these findings to your own work?

If you answer these questions they will form the basis of your written review. Try to answer these as you go along and make notes on what you are reading.

Note taking

Taking notes and making critical comments is more useful than merely writing a summary of what you have read. This is certainly a time consuming exercise but will be useful later on when you start to write up your review.

Structure of the literature review

You want to ensure that your literature review is a coherent piece of work and to that end the writing up of your review must be planned and structured well.

The first task is to make sense of the notes already made which now must be arranged. It is important that the ideas from your reading of articles are presented in an order that makes sense in the context of your research project.

Structural tips

A number of reviews I have read contain a common error: the tendency to present material from one author, followed by information from another, and so on. By linking ideas this can be avoided. You will need to identify common themes and categorise the work read into groups of ideas. You could group authors who draw similar conclusions and other authors who disagree. Try not to just describe the work you have read but make comments as to how the work has been used and what it means for you in your own work. By linking what you have read to your study you are ensuring that the literature review is related to the hypothesis and methodology to follow. A summary of what the literature means and implies will clearly show you have thought about your reading in the light of what is to follow.

Starting to write the literature review

You will probably have a lot of material by now and will want to know how to put it together and whether you really have enough.

When beginning to draft your work use the notes you have already compiled and you will find you already have a head start with respect to the writing up. You will also find you have a greater knowledge of the subject than you started with and can make a decision as to whether you need to read any more or whether you can actually start now to write up what you know.

Start on a small section of the review and just remember that you can add to this review as you go along with other parts of your study.

Constructing your argument

A well-argued literature review will show:

- A clear relationship between your arguments and the evidence.
- Opinions which are supported by facts from the literature.
- Citations and quotations used where relevant.
- Acknowledgement opposing viewpoints.
- A clearly structured review with a statement in the introduction which makes the argument clear.
- A rationale for the choice of your materials is given.

Remember – A cohesive literature review presents a clear line of argument. If it is still not clear then you have not read enough.

Academic language

The use of so-called academic language can be a real worry for students, but you need not get too stressed about it. Here are some pointers to help.

One of the basic qualities of academic language is that it should be objective and fair. When you discuss other's work you must avoid strong or emotive language and apply a respectful account of what you have read. In dealing with work that you considered 'nonsense', or 'poorly carried out' you would be wise to adopt a neutral tone and perhaps refer to 'inconsistency that has weakened the validity of the results'. Less personalised comments are the best approach.

When you are convinced that there are shortcomings in the research politely point this out by using convincing and decisive comments. The use of the words 'maybe' or 'perhaps' should be used sparingly in order to maintain a confident tone to your findings.

The following checklist may prove useful to you in your assessment and any research you may undertake in the future.

A final checklist

The skills required to carry out an empirical study in practice

The text thus far identifies all you need to carry out a research study in your own area of practice. In selecting a suitable method you might need to consider the following.

Without a research method you will not be able to collect data, so methods are the 'tools of the trade' you need to employ.

The design and selection of an appropriate method will determine the quality of the findings. You need to think about the aims and objectives of your research and what evidence you need to collect in order to achieve that aim. It is also appropriate at the outset to think about where and from whom that data will be collected. The means of

Selection of sources	Tick
What is the purpose of the review and have you identified it?	
How did you go about it and have you justified your choices?	
Have you justified your choice of materials and stated why you discarded others?	
Have you rationalised what years you excluded?	
Have you emphasised recent developments in the subject under study?	
Have you focused on primary sources with only selective use of secondary sources?	
Is the literature you have selected relevant? How do you know?	
Is your reference data complete?	
Critical evaluation of the literature	
Have you organised your material according to issues?	
Have you organised the material in a logical way ?	
Does the amount of detail included on an issue relate to its importance?	
Have you critically evaluated design and methodology?	
Have you shown results which were conflicting or inconclusive and suggested possible reasons?	
Have you shown the relevance of each reference to your research?	
Interpretation	
Can you say that the reader's understanding has been enhanced by your summary of the current literature?	
Does your research design reflect the methodological implications of the literature review?	

(Adapted from Worcester University checklist)

collection should also be determined at this stage. You also need to consider the ethical implications of your research and this is referred to as research governance.

Summarising your study plan.

Step 1 – Decide what you are interested in studying.

Step 2 – Devise your aims and objectives. What are you trying to find out and how will you do this?

Step 3 – Decide on the evidence you need to collect.

Step 4 – Where will you collect and who will your sample be?

Step 5 – Select an appropriate method.

Step 6 – How will you collect the evidence?

Step 7 – Are there any ethical implications of your study you need to account for?

The last point is very important, so let's address this now.

Research governance and ethics

Any research carried out in the field of Health and Social Care is subject to the DoH Research Governance Framework for Health and Social Care (the first issue came out in 2001, the second edition was published in April 2005, with subsequent amendments).

This framework ensures that there is:

■ A quality framework in place.

■ Public confidence in quality research.

■ Principles of good practice.

■ Monitoring and regulation, for example through funding bodies; National Patient Safety Agency (for reporting adverse effects). (Department of Health (2005) *Research Governance Framework For Health and Social Care*. London, Department of Health)

In addition to the above, the Economic and Social Research Council (ESRC) have developed a framework for Research Ethics to ensure that all research is carried out to a high ethical standard.

If you are planning to conduct research in an academic or professional setting, you need to be aware of the ethics involved. First of all you need to ensure you have the permission of the people participating to conduct research involving them. Anything in the research design that is potentially harmful needs to be carefully considered. For example, this might be something as simple as being careful how you word sensitive questions during interviews.

Any research undertaken must be conducted in an objective way and you must make sure your own personal biases and opinions do not get in the way of your research. The following may help to ensure you conduct ethical research.

Anonymity of the participants must be addressed and you need to ensure your participants know whether your research results will be anonymous or not.

The sample chosen needs to be one which will produce good quality data and should not be purely based on easy-to-access groups.

You may have to contact an ethical committee to gain approval to carry out research and should check your institutions policies on this

The final reporting of your findings needs to be accurate and fully represent what you observed or what you were told.

Practising within an ethical framework means adherence to a number of ethical principles (Singleton, J., and McLaren, S., (1995) and Burkhardt and Nathaniel (2007).)

These are:

Autonomy – the individual's right to be self-governing and to make decisions that apply to their lives. In a research setting this means that people should be able to choose whether or not they wish to participate.

Beneficence – benefits to the individual should be promoted. This principle refers to doing what is good. An example of 'doing good' is found in the health profession when the health of an individual is improved by treatment from a practitioner.

Non-maleficence – the need to do no harm. As health professionals this ethical principle demands that we do not provide ineffective treatment. Unfortunately so many treatments whilst beneficial do carry risk and the issue to bear in mind here is whether the benefits outweigh the risk.

In terms of research studies one would need to declare the risks as well as potential benefits of an intervention.

Justice – this ethical principle states that ethical research should prescribe actions that are fair to those involved.

Veracity – telling the truth and in the context of research; this requires the researcher to be open and unambiguous in their work.

Confidentiality – protecting the individuals right to privacy.

Fidelity – the principle of faithfulness and keeping promises.

The whole issue of ethical research came about as a result of The Nuremberg Code which was formulated in 1947 after the Nazi war criminals were put on trial in the International Court at Nuremberg. The dreadful crimes committed in the name of research came to light after the Second World War and resulted in a code of practice (Katz, J, 1972).

This code specifies how research is to be conducted in an ethical manner. One of the main changes was do with consent. Research subjects in the Nazi War camps were unable to withdraw from studies and many died as a result of inhumane research experiments. All participants in research now must agree to be part of the research and should consent to being a subject. This consent needs to be 'informed' which means the subject needs to have knowledge and understanding of the study to be conducted and have full details of any potential harmful effects.

In some cases no consent is required to lawfully involve a person in research. For example in any research where data that has been anonymised and cannot be traced back to individuals then Confidentiality and Data Protection laws do not apply.

A good study to look at is that carried out by Stanley Milgram in 1963 – see the study in Atkinson, R. et al (2002) *Introduction to Psychology*. Harcourt Brace, USA. This study used deception to enable the research to be carried out. What do you think of this?

The Helsinki Declaration (1975) Guidelines, originally adopted in 1964, outlines clinical trial procedures and requires researchers to ensure patient safety, consent and use ethics committee reviews when using human subjects.

The world events which have shaped our understanding of ethics in research have served to identify the good practice by which we should conduct our studies. The terrible experiments carried out in the war have brought about the implementation of ethical standards in scientific research. In addition to changed standards we also have ethical committees who ensure that researchers consider all relevant ethical issues when conducting research.

Guidance on research ethics provided in a government paper states;

The dignity, rights, safety and well-being of participants must be the primary consideration in any research study.

The right to be treated with respect applies in all aspects of health care and research is no exception.

Summary

Evidence-based practice (EBP) impacts upon the service user and as such has become a common expectation for all health and social care practitioners. In this chapter we have explored how EBP has become part of the NHS agenda and through the implementation of Clinical Governance in 1998 has introduced a framework for accountability. The impact upon the service user and staff has been development of quality services, high standards of care and the creation excellence in clinical care environments (DoH, 1998).

The link to research has also been addressed. As this chapter has shown, research involves systematic investigation to discover facts or relationships and enables us to make conclusions using scientific methods. Evidence-based practice is about using that research to make professional judgements and applying our informed and enhanced knowledge to making care decisions. Therefore knowledge of how to undertake research is crucial for the health professional and the chapter has supplied some pointers as to the use of research methodologies, methods and analytical techniques. One of the most useful tools at your disposal is how to carry out a critical review of relevant literature and the simple checklist provided may help in your assessment.

At this stage in your degree work you are not expected to undertake a full research study but the chapter has highlighted some of the things you need to be aware should you need to do so in the future. The ethical guidelines and a quick look at how these must be central to any research was covered briefly but is by no means definitive. You are asked to seek out further information to ensure a greater understanding.

The final activity here is designed to help you with your assessment in this particular module. There will be no answers provided.

Summary assignment

Prepare a report critically reviewing literature relevant to an issue in your work base.

Propose a methodology and method that would enable you to explore the identified issues in your practice.

References

Acheson, D. ((1988)*Public Health In England: The Report of the Committee of Inquiry into the Future Development of Public Health Function* (Chairman:Sir Donald Acheson) HMSO, London.

Atkinson, R.L., Atkinson,R.G., Smith.E.E., Bem,D.J. (2002) *Introduction to Psychology*. Harcourt Brace, USA.

Burkhardt, M. A. and Nathaniel, A.K., (2007) *Ethics and Issues in Contemporary Nursing* (3rd Edition). Delmar, New York. Thomson Learning.

Carnwell, R. (2000) Essential difference between research and evidence-based practice. *Nurse Researcher.* **8** (2):, 55–68

Cochrane Centre (2003) *UK Cochrane Centre: 2003 Annual Report* downloaded from: http://www.cochrane.co.uk/ Annual%20Report%202003 – 21/11/04.

Cohen, L., Manion, L. and Morrison, K., (2000) *Research Methods In Education*. Routledge, London.

Cormack, D. (2000) *The Research Process in Nursing*. 4th Edition. Blackwell Science, Oxford, London, Edinburgh.

Department of Health (2005) *Research Governance Framework For Health and Social Care. HMSO, London.*

Department of Health (access at: http:// www.dh.gov.uk/en/ Publicationsandstatistics/Publications/ PublicationsPolicyAndGuidance/ DH_4108962).

Department of Health (1998) 'A first class service: quality in the NHS'. Stationery Office, London.

Erikson-Owens and Kennedy (2001) 'Fostering evidenced-based care in clinical teaching'. *Journal of Midwifery and Womens Health.* **46**, 137–145

Glaser and Strauss.

Katz, J. (1972) *Experimentation with Human Subjects*, Russell Sage, New York: pp. 305–6.

Singleton, J. and McLaren, S. (1995*) Ethical Foundations of Health Care.* London, Mosby, http://cks.library.nhs.uk/home http://www.jr2.ox.ac.uk/bandolier/index. html http://www3.interscience.wiley.com/cgi- http://newsvote.bbc.co.uk/mpapps/ pagetools/print/news.bbc.co.uk/1/hi/ health/180895...accessed 8/10/10

Further reading

Becker S., Bryman A. (2004) *Understanding Research for Social Policy and Practice*. 1st Edition. The Policy Press, Bristol.

Bowling, A. (2002) *Research Methods in Health: Investigating Health and Health Services*. (2nd Edition). Open University Press, Buckinghamshire.

Burns, N. and Grove, S.K. (1987) *The Practice of Nursing Research. Conduct, Critique and Utilisation.* W.B.Saunders, Philadelphia.

Clarke, A.M., (1998) 'The qualitative-quantitative debate: moving from positivism and confrontation to post-positivism and reconciliation.' *Journal of Advanced Nursing.* **27**, 1242–1249.

Coolican, H. (1999) *Research Methods and statistics in Psychology.* Hodder and Stoughton, London.

Denscombe, M. (2002) *Ground Rules for Good Research: A 10 point Guide for Social Researchers.* Open University Press, Buckingham.

Denscombe, M. (2003) *The Good Research Guide for Small-scale Social Research Projects,* 2nd Edition. Open University Press. Buckingham.

Department of Health (1993) *Research for Health.* Department of Health, London.

Dey, J. (1993) *Qualitative Data Analysis: A User Friendly guide For Social Scientists.* Routledge, London.

Economic and Social Research Council(2002) *Research Ethics Framework.* HMSO, London.

Gomm, R. and Davies, C. (2000) *Using Evidence in Health & Social Care.* Sage Publications, London.

Holliday A. (2001) *Doing and Writing Qualitative Research.* Sage Publications, London.

Kerr, A.W., Hall, H.K. and Kozub, S.A. (2005) *Doing Statistics With SPSS.* 2nd Edition. Sage Publications, London.

Knight PT. (2001) *Small Scale Research: Pragmatic Inquiry in Social Science and the Caring Professions.* Sage Publications, London.

Lincoln Y.S., and Guba, E.G., (2000) 'Paradigmatic controversies, contradictions, and emerging confluences.' In Denzin, N.K., and Lincoln, Y.S., (Eds.) *The Handbook of Qualitative Research.* Sage Publications, Inc, Thousand Oaks, CA. pp. 163–188.

Lincoln Y and Guba EG (1985) *Naturalist Inquiry,* Sage Publications, Newbury Park, CA.

Oppenheim, A. N., (1992) *Questionnaire Design, Interviewing And Attitude Measurement.* Pinter Publishers, London.

Robson, C., (2002) *Real World Research: Resources for Social Scientists and Practitioner-Researchers.* Blackwell Publishing, Oxford.

Sallah, D. and Clark, C. (2005) *Research and Development in Mental Health Theory, Framework and Models.* Churchill Livingstone

Tesch, R. (1990) *Qualitative Research: Analysis Types and Software Tools.* The Falmer Press, Basingstoke.

Thompson, C., McCaughan, D., Cullum, N., Sheldon, T., Thompson, D. and Mulhall, A. (2001), *Nurses Use of Research Information In Clinical Decision Making: A Descriptive And Analytical Study: Final Report.* NCC SDO, London.

Walliman NSR. (2000) *Your Research Project: A Step-by-Step Guide for the First-Time Researcher.* Sage Publications, London.

Useful websites

www.elsc.org.uk

www.nlh.nhs.uk

www.sosig.ac.uk

www.nmap.ac.uk

www.omni.ac.ukl

http://gateway.uk.ovid.com/athens/ (requires ATHENS password)

www.pubmed.com (requires ATHENS password)

http://bmj.com

http://www.jr2.ox.ac.uk/bandolier/

http://www.dh.gov.uk

9

Team working

In order to provide effective health and social care it is essential to work in collaboration and partnership with others either in the same team or across a range of different agencies and disciplines within the care sector. The most important person in your team will be the service user and they need to be central in any team working. You will be involved in several different teams in your work setting; this chapter will help you work more effectively in those teams. The chapter will introduce you to team function and the roles that are adopted in teams. It will examine models of leadership relevant to the health and care sector. You will be encouraged to examine strategies of team working and leadership in order to identify your own strengths, responsibilities and learning needs and to reflect on best practice within the care context. A range of practical skills and suggestions relevant to team working will be discussed. Team working means taking

responsibility for your own work as well as respecting the contributions of all your colleagues and good communication is essential to effective team working, therefore this chapter relates closely to Chapter 2.

Learning outcomes

By the end of the chapter you will be able to:

■ Show styles and theories of leadership and management

■ Help the student reflect on their own experiences of team working

■ Show how team working is effected by national policy initiatives

■ Understand team working in different health and social care settings

■ Explore practical strategies for effective team working.

A team is a group of people who work together. A group is a collection of two or more people who communicate together because they have interests in common. Wheelan (2005) acknowledges that from the beginning of human history, people have utilised work groups to generate new ideas, get things done and nurture individuals. A team has similarities to a group, however a team needs to be coordinated and team members need to be able to communicate and collaborate effectively. Pearson and Spencer (1997) suggest that teams are formed because of a belief that having people work on shared goals interdependently will lead to synergy; the aggregate of individual's performances will be exceeded by the work group's performance. It is more successful to bring together people with diverse skills and

knowledge. For example the skills of doctors, nurses, occupational therapists and physiotherapists working together in an orthopaedic ward to best meet the needs of the patients on the ward. This is called a multi-disciplinary team (MDT).

This style of working is a relatively recent phenomenon in health and social care. In the past groups of staff from the same discipline rarely communicated with other specialists around patient issues. This often led to a duplication of service provision or no provision at all. In the last 20 years there has been a greater push towards multidisciplinary team working; that is groups of people from different professions working together with the patient at the centre. The Laming report (2003) highlighted the importance of working closely with people from other professional groups and agencies. The improvement in collaborative working has also been promoted by the housing of people from different professions in one building. It is a simple fact that when people work physically close together they communicate more, know each other better, understand each other's values and procedures better and therefore work more effectively together. However in some circumstances teams may perform less effectively than individuals working alone. Teams may take more time to achieve a task as they may become sidetracked with unimportant issues, take too much time discussing small details or get caught up in team conflict. One of the advantages of teamwork is the abundance and quality of ideas, however over time some teams may start to think in the same way and the ideas from individuals could become subsumed into the team view. Teams in health and social care vary in size and complexity; they deal with difficult and demanding personal issues that can take a toll on the health of the individual team

members. Martin *et al.* (2010) argue that teams in health and social care often work with ambiguous and sometimes contradictory objectives of meeting the demand and giving the best possible care while staying in the budget. An effective team supports its individual team members.

The NHS – organisation and structure

The National Health Service (NHS) is one of the largest employers in the world, and is the biggest in Europe, with over 1.3 million staff. Within this huge organisation there will be many different types of teams working to achieve the best health for service users from a range of diverse sectors. There are more than 300 different careers within the National Health Service. If you choose to work in the NHS you can guarantee that you will work as part of a team (NHS jobs 2010).

The diagram below outlines the structure of the NHS in England since April 2002.

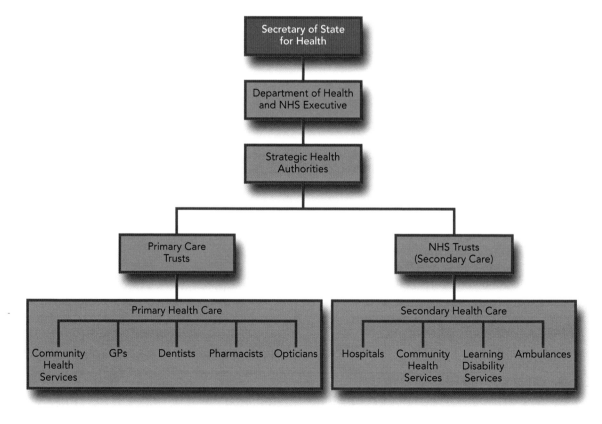

Figure 9.1 Structure of the National Health Service
(Office of Health Economics 2009)

Structure of the National Health Service

At the top of the picture is the Secretary of State for Health, the government minister in charge of the Department of Health, responsible for the NHS, social work and social care in England and appointed by the Prime Minister. The Department of Health and the NHS Executive are responsible for the overall planning of the health service and responsible for taking forward health and social care policies. Under the Department of Health are 28 Strategic Health Authorities which provide the link between the Department of Health and the NHS and plan health care for the population of the region they cover.

Health services are divided between 'primary' and 'secondary'. Primary care services include general medical practitioners (GPs), dentists, pharmacists, opticians, district nurses, practice managers, community midwives and numerous other services. These are provided locally, near to where patients live, often in the local high street or even in patients' own homes. Primary health care has been defined by the World Health Organization (WHO 1978) as 'the first level contact of individuals, the family and the community with the national health system which brings health care as close as possible to where people live and work'. The more specialised services, which we use less often and are provided in fewer locations, are called 'secondary care'. This includes not only hospitals but also ambulances and specialised health services for the mentally ill and the learning disabled.

Services are provided by NHS Trusts and supply secondary care. Primary Care Trusts provide primary care services. But they also have a second, very important role. Primary Care Trusts are responsible for buying almost all of the health care, both primary and secondary, required by the local populations they serve. They are allocated funds each year by the Department of Health to do this and they must decide how much to spend on which health care services for the local population (Office of Health Economics, 2009).

However, this structure will be replaced after 2011 by a more streamlined NHS. The White Paper 'Equity and excellence: liberating the NHS' 2010 states:

> As a result of the changes, the NHS will be streamlined with fewer layers of bureaucracy. Strategic Health Authorities and Primary Care Trusts will be phased out. Management costs will be reduced so that as much resource as possible supports frontline services. The reforms build on changes started under the previous Government. (Department of Health, 2010)

How does this system work?

Imagine that you are unwell. You visit your General Practitioner (GP) who diagnoses your illness and if necessary either gives you a prescription or arranges for you to see a specialist at a hospital for a better diagnosis. You may then need to be treated in hospital either as a day patient or as an inpatient. Throughout this sequence you receive the medical care which the professionals – the GPs, hospital doctors and nurses consider your need.

Activity 9.1

Follow a journey of someone you know who has needed health care recently. It might be a parent or friend or relative. Identify all the staff they might have come in contact with along the way.

Try and work out where, on the diagram above each person is located, for example G.P. receptionist = Primary Health care, GP practice.

What ever the changes in the provision of health it will always be a challenge for the NHS to balance services for preventing ill health, promoting health and curing illness with the need to manage a budget; Quinney, (2006) states that this is also the case in social care.

How social care is delivered

Department of Health National Archives (2010) explain the Department of Health shapes the delivery of adult social care services through leadership, policy and guidance. Local councils with social services responsibilities commission public, private and voluntary sector providers to deliver services that meet the needs of their local population.

The role of the Social Care, Local Government and Care Partnerships Directorate

The Directorate provides professional leadership and advice on all aspects of social care policy in order to promote effective and equitable delivery of services, and a clear vision for the future of social care. The Department also consults with people who use services, carers and stakeholders, and actively engages those in government to develop and improve evidence-based social care policies.

The role of local councils with social services responsibilities

Local councils with social services responsibilities, in conjunction with their partners, are responsible for identifying the needs of their local population and commissioning services to meet them. In order to do this, councils work through a number of partnerships and frameworks. The key responsibility for adult social services rests with the Director of Adult Social Services, which is a statutory post in local authorities with social services responsibilities.

The delivery of adult social care services

Adult social care is delivered by over 25,000 providers, the majority of these providers are small and the ten largest providers only own a quarter of the private residential market between them.

Public sector – there is still a small remnant of services that councils provide directly. This equates to 9 per cent of care homes and 17 per cent of domiciliary agencies. Councils also provide nearly 80 per cent of adult placement schemes, although the carers themselves are not local authority employees.

Private sector – the majority of adult social care providers are private sector. Two thirds of care homes and over 70 per cent of domiciliary agencies are operated by the private sector. Many of these providers sell their services to councils as well as to private individuals.

Voluntary sector – the voluntary sector is also a key service provider.

In the White Paper 'Equity and excellence: liberating the NHS' (2010) the emphasis is still on collaborative working within the public sector as stated below

> The Department will continue to have a vital role in setting adult social care policy. We want a sustainable adult social care system that gives people support and freedom to lead the life they choose, with dignity. We recognise the critical interdependence between the NHS and the adult social care system in securing better outcomes for people, including carers. We will seek to break down barriers between health and social care funding to encourage preventative action. (Department of Health, 2010)

The government White Paper 'Our health, our care, our say a new direction for community services' sets out a number of key priorities for health and social care. The responses address key statements posed by local communities in relation to the delivery of health and social care services.

The statement:

> There should be more co-ordination between the health service, social care and the local authority. There needs to be more communication between them.

> One of our main aims for the future is to make sure that health and social services will work together and share information to give 'joined-up' care to the people they work for. Services will share information about the people in their care so that health, housing,

benefits and other needs are considered together. By 2008, anyone with long-term health and social care needs should have an integrated Personal Health and Social Care Plan, if they want one. All Primary Care Trusts and local authorities should have joint health and social care managed networks and/or teams for people with complex needs. We will also be building modern NHS community hospitals, which will offer integrated health and social services. (Department of Health, 2006)

It has been suggested that health and social care professionals work together at three levels (Department of Health, 1998).

■ Strategic – planning and sharing information.

■ Operational management – policies that demonstrate partnership.

■ Individual care – joint training and a single point of access to health care.

It is important for effective working in health and social care that people want to collaborate together; in order to do this the organisational structures need to be in place (Day, 2006). Effective team work enhances patient care and safety as members of the team coordinate and communicate their activities and have the patient at the centre of the care. Many people working in the NHS would believe that they have always worked in teams, and although the importance of teamwork has long been recognised in health and social care settings it has not always been achieved.

Examples of problems in teamwork

Two high profile legal cases highlight a problem of team working in health and social care. In June 1998 the Secretary of State announced a Public Inquiry into the management of children receiving cardiac surgical services at Bristol Royal Infirmary. Concerns had been raised about the surgery following a higher than expected number of deaths of children. More children died in Bristol than anywhere else in the country following the same operation. However the Bristol Royal Infirmary inquiry (2001) supports our earlier statement that earlier teams consisted of individuals from one group of professionals, such as a team of nurses or a team of occupational therapists with a senior person being in charge. The inquiry recommended that skills in communication with patients and colleagues and the development of team work and effective leadership should be paramount and there should be a greater focus on MDT working.

The final statement revealed that effective team work did not exist, relations between various professionals were on occasions poor and there was a lack of clinical leadership. It could be said that professionals felt safe with this model. It's also convenient from an administration point of view.

The inquiry revealed that this model didn't always suit the patient. They suggest that a multiprofessional team should share responsibility. Leadership should be based on ability and the task rather than a title or professional qualification. Team work is the collective, collaborative effort of all those concerned with the care of the patient. Patients do not belong to any one profession, they are the responsibility of all who take care of them. (Bristol Inquiry 2001)

Integration is seen as the assimilation of organisations and/or services into single entities, allowing for greater transparency between partners as well as enhanced benefits for service users.

Integration of both NHS and Local Government Adult Services is at the heart of national policy. The development of commissioning in this area is a high priority for many Primary Care Trusts and councils in the UK (Maslin, Prothero and Bennion, 2010).

Activity 9.2

How might effective team work improve NHS and local government services integration?

The second high profile case is the Lord Laming inquiry into the death of Victoria Climbie (2003). On 12 January 2001 Marie Terez-Kouao and Carl John-Manning were convicted of Victoria Climbie's murder. An inquiry to establish the circumstances leading to and surrounding the death of Victoria Climbie was commissioned. Part of the inquiry was concerned with how social services, health and the police cooperated with each other and local education and local authorities. (For full details of the report please refer to www.publications. education.gov.uk.) Recommendations 14, 15, 16 are all concerned with team working, communication and interagency working.

The Victoria Climbie inquiry (2003) advised that at a local level the future of social care lies with those managers who can demonstrate the capacity to work effectively across organisational boundaries. Such boundaries will always exist. Those able to operate flexibly need encouragement in contrast to those who persist in working in isolation and making decisions alone. Improvements to the way information is exchanged within and between agencies is imperative if children are to be adequately safeguarded. The NHS plan (2000) had a major impact on working within the NHS and social care sectors. It suggested a more integrated way of working, with the patient at the centre of the team. Patients were given new powers and more influence over the way the NHS functions them which gave a stronger voice in the decision making process. Reforms were put in place to give greater choice and control over care as well as access to far more information about the quality of that care. Very often teams are resistant to change because it takes them out of their comfort zone and they feel secure in what they know. The NHS plan (2010) criticises some teams for caring more about the structures and systems of the organisation than the patient experience. The NHS plan is promoting greater collaboration with other agencies in joint teams and to implement such arrangements will require clear leadership and flexibility from staff.

Examples of health and social care teams

Activity 9.3

What teams operate in your working environment? Write down a list of the teams that you come into contact with and the roles of the people within them?

Ward team:

- Nurses
- Doctors
- Ward clerks

Community Team:

- Nurses
- Occupational therapists
- Physiotherapists
- Speech therapists
- Social workers

Nursing home:

- Owner/manager
- Registered manager
- Deputy manager
- Care workers
- Catering staff
- Administrators
- Cleaners

Team working is affected by the relationships between the people who work together. Teams vary in terms of how the team influences a team member's decisions at work. In some teams the other members have a lot of influence over an individual practitioner's clinical decisions; whereas in other teams the individual makes most clinical and day-to-day decisions alone. Mathias and Thompson (1997) suggest that inter-professional working can range from making a referral

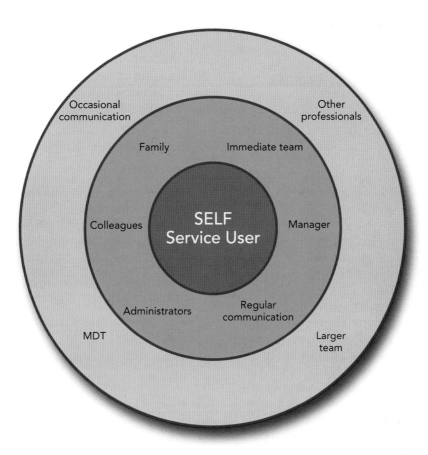

Figure 9.2 Team communication

to another professional through to doing joint assessment and working together as co-therapists.

Activity 9.4

Who do you communicate most with in your team?

Draw concentric rings and place the members of your wider team within the concentric rings. Place the people with whom you have most contact in the inner ring.

Does the communication you have with people in the inner ring differ in any way from the communication you have with people in the outer rings?

You may have identified a number of different teams with whom you have contact, and these could include the following teams.

Community teams

Pearson and Spencer (1997) suggest that the conditions in a complex community team are not always good for building inter-professional relationships. The full range of professionals may not meet together at the same time and the team has too many members to be an effective size. Boundary crossing is taking responsibility for the business of another profession and flexible working is taking and carrying out advice from another professional. Developments in electronic communication have had a significant impact on how team members and different teams interact, and the communication will differ from teams who regularly communicate face to face.

Practice teams

The staffing in practice teams is usually smaller than in community teams, and the team is more stable and predictable. Communication in practice teams may be more regular and predictable.

Service user involvement

There are different terms used to describe people who use the health and social care services. Traditionally the term 'patient' was used and is still used in inpatient hospital care. When working in mental health services I used the term 'client' and sometimes the term 'customer' is used. Martin *et al.* (2010) say that 'service user' is considered a more neutral term. They say that service users are the ultimate customers and they are at the centre of designing and delivering health and social care services. Reforms to the United Kingdom's National Health Service include efforts to change the relationship between patients and professionals. Service users are being encouraged to exercise greater control over their own health care and to become more involved in the development of health services. The Department of Health promotes the involvement of service users and the public in decisions about the planning, design, development and delivery of local services, with the promise that this will lead to improved services and better outcomes for patients. Service users see themselves as having a particular role to play in health and social care, as 'experts in their own experience'. However Branfield and Beresford (2006) argue that 'service users feel that their knowledge is generally not valued or taken seriously by professionals, policy-makers and services. The closed culture of health and social care services and their own inadequate resources restrict service users' capacity to develop and share their knowledge'.

Changing relationships within teams

Nurses have traditionally played a supporting role to doctors. Although this culture is still operating the relationship is more complex; nurses are not always subservient to doctors and are able to influence care for service users (Baggott, 2004). When someone is part of a multidisciplinary team the lines of accountability become complicated. The NHS Plan aimed to break down the old boundaries between staff and extended the roles of non-medical staff. Baggott (2004) notes that professional rivalries and the desire to promote territory are still strong in some teams; each profession has a different set of values and their values affect the perspective they have on what needs to be done.

Barriers to team working

These include:

- The divide between social care staff working along side medical staff illustrated by geographical boundaries, communication boundaries and status inequalities.

- The mismatch of cultures, behaviours and understanding of services.

- The lack of understanding of each others' roles.

- The lack of clarity regarding management roles and responsibilities.

- Lack of control given to team managers.

- People not being fully committed to team working.

Benefits of team working

These include:

- Increased job satisfaction.

- Greater team working.

- Development of a shared culture.

- Improved communication.

- Enhanced cooperation with other agencies.

- Speed of response from referral to assessment.

Team work roles

It is important for effective team work for all team members to relate well to each other and to do this it may be a good idea if they are similar people. However it is also important to have a balance of personality types and a mix of ages, gender and skills. Belbin (1981) carried out research to see what variety of roles were needed in an effective team. He wanted to control the dynamics of teams to discover if and how problems could be predicted and avoided.

The research revealed that the difference between success and failure for a team was not dependent on factors such as intellect, but more on behaviour. The research team began to identify separate clusters of behaviour, each of which formed distinct team contributions or Team Roles.
(Belbin 2010)

Belbins nine team roles

Plant

Characteristics: Plants are innovators and inventors and can be highly creative. They provide the seeds and ideas from which major developments spring. Usually they prefer to operate by themselves at some distance from the other members of the team, using their imagination and often working in an unorthodox manner. They tend to be introverted and react strongly to criticism and praise. Their ideas may often be radical and may lack practical constraint. They are independent, clever and original and may be weak in communicating with other people on a different wave length.

Function: The main use of a Plant is to generate new proposals and to solve complex problems. Plants are often needed in the initial stages of a project or when a project is failing to progress. Plants have usually made their mark as founders of companies or as originators of new products. Too many Plants in one organisation, however, may be counterproductive as they tend to spend their time reinforcing their own ideas and engaging each other in combat.

Monitor evaluator

Characteristics: Monitor Evaluators are serious-minded, prudent individuals with a built-in immunity from being over-enthusiastic. They are slow in making decisions preferring to think things over. Usually they have a high critical thinking ability. They have a capacity for shrewd judgements that take all factors into consideration. A good Monitor Evaluator is seldom wrong.

Function: Monitor Evaluators are best suited to analysing problems and evaluating ideas and suggestions. They are very good at weighing up the pros and cons of options.

To many outsiders the Monitor Evaluator may appear as dry, boring or even over-critical. Some people are surprised that they become managers. Nevertheless, many Monitor Evaluators occupy strategic posts and thrive in high level appointments. In some jobs success or failure hinges on a relatively small number of crunch decisions. This is ideal territory for an Monitor Evaluator; for the person who is never wrong is the one who scores in the end.

Coordinators

Characteristics: The distinguishing feature of Co-ordinators is their ability to cause others to work towards shared goals. Mature, trusting and confident, they delegate readily. In interpersonal relations they are quick to spot individual talents and to use them in the pursuit of group objectives. While Co ordinators are not necessarily the cleverest members of a team, they have a broad and worldly outlook and generally command respect.

Function: Co-ordinators are well placed when put in charge of a team of people with diverse skills and personal characteristics. They perform better in dealing with colleagues of near or equal rank than in directing junior subordinates. Their motto might well be 'consultation with control' and they usually believe in tackling problems calmly. In some organisations Co-ordinators are inclined to clash with Shapers due to their contrasting management styles.

*Co-ordinator is referred to as 'Chairman' in the book: *Management Teams – Why They Succeed or Fail*, R. Meredith Belbin, 1981; Butterworth Heinemann.

Resource investigator

Characteristics: Resource Investigators are often enthusiastic, quick-off-the-mark extroverts. They are good at communicating with people both inside and outside the company. They are natural negotiators and are adept at exploring new opportunities and developing contacts. Although not a great source of original ideas, the Resource Investigator is effective when it comes to picking up other people's ideas and developing them. As the name suggests, they are skilled at finding out what is available and what can be done.

They usually receive a warm reception from others because of their own outgoing nature. Resource Investigators have relaxed personalities with a strong inquisitive sense and a readiness to see the possibilities in anything new. However, unless they remain stimulated by others, their enthusiasm rapidly fades.

Function: Resource Investigators are good at exploring and reporting back on ideas, developments or resources outside the group. They are the best people to set up external contacts and to carry out any subsequent negotiations. They have an ability to think on their feet and to probe others for information.

Implementer

Characteristics: Implementers have practical common sense and a good deal of self-control and discipline. They favour hard work and tackle problems in a systematic fashion. On a wider front the IMP is typically a person whose loyalty and interest lie with the Company and who is less concerned with the pursuit of self-interest. However, Implementers may lack spontaneity and show signs of rigidity.

Function: Implementers are useful to an organisation because of their reliability and capacity for application. They succeed because they are efficient and because they have a sense of what is feasible and relevant. It is said that many executives only do the jobs they wish to do and neglect those tasks which they find distasteful. By contrast, an Implementer will do what needs to be done. Good Implementers often progress to high management positions by virtue of good organisational skills and competency in tackling necessary tasks.

*Implementers are referred to as 'Company Workers' in the book: *Management Teams - Why They Succeed or Fail*, R. Meredith Belbin, 1981; Butterworth Heinemann.

Completer finisher

Characteristics: Completer Finishers have a great capacity for follow-through and attention to detail. They are unlikely to start anything that they cannot finish. They are motivated by internal anxiety, yet outwardly they may appear unruffled. Typically, they are introverted and require little in the way of external stimulus or incentive. Completer Finishers can be intolerant of those with a casual disposition. They are not often keen on delegating, preferring to tackle all tasks themselves.

Function: Completer Finishers are invaluable where tasks demand close concentration and a high degree of accuracy. They foster a sense of urgency within a team and are good at meeting schedules. In management they excel by the high standards to which they aspire, and by their concern for precision, attention to detail and follow through.

Team workers

Characteristics: Team workers are the most supportive members of a team. They are mild, sociable and concerned about others. They have a great capacity for flexibility and adapting to different situations and people. Teamworkers are perceptive and diplomatic. They are good listeners and are generally popular members of a group. They operate with a sensitivity at work, but they may be indecisive in crunch situations.

Function: The role of the Teamworker is to prevent interpersonal problems arising within a team and thus allow all team members to contribute effectively. Not liking friction, they will go to great lengths to avoid it. It is not uncommon for Teamworkers to become senior managers especially if divisional managers are dominated by Shapers. This creates a climate in which the diplomatic and perceptive skills of a Teamworker become real assets, particularly under a managerial regime where conflicts are liable to arise. Teamworker managers are seen as a threat to no one and therefore the most accepted and favoured people to serve under. Teamworkers have a lubricating effect on teams. Morale is better and people seem to co-operate better when they are around.

Shaper

Characteristics: Shapers are highly motivated people with a lot of nervous energy and a great need for achievement. Usually they are aggressive extroverts and possess strong drive. Shapers like to challenge others and their concern is to win. They like to lead and to push others into action. If obstacles arise, they will find a way round. Headstrong and assertive, they tend to show strong emotional response to any form of disappointment or frustration. Shapers are thick skinned and argumentative and may lack interpersonal understanding. Their's is the most competitive team role.

Function: Shapers generally make good managers because they generate action and thrive under pressure. They are excellent at sparking life into a team and are very useful in groups where political complications are apt to slow things down; Shapers are inclined to rise above problems of this kind and forge ahead regardless. They are well suited to making necessary changes and do not mind taking unpopular decisions. As the name implies, they try to impose some shape or pattern on group discussion or activities. They are probably the most effective members of a team in guaranteeing positive action.

Specialist

Characteristics: Specialists are dedicated individuals who pride themselves on acquiring technical skills and specialised knowledge. Their priorities centre on maintaining professional standards and on furthering and defending their own field. While they show great pride in their own subject, they usually lack interest in other people's. Eventually, the Specialist becomes the expert by sheer commitment along a narrow front. There are few people who have either the single-mindedness or the aptitude to become a first-class Specialist.

	Team role	Strengths	Allowable weaknesses
Action oriented roles	**Shaper**	• Challenging, dynamic, thrives on pressure • The drive and courage to overcome obstacles	• Prone to provocation • Offends people's feelings
	Implementer (company worker)	• Disciplined, reliable, conservative and efficient • Turns ideas into practical actions	• Somewhat inflexible • Slow to respond to new possibilities
	Completer finisher	• Painstaking, conscientious, anxious • Searches out errors and omissions • Delivers on time	• Inclined to worry unduly • Reluctant to delegate
People oriented roles	**Coordinator** (Chairman)	• Mature, confident, a good chairperson • Clarifies goals, promotes decision-making, delegates well	• Can often be seen as manipulative • Offloads personal work
	Team worker	• Cooperative, mild, perceptive and diplomatic • Listens, builds, averts friction	• Indecisive in crunch situations
	Resource investigator	• Extrovert, enthusiastic, communicative • Explores opportunities • Develops contacts	• Over-optimistic • Loses interest once initial enthusiasm has passed
Cerebral roles	**Plant**	• Creative, imagination, unorthodox • Solves difficult problems	• Ignores incidentals • Too pre-occupied to communicate effectively
	Monitor evaluator	• Sober, strategic and discerning • Sees all options • Judges accurately	• Lacks drive and ability to inspire others
	Specialist	• Single-minded, self-starting, dedicated • Provides knowledge and skills in rare supply	• Contributes only on a narrow front • Dwells on technicalities

Figure 9.4 The Management Network (2003)

Function: Specialists have an indispensable part to play in some teams, for they provide the rare skill upon which the organisation's service or product is based. As managers, they command support because they know more about their subject than anyone else and can usually be called upon to make decisions based on in-depth experience.

Activity 9.5

Identify the roles that Belbin described in a team meeting in your workplace.

Tuckman group process

Tuckman's (1965) theory on how groups develop over time is relevant to team working because it demonstrates a process which people go through when forming a team.

Tuckman suggested a mnemonic for common stages of group development. He said that groups go through stages of Forming, Storming, Norming and Performing. More recently, a fifth and final stage was added called Mourning or Adjourning (businessballs 2010).

Forming

This stage is most likely to happen if a team is new, however it may also happen if several new people arrive at the same time.

The members of the team are new to each other. They're unsure of each other and unsure of the purpose of the team. Their first responsibility is to become a team. Individual team members are looking for direction and rely heavily on the team leader as individual roles are unclear. Team members are anxious and look to the team leader for direction and support.

However, if a team leader is too directive at this stage it may result in team members only relating to them and not forming a team together. This will slow down the process of achieving team cohesion.

Storming

Tuckman argues that storming is the next stage. This stage occurs as team members become more familiar with each other. The team leader may be challenged at this stage. Personality clashes and differences of opinion are likely at this stage. The atmosphere of the group has changed and feels uncomfortable. It is likely that a scapegoat will emerge. This is often the team leader because team members find it easier to blame the team leader for all of the problems within the team.

A scapegoat is someone who is perceived to be different from the rest of the team, and the problems of the team are transferred to the scapegoat rather than carried by the team as a whole.

Although storming is an uncomfortable stage it is one of the most important. It could be argued that we never truly have an honest and trusting relationship unless we allow ourselves to disagree.

Norming

During this stage the team begins to find mutual direction and a consensus emerges, partly because of the creative ideas which have been thrown around during the storming stage and partly because team members want to move away from the storming stage. This stage feels more harmonious and less superficial than the forming stage.

This stage can feel complacent but if the storming stage has been allowed to occur the team can feel positive and intimate.

Performing

The team starts to fully apply themselves to the task. They get on with the work that needs to be done. They may take on new activities and because they know each other quite well they feel safe to take on different roles and activities.

Mourning/Adjourning

This stage occurs when a team comes to an end. This may happen when members of the team leave or new members join. If you're about to leave your team it is likely that you'll go through a stage of mourning. You will look back and review events from the past and you will look forward with excitement and fear to future challenges. It is natural at this stage to experience negative feelings for the team as a way of coping and feeling better about leaving them.

All groups develop and change and Preston-Shoot (2007) states that groups may be at different stages for different tasks. He says that the duration of any stage relates more to the groups;' history, their function and the personalities within them.

Schiller

Schiller (2003) has identified five stages that a team goes through. The stages are characterised in the following way.

Pre-affiliation

Team members get to know each other and find positive ways of relating.

Mutuality

Team members learn more about each other and develop greater respect for the members.

Challenge

Team members feel comfortable enough with each other and challenge the opinions of other team members without fear of rejection.

Change

This stage is about action and achieving the task.

Termination

This is the end of the team.

You may have noticed that the main difference lies with the interpretation of the Storming (Tuckman) or Challenge (Shilller). Tuckman argues that teams only start to perform after storming has occurred and team members only get to know each other during the storming process.

However, according to Shiller's model, team members only argue and challenge each other after they have got to know each other and feel safe enough to avoid rejection.

Leadership and management

A key factor in developing good team working may be the personality of the team managers and their ability to develop positive relationships with a wide range of staff from different disciplines. This requires the ability to communicate effectively with people at all levels within the organisation.

It is easy to confuse leadership and management as the same thing. However, most recent theories would disagree with this and see management as mostly about process and leadership as about behaviour. Management is concerned with developing systems which relate to organisational aims and objectives and communicating those systems across the organisations.

Leadership is very much about the behaviour and the personal style of the person leading. A question is often asked whether leaders are born or are they made. Martin *et al.* (2010) suggest in the early 20th century it was thought that people were born to leadership. They looked for personality traits and found examples such as high energy levels, tolerance of stress and self-confidence. Gordon Allport (1936) was the founding father of the Trait theory. This theory suggests that people possess certain characteristics which make them good leaders. The theory purports that 'leaders are born rather than made'. This assumes that if you can identify those characteristic in a person then we could identify who might be an effective leader. However, behavioural theories suggest that leadership is about learning to display the appropriate behaviours. Contingency theories, on the other hand, focus on the flexibility of the leader to adapt in response to different situations. Fielder (1967) argued that different leadership styles might be appropriate in different circumstances and an effective leader chooses an appropriate style depending on the context (Martin *et al.* 2010). Adair (1983) has been influential around theories of leadership and management, he identified three key roles a leader must adopt when approaching a task; these are achieving the task, develop team members and develop and maintain the team. In order to achieve the task team members require an understanding of the task and resources to achieve the task. The development of the team and the maintenance of the team is a crucial role and the development of individual team members is needed to ensure that individuals can perform in the team (Martin *et al.* 2010). Good leaders possess qualities which generate enthusiasm and commitment in others. These qualities include trust, respect and honesty. Wheelan (2005) states that the social skills needed in different leadership roles vary; and leaders need to adjust their styles at different times to facilitate the group process. At the forming stage Wheelan (2005) recommends being directive and working to reduce the team members' anxiety, providing positive feedback and facilitating an open discussion of goals. It is also a good idea to work on the physical environment of the workplace and organise the resources needed to do the job well. Later, in the process of the team development when the team are demanding more participation, they may resent the undue influence from the leader. They may challenge the leader's competence and it is important that the leader does not take the attacks and challenges personally and seek revenge and retaliate. At the later stages the team members can be involved in the leadership roles, they can be encouraged to work in sub-groups to achieve a task; leaders can relax as team members take more responsibility. Hawkins and Shohet (2009) cite the work of Rioch *et al.*'s (1976) dialogues for therapists and argue that having knowledge and understanding about group theories is not enough and that the person leading the group must learn how to facilitate positive group behaviour and know how to confront the group process.

Kouzes and Posner (2003) also proclaim that good leaders lead by example with consistent values. They will celebrate 'small wins' and breakdown barriers which stand in the way of achievement.

- ■ A good leader will also inspire a shared vision and enlist the commitment of others.

- ■ A good leader will promote collaborative working which builds trust and empowers others.

- ■ A good leader recognises others' achievements and celebrates accomplishments.

Not everyone agrees that leaders are born rather than made. Some theorists argue that it is possible to learn how to become a good leader by learning to behave in a manner which makes you a 'good' leader. For example – a person without courage can learn to become more courageous. Bennis and Goldsmith (2003) have identified a number of myths about what makes a good leader;

Activity 9.6

Have you ever found yourself in awe of someone at work for their ability to lead on certain situations? It might be an inspiring manager or a support worker or even one of the agency staff. Have you ever wondered what it is about this person that makes then stand out from the crowd?

It might be that they possess certain characteristics which identify them as good leaders.

Write down what you believe to be the characteristics of a good leader

The Leadership Challenge model by Kouzes and Posner (2003) identifies character traits that are generally associated with good leaders.

> Honest
> Inspiring
> Forward-looking
> Competent
> Intelligent
> Dominance
> Consciousness
> Enthusiastic
> Sense of humour
> Integrity
> Courage
> Visionary

- ■ 'Leaders are charismatic' – most leaders are ordinary.

- ■ 'Leaders can exist only at the 'top' – leadership is relevant at all levels from bottom up.

- ■ 'Leaders control, direct and manipulate' – they believe that transformative leaders align the energies of others behind an attractive goal

Some people are more attracted to leadership than others. Most people don't seek to be a leader, but many more people are able to lead, in one way or another and in one situation or another, than they realise. People who want to be a leader can develop leadership ability. Leadership is not the exclusive preserve of the wealthy and educated. Leadership can be performed with different styles. Some leaders have one style, which is right for certain situations and wrong for others. Some leaders can adapt and use different leadership styles for given situations. Levin's (1939) classic description of leadership styles remains largely unchanged and is still relevant to team leadership today. He identified three very different leadership styles.

Leadership styles

Autocratic

This leader makes decisions on their own without consulting the team. They expect the team to follow the decision exactly. The task therefore takes the least amount of time and instructions tend to be clear and concise. However this style of leadership causes dissatisfaction within the team as the team members may have ideas but they are not consulted and therefore feel less involved and committed to the task. This could be a good leadership style in situations that require immediate action. In a health and social care setting when a person is in acute distress and requires immediate attention decisions have to be made quickly.

Democratic

The democratic leader involves the team in the decision making process so the final decision feels as if it is owned by the whole team. The democratic style is the most popular style of leadership and strengthens the team approach. One problem with this style is when the members of a team have vastly different opinions and therefore the time it takes to make a decision is lengthy. In this case an effective leader would make the final decision in a collaborative way.

Laissez-faire

This leadership style allows the team to make decisions and get on with the tasks. Laissez-faire works best when people are capable and motivated in making their own decisions, and where there is no requirement for a central coordination, for example in sharing resources across a range of different people and groups. One of the problems of adopting this style is when they go off-task an outcome is never achieved. The team may get impatient with the amount of time it takes to make a decision.

Activity 9.7

Describe a situation when these leadership styles are used in a health and social care setting. What is the effect on the team?

Part of a manager's role is to encourage others to work effectively. An effective team works towards the same goals and the team members will cooperate with the decisions made. When properly managed and developed, team work improves processes and produces results quickly and economically through the free exchange of ideas and information (*Department of Trade and Industry 2005*).

Some of the areas that motivate people to work in health and social care are highlighted by Martin *et al.* (2010) and include making peoples lives better and improving people's quality of life. Health and social care staff also value team work and mutual support.

Meetings

Meetings are important to effective teams in a number of different ways. A meeting is an opportunity to communicate the team's goals to the whole team, it is where the team get to know each other and it is also where people discuss and make action points. Day (2006) suggests that the success of a meeting can depend on the way it is chaired. It is important to start the meeting on time and open with introductions. It is also important to remind the people attending the meeting of the purpose of it. It may also be a good idea to remind people of the fire exits and house keeping arrangements if people are new to the building. The chairperson needs to encourage participation from the entire

The characteristics of high performance teams

1. Members are clear about and agree with the team's goals.

2. Tasks are appropriate to team versus individual solution.

3. Members are clear about and accept their roles.

4. Role assignments match members' abilities.

5. The leadership style matches the team's development level.

6. An open communication structure allows all members to participate.

7. The team gets, gives and utilises feedback about its effectiveness and productivity.

8. The team spends time defining and discussing problems it must solve or decisions it must make.

9. Members also spend time planning how they will solve problems and make decisions.

10. The team uses effective decision-making strategies.

11. The team implements and evaluates its solutions and decisions.

12. Task-related deviance is tolerated.

13. Team norms encourage high performance, quality, success and innovation.

14. Sub-groups are integrated into the team as a whole.

15. The team contains the smallest number of members necessary to accomplish its goals.

16. Team members have sufficient time together to develop a mature working unit and to accomplish the team's goals.

17. The team is highly cohesive and cooperative.

18. Periods of conflict are frequent but brief, and the group has effective conflict management strategies.

(Wheelan 2005, p. 40)

group using open questions and occasionally directing attention to one person in particular. It is very important to come away from the meeting with some action points; it can be very irritating to attend a meeting, have lots of discussion but no decisions made. The chair person needs to facilitate the team into making appropriate decisions. Day (2006: 91) suggests some ground rules for team members;

- Be prepared for the meeting.
- Attend the meeting on time.
- Start and end the meeting on time.
- Respect and value the diversity of team members.
- Participate in the meeting.
- Actively listen to the discussions.
- Make decisions by consensus.

Coaching

One significant strand to underpin these factors will be the use of coaching as a strategy to enhance team performance. Downey (2003) describes coaching as: 'the art of facilitating the performance, learning and development of another.'

Downey also argues that coaching can be a series of conversations that assist a person in performing closest to their potential.

Clutterbuck and Megginson (2006) have identified four main styles that people who coach have defined themselves. These are; Assessor, Tutor, Demonstrator and Stimulator. The styles sit on a continuum between Directive and Non-directive, Assessor and Tutor tend to be more Directive whilst Demonstrator and Stimulator tend to be more Non-directive. They argue that managers providing coaching need to be able to move between one style and another fairly effortlessly. In order to be successful a high degree of reflection is required and the ability to recognise when and how to use the styles.

The GROW model is an appropriate framework for any coaching session. The model was developed by Whitmore (2002) and adapted by Alexander and Renshaw

Figure 9.5 GROW model (Whitmore/adapted by Alexander and Renshaw 2005)

(2005). The model offers an excellent framework for structuring a coaching session. It is particularly useful for beginners, helping them to see the wood for the trees and keep the session on track.

BOOST feedback

- **Balanced**: focus not only on areas for development, but also on strengths.
- **Observed**: provide feedback based only upon behaviours that you have observed.
- **Objective**: avoid judgements and relate your feedback to the observed behaviours, not personally.
- **Specific**: back up your comments with specific examples of observed behaviour.
- **Timely**: give feedback soon after the activity to allow the learner the opportunity to reflect on the learning.

Figure 9.6 Boost feedback

Using supervision

Hawkins and Shohet (2009) suggest supervision is an important part of taking care of the team members and it can be carried out individually or in a group. Supervision involves education, support, self-development and self-awareness, however in many teams in health and social care it is ignored. Supervision is viewed by some team members with suspicion and a lack of trust. Team members may think that they are being judged, they may feel defensive and uncomfortable in a one-to-one relationship. Team members may have

problems with authority or there may be a conflict in the direction the supervisor and supervisee want to take.

Many people in the helping professions feel stressed at some point in their careers. 'Burn out' is a phrase that is often used and means the constant emotional pressure has taken it's toll and people feel that they can no longer help people in need. The main advantage of supervision is to enable the team members to continue to learn and move forwards at work it can also help people use their resources better.

A dysfunctional team does not look after the team members and if it is not looking after itself it will not adequately look after it's patients. Dysfunctional teams make people less happy and more stressed; people concentrate on the team's problems and not on their work. Gorman (1998) states that teams become dysfunctional because of a mixture of internal neglect and external change. Once a team becomes dysfunctional it is difficult to break out of the patterns of working. The following practical suggestions may help.

Assertiveness

Honesty and assertiveness are essential skills for effective team working. Acting in an assertive manner means that you state your feelings and what you want from a situation and take account of other people's feelings and what they want. Some people are naturally assertive; however, for most of us assertiveness is a set of skills we have to learn. There are four different types of behaviours we could adopt in a difficult situation. Assertive behaviour involves standing up for your own rights in any given situation in such a way that you do not violate the rights of other people it involves expressing your needs, wants, views and feelings in a direct, honest and appropriate way. It involves allowing others to choose for their selves and negotiating at an adult level and involves putting yourself up and not putting others down.

Aggressive behaviour is when we are very aware of what we want. We are determined to win at any cost. When faced with a difficult situation we respond with outright attack. We resort to verbal or physical abuse and other people are frightened of us. Passive behaviour which means that we try and avoid confrontation; we might choose to opt out and avoid taking responsibility. When we are passive, we allow other people to make decisions on our behalf but we end up feeling unhappy with the outcome. We tend to say yes to requests even though we might not want to.

The final type of behaviour is manipulative, also called indirectly aggressive or passive aggressive. We may say yes to any task that is requested of us but find some way of avoiding doing the task at the last minute and let people down. When we want something done we do not ask directly but persuade people by making people feel guilty. It is possible to learn how to sound assertive but use the skills to get what we want; this is not true assertive behaviour it is manipulative behaviour winning at the cost of others rights.

We could be aggressive – when we're being aggressive we are very aware of what we want. We are determined to win at any cost. When faced with a difficult situation we respond with outright attack. We resort to verbal/physical abuse and other people are frightened of us.

We could be Passive – which means that we try and avoid confrontation. We might choose to opt out and avoid taking responsibility. When we are passive, we allow other people to make decisions on our behalf but we end up feeling unhappy with the outcome. We tend to say yes to requests even though we might not want to.

The fourth type of behaviour is manipulative, indirectly aggressive or passively aggressive. We may say 'yes' to any task that is requested of us but find some way of avoiding doing the task at the last minute and let people down. When we want something done we do not ask directly but persuade people by making people feel guilty.

Assertive Janet

Janet is the manager of the nursing home and she is chairing the team meeting. Her tone of voice is sincere, clear, rich and warm. She uses open and relaxed gestures to emphasise the points, she smiles when she is relaxed and frowns when angry. She uses few awkward hesitations and emphasises key words at a steady and even pace.

Aggressive Alison

Alison comes across loudly and forcibly. She is 50 years old and has recently been appointed to the role of senior care worker. She tends to the one who represents the group even though she has never been asked. She has a tendency to over react to management decisions and takes offence easily. In her position she asks junior staff to do tasks that she should be doing herself and if they dare to complain she shouts them down.

Her tone of voice is sharp, loud and very threatening. She becomes very sarcastic if crossed. She stands over the person when carrying out tasks with her hands on her hips and feet apart. When asking someone to do something she gestures a lot and uses a lot of pointing. When someone agrees to do what she has asked she delivers rather hard slaps on the back.

Passive Patricia

Patricia is often picked on by Alison because she's easy to persuade to take on tasks that Alison would rather not do herself. Alison and Patricia can often be found together. Alison likes to control people and Patricia finds it easier for someone else to make decisions. Her posture is slumped; she avoids eye contact and has a nervous smile. She is constantly wringing her hands and covering her mouth when she speaks.

However, Patricia complains to other members of the team about Alison. She wonders why Alison bullies her so much and feels unhappy about the things she is asked to do although would never say this to Alison.

The other people in the team feel sorry for Patricia but are infuriated by her and wish that she would take more control of the situation. They are fed up of listening to her hard luck stories and the way she puts herself down. They are also fed up of hearing her childlike and monotonic voice complain about the situation.

Imogen

Imogen is indirectly aggressive. She appears to get on with every one in the team especially the manager. Whereas Alison is threatening cold and strident, Imogen is smarmy and over sweet, she may appear to think highly of others but they can often detect an undercurrent of disapproval. Her attack is concealed, unlike that of Alison, and she will often deny her feelings and wriggle away. She manipulates people in all sorts of ways to get what she wants. Her tone of voice is exaggerated and dramatic, she may appear over chummy, her gestures are patronising – touching or patting, she may appear over nice and can be quite smarmy.

Activity 9.8

Do any of these behaviour patterns strike you as familiar? If they did do you recognise them in yourself and or others?

Observe your own behaviour and notice how Alison interacts with Patricia in you. See how you may swing from aggressive to passive and back again; this seesaw is a common problem.

Examples of assertive aggressive and passive behaviour

The manager in charge of duty asks you to complete some additional work which you know will make you late going to collect your daughter from school. You are the best person to do the work but you really need to leave on time.

Assertive behaviour

'I understand that you would like this work completed by the end of the day but I do not see that I can complete it by the end of my shift'.

Aggressive behaviour

'What! You know perfectly well that my shift finishes in a hour there is no way that I can do that as well'.

Passive behaviour

'Well umm... I don't really think I can do this but I suppose that if I phone my Mum and took other things home then I could fit it in... I don't mind... Err, all right I'll manage it'.

Manipulative behaviour

Large sigh ... 'Well I know you ask me because I am the only reliable person around here and I am sure that you have not noticed that you are letting the others get away with it'.

Dealing with conflict

Conflict within teams is a common occurrence and can disrupt performance in

Assertive
- Being gently direct
- Saying what you want
- Saying 'No' when required
- Choosing for yourself
- Allowing others to choose for themselves
- Negotiating at an adult level
- Not putting others down

Aggressive
- Being pushy
- Bulldozing others
- Not respecting the rights of others
- Showing anger
- Choosing for others
- Putting other people down
- Over-reacting

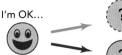

Passive
- Being over-apologetic
- Not saying what you want
- Giving in when you don't want to
- Not respecting your own rights
- Allowing others to choose for you and put you down

Manipulative
- Being manipulative
- Talking other people into doing what they don't want to do
- Appearing to boost them up but in fact putting them down
- Choosing for others though they don't realise it straight away

Figure 9.7 Four approaches to dealing with others
Picture by Lee Badham, University of Worcester

a major way. The fact that conflict exists, however, is not necessarily a bad thing: as long as it is resolved effectively, it can lead to personal and professional growth. If managed well, conflict can be creative and productive and creative solutions to difficult problems can often be found through positive conflict resolution.

There are two types of conflict:

Task-based conflict – disagreements in relation to approaches to work, processes and structural issues within the team and the organisation.

Relationship-based conflict – conflicts between individual members of the team that generally stem from differences in personal values and beliefs.

Activity 9.9

Identify all the possible causes of conflict within a team.

This could be a work team or a team outside of work to which you belong.

You may have written things like:

- Lack of clarity around team roles and responsibilities.
- Unfair distribution of work.
- Lack of clear vision.
- Lack of understanding of the role of others.
- Poor communication.
- Poor leadership.
- Unfair treatment by manager.
- Poor decision-making.

If conflict is badly managed then ineffective teams start to emerge. This is because people start avoiding each other, rifts occur as people begin to take sides and, most of all, dysfunctional teams could lead to poor and in effectual care of service users, clients and patients.

Larson and LaFasto (2001) suggest that the most effective way of solving conflict in a team is for the people concerned to have constructive conversation. This will allow

each person to see the perspective of the other person and to gain some understanding about the way the other person feels about the situation. The conversation must result in each party committing to making improvements in the relationship.

These conversations might be initiated by the people themselves or they may require the services of a neutral facilitator.

Larson and LaFasto (2001) have developed a CONECT model for resolving conflict by conversation:

- **C**ommit to the relationship – individuals should begin by discussing the relationship, and not the problem causing concern. Each person should say why they feel change should occur and what they hope to gain. This is a very positive approach.

- **O**ptimise safety – both parties must commit to maintaining confidentiality and create an atmosphere of trust.

- **N**eutralise defensiveness – in order to prevent a defensive response, each person should explain what they have observed, how it made them feel, and the long term effects of the other person's actions.

- **E**xplain each perspective – each person should have the opportunity to explain their view of the issue.

- **C**hange one behaviour – each person should commit to changing one behaviour.

- **T**rack the change – the individuals will decide how improvements will be measured and agree to meet to discuss whether changes have been successful.

Thompson (2006) recommends the RED approach to managing conflict. He states that situations involving conflict tend to have a high degree of tension associated with them.

R stands for Recognise the conflict; do not sweep it under the carpet.

E stands for Evaluate the conflict; to see how detrimental it would be if it was allowed to develop.

D stands for Deal with the conflict; keep open communication.

Thompson (2006) suggests that we need to avoid the two destructive extremes; either pretending the conflict does not exist or over reacting.

This next section provides you with a number of practical ways of managing conflict.

- Join with the other person towards a win/win outcome. Often in a conflict situation the people tend to be against each other rather than with each other. This tends to lead to non-assertive win/lose way of dealing with conflict. When two people join with each other they respect each other and the differences between them. They are prepared and committed to work towards an outcome which is mutually acceptable.

- Keep a clear picture of the person and yourself separate from the issue. Often in a conflict situation a person identifies herself and the other person with the issue which can lead to confusion and to both people insulting each other.

- Make clear 'I' statements. By making clear 'I' statements a person takes responsibility for herself and avoids blaming and accusing the other person for how she feels and what she thinks.

- Be clear and specific about your perception of the conflict and your desired outcome. It is important for both people to define and share their perception of the conflict and their desired outcomes. This way, both people have heard and begin to understand each other.

- Take one issue at a time. Avoid confusing an issue with another issue and using examples from the past to illustrate your point. Using the past can lead to distortion and manipulation since the other person is likely to have forgotten or to have remembered it very differently.

- Look and listen to each other. Often in a conflict situation both people avoid looking directly at each other and stop listening to each other. We need to look and listen to each other so that we can respond appropriately.

- Ensure that you understand each other. If you are unclear and confused about the issue, ask open questions and paraphrase back what you think you hear.

- Word storm creative ways of sorting out the conflict. Word storming involves both parties imagining all the ways in which they could sort out the conflict. Every suggestion must be written down even though it may seem impractical. When you have made the list, go through it with each other and see if you can sort out the conflict.

- Choose a mutually convenient time and place. Choose a place where both parties feel comfortable. It is also useful to set a time limit.

- Acknowledge and appreciate one another. Acknowledge and appreciate one another and what you do away from the conflict.

In conflict resolution it's only when people's needs are discovered that a solution can be found. In conflict resolution, it is best, if possible, not to compromise but to find a solution. Compromise means that people's needs are still not fully met which could lead to resentment (West, 2004). Anger is one of the predominant and uncomfortable feelings when dealing with conflict; the following list has some helpful strategies for dealing with indirectly expressed anger. A common setting for anger episodes is at work with colleagues and supervisors (Chave, 2003).

How to deal with different types of indirectly expressed anger

Displacement

This involves diverting anger from one target to another. The simplest example would be slamming doors or breaking objects (sometimes 'accidentally') rather then expressing anger to the offending person. Anger is also commonly displaced from people of whom one is afraid onto more vulnerable people who are more easily attacked. Aggression towards children may often be of this type though it may be justified as 'discipline'.

Dealing with displacement Here the anger is not very disguised and a direct approach offering sympathetic discussion is reasonable.

Withdrawal

This may be physical withdrawal such as walking out, sulking or giving the 'cold shoulder', or more psychological withdrawal involving becoming distant or uncommunicative. There is a strong element of attacking the other person by arousing his guilt, as the offence he has committed may not be made clear. If he asks, 'What have I done?' the response may be 'Nothing', 'Leave me alone' or 'Go away'.

Dealing with withdrawal Avoid feeling guilty. Do not reward the behaviour by giving attention. Wait until communication is re-established and again make a direct approach.

Guilt rousing

This involves subtly making the other person feel guilty by criticism which can be justified as reasonable. For example, a husband might criticise his wife's housekeeping and mothering in such a way that she begins to feel guilty about having a part-time job.

Dealing with guilt rousing Avoid being made guilty. Give clear messages that these tactics will not succeed. Don't get angry. Try to confront the issue underlying the resentment, for example 'Do you really think I am a rotten mother, or do you think I shouldn't be going out to work?'.

Being uncooperative

Making life difficult for other people in small ways is a common way of expressing anger. For example, being late, leaving clothes lying about, forgetting important things, losing things, misinterpreting messages or promising to do things but not actually doing them.

Dealing with being uncooperative Set up clear agreements and limits, for example 'Meet me at 7.00 p.m. If you aren't there by ten past I'll go without you'. 'From Friday I'm not washing anything that isn't put in the basket'. Ask for the 'forgettor' to repeat or write down what is to be remembered.

Failure to learn

Repeating behaviour which offends, despite continually being told about it, is another way of being angry. A simple example might be always putting sugar in the tea of someone who doesn't take sugar, despite being told about it.

Dealing with failure to learn Ask the person to agree clearly in advance what will happen, for example 'You won't put sugar in my tea, will you?' Set limits, such as 'I can't drink this as it has got sugar in it'. Don't simply accept the situation without complaint.

Undermining

This involves stressing the dangers or negative aspects of any plan so as to undermine the person's confidence that it will go well, or to sow doubts in their mind about their ability to carry it through. For example, if a daughter wishes to learn to drive so as to be more independent, she might be told of the expense, the difficulty, the dangers of driving, the low pass-rate for driving tests, situations in which driving instructors have sexually assaulted female pupils, and so on.

Dealing with undermining Don't accept the doubts which are sown. Confront the person, for example 'It sounds as if you don't want me to learn to drive – why is that?'

Helplessness

Some people require continuous help and support. They seem unable to do anything for themselves, and if forced into a position of having to be responsible for something, they immediately make a mess of it. They absorb immense amounts of time and energy from others. Sometimes illness is used in this way, the 'sick' being immune to blame as they 'can't help it'.

Dealing with helplessness Set very clear limits to what you will tolerate. Don't be put off by tears and pleading. If the helpless person is going to make a mess of something, make sure it is something of theirs not yours and don't rush to their aid.

Killing with kindness

There are many apparently 'kind' acts which are actually veiled aggression. An example might be offering sweets to someone you know is on a diet, or insisting that someone who has been ill stays in bed when they have been instructed to take exercise as part of their recovery programme. Hiding bills so as 'not to worry' someone or praising them for an inferior performance are other examples.

Dealing with killing with kindness Be independent. Reject offered help you don't need. Be prepared to offend.

Sarcasm and gossip

Hurtful comments disguised as humour, practical jokes and gossip can also be used to express anger. An example would be giving sensitive information 'in confidence' to someone who you know will broadcast it to everybody else.

Dealing with sarcasm and gossip Deal with sarcasm in some of the ways suggested for dealing with criticism in the previous workshop. Be careful whom you give personal information to. Let a gossip know you do not like what they do.

Sabotage

This means apparently doing the right thing but ensuring that it is spoiled. Forgetting the plane tickets for a holiday you don't want to go on, or feeling sick in the middle of a concert you don't want to be at may be presented as unfortunate accidents, but succeed in spoiling everybody else's pleasure.

Dealing with sabotage Again set clear limits. Confront saboteurs. Don't trust them with things they can sabotage (for example make sure you have your own plane ticket so they can't forget it).

Holier than thou

Some people who profess to exist on a 'higher plane' than the rest of us can aggressively produce feelings of inferiority. For example, people who are very 'intellectual' or 'cultured' can subtly despise the ideas or taste of others. Those with strong religious or moral views can give the impression that they are not bothered by the petty concerns of their less enlightened fellows.

Dealing with holier than thou Do not be seduced into feeling guilty or inferior. Trust your own feelings and don't get into a competitive game of one-upmanship.

Non-rewarders

This involves never giving any praise for anything so that the other person's confidence in their ability is gradually undermined. There may be no obvious criticism but the long-term effect is much the same.

Dealing with non-rewarders Demand comment, for example 'What did you think of that?', 'Did you think I did that well or badly?', 'What do you mean "so-so"?'.

Adapted from Anger Management, Mia 2011)

General advice on dealing with indirectly expressed anger

Be clear that you are dealing with indirectly expressed anger. Your own feelings of anger are the best guide to this, but the aggressive intent is likely to be denied and the behaviour justified as well-intentioned.

Ask yourself if you are somehow dominating or otherwise preventing the person from expressing his anger directly. Make sure that it is his problem and not yours.

Ask yourself if you are not more comfortable with indirectly expressed anger. Think about how you would feel and handle the situation if the anger were expressed directly. Make sure it is not your own sensitivity to criticism which has driven the anger underground.

Try to bring the hidden anger to the surface and be ready to discuss it.

Do not respond angrily in return. Make it obvious that you are prepared to accept the other person's feelings and discuss problems calmly.

Do not be surprised if a mass of hidden resentment emerges.

Set clear limits for behaviour you will tolerate and make sure the other person understands them.

Work out what you will do if the person infringes these limits and act on it consistently.

In general avoid colluding with indirect expressions of anger. Not colluding may be uncomfortable but avoids the long-term frustrations to which collusion leads.

Adapted from dealing with anger in relationships (Chave 2003).

Guidelines for responding to criticism assertively

No-one is invulnerable to criticism. When criticised, most of us react in one of three ways:

- We take unfair criticism to heart.
- We react aggressively with a counter-attack.
- We avoid criticism by passive or ingratiating behaviour (University of Cambridge Counselling Service, 2010).

Listen to the criticism carefully, rather than rejecting it or arguing with the person.

Ask yourself whether the criticism is valid/invalid and/or whether it is in the form of a put down.

If the criticism is valid:

- Acknowledge that it is true.
- If it is generalised then ask for more specific information.
- Ask other people for information, whether or not they experience you in a similar way.
- Decide whether or not you are going to change your behaviour as a consequence of the criticism.
- Thank the other person for giving you the criticism.

If the criticism is invalid:

- Say so and assert yourself positively e.g. 'You are very careless in your work'. 'No that isn't true I am usually careful in my work'.
- When criticisms are made of you that are invalid affirm yourself.

If the criticism is valid and in the form of a put down:

- Acknowledge that it is true!

- Challenge the put down and assert yourself positively.
- It is important with put downs to respond assertively and to confront the put down. E.g Typical of you – you are always so careless in your work. 'Yes I have been careless today. However, I am usually careful in my work and I don't like your put downs'.

If the criticism is invalid and in the form of a put down:

- Say so. Challenge the put down and assert yourself positively. For example, 'No that isn't true, I am careful in my work and I don't like your put down'.

When negotiations break down an aggressive or violent response can be the likely outcome. It is therefore important to try and anticipate likely aggressive responses, diffuse tense situations and respond positively and supportively (Thompson, 2009).

Negotiation Skills

The negotiating process is almost an unconscious act. We spend our day constantly negotiating with other people. This might be as simple as negotiating a meeting time or date or a more complicated negotiation that might involve a plan of care.

Steps to successful negotiation

Successful negotiation is linked to assertiveness and we aim to negotiate successfully in an open and flexible manner in order to achieve a successful outcome. Sussex and Scourfield (2004) identify seven key negotiating skills in their checklist:

1. Am I clear about what I am trying to achieve?
2. Am I clear what my fallback position is?
3. What will I do if I am pushed beyond my fallback position?
4. How will I conduct my negotiation – what arguments will I use?
5. Have I got a case which can clearly be seen to promote client care?
6. How will I negotiate in a way that is assertive and not aggressive, manipulative or passive?

7. Am I being open, flexible and reasonable?

While we have these points in mind we also have to consider the following points:

- Empathise with the other person; this is about really trying to find out what it feels like to be in the shoes of the other person.

- Seek clarification; make sure that you fully understand the other person's position, their reasoning and their needs.

- Keep calm; remember to stick to the issues and don't take things personally.

- Be prepared; prepare your information in advance and gather any facts and figures that may support your case.

- Keep to the point and don't be sidetracked by history and by future issues.

- Offer a compromise.

Thompson (2009) suggests that negotiation involves a set of skills that can be developed through practice and reflection. For more information about reflection see the communication chapter. If we aim to negotiate in a way that shows us to be open, flexible and reasonable then this will be conducive to effective collaborative working.

Summary

This chapter commenced by explaining the organisation and structure of the NHS and Social Care and exploring how the different systems work. The chapter goes on to give examples of health and social care teams and understand team communication. The benefits and barriers of team working have been explored and different roles in teams were explained. The chapter introduced the concepts of leadership and management and explored some leadership styles and theories. The middle section of the chapter explored components of effective teams and discussed the importance of meetings, coaching and using supervision. The final section introduced practical skills for dealing with problems in teams. This section suggested some useful skills for dealing with conflict and suggestions for

how to deal with different types of indirectly expressed anger. Finally guidelines for responding to criticism assertively were explained and skills for using negotiation effectively were explored. The most important concept in this section is the importance of honestly and being assertive; many problems in team working occur when we avoid honest communication.

References

Adair, J. (1983), *Effective Leadership*. Pan Books, New York.

Allport, G.W. and Odbert, H.S. (1936). Trait-names: A psycho-lexical study. *Psychological Monographs,* **47** (211).

Alexander and Renshaw (2005) *Supercoaching*. Random House Business Books

Baggott, R. (2004) *Health and Health Care in Britain*. 3rd edition. Palgrave Macmillan, London.

Belbin, M. (1981) *Management Teams: Why They Succeed or Fail*. Heinemann, London.

Bennis and Goldsmith (2010) *Learning to Lead*. 4th Edition Basic Books

Branfield, F. and Beresford, P. (2006) Making user involvement work: supporting service user networking and knowledge http://www.jrf.org.uk/publications/making-user-involvement-work-supporting-service-user-networking-and-knowledge accessed 20.11.10.

Carnwell, R. and Buchanan, J. (2005) *Effective Practice in Health and Social Care: A Partnership Approach* Open University Press, Berkshire.

Chave, P. (2003) Dealing with Anger in relationships.

Clutterbuck, D. and Megginson, D. (2006) *Making Coaching Work*. CIPD, London

Day. J. (2006) *Interprofessional Working*. Nelson Thornes, Cheltenham.

Department of Health (2001) 'Shifting the balance of power: the next steps'. www.dh.gov.uk/assetRoot/04/07/35/54/04073554.pdf. accessed 20.11.10

Department of Health (2005) 'Creating a patient-led NHS'. www.dh.gov.uk/

assetRoot/04/10/65/07/04106507.pdf.
accessed 20.11.10

Department of Health (2006) Our health,
our care, our say: a new direction for
community services http://www.dh.gov.uk/
prod_consum_dh/groups/dh_
digitalassets/@dh/@en/documents/
digitalasset/dh_4127604.pdf

Department of Health (2006) 'Our health, our
care, our say: a new direction for community
services'. White paper. www.dh.gov.uk/en/
Publicationsandstatistics/Publications/
PublicationsPolicyAndGuidance/
DH_4127453. accessed 20.11.10

Department of Health (2010a) 'Equity and
excellence: Liberating the NHS' http://
www.dh.gov.uk/en/MediaCentre/
Pressreleases/DH_117360 accessed 20.11.10

Department of Health National Archives
(2010b) 'How social care is delivered'.
http://webarchive.nationalarchives.gov.
uk/+/www.dh.gov.uk/en/SocialCare/
Aboutthedirectorate/
Howsocialcareisdelivered/index.htm
accessed 20.11.10.

Department of Health (2010c) 'Equity and
excellence: Liberating the NHS'. http://
www.dh.gov.uk/prod_consum_dh/groups/
dh_digitalassets/@dh/@en/@ps/
documents/digitalasset/dh_117794.pdf.

Fiedler, F. E. (1967). *A Theory of Leadership
Effectiveness*. McGraw-Hill, New York.

Hawkins, P. and Shohet, R. (2009)
Supervision in the Helping Professions. 3rd
Edition. Open University Press, Berkshire.

Gorman, P. (1998) *Managing Multi-
Disciplinary teams in the NHS*. Kogan,
London.

Kouzes, J. M. and Posner, B. Z. (2003) *The
Leadership Challenge* 3rd edition. Jossey-
Bass, San Francisco.

LaFasto and Larson (2001) *When Teams
Work Best: 6,000 Team Members and
Leaders Tell What it Takes to Succeed*. Sage,
London.

Lewin, K., Lippit, R. and White, R.K. (1939).
'Patterns of aggressive behavior in
experimentally created social climates'.
Journal of Social Psychology, **10**, 271–301

Maslin-Prothero S. E. and Bennion A. E.
(2010) Integrated team working.

International Journal of Integrated Care,
April.

Martin, V., Charlesworth, J. and
Henderson, E. (2010) *Managing in Health
and Social Care*. 2nd Edition. London,
Routledge.

Mathias, P. and Thompson, T. (1997)
*Interprofessional Working in Health and
Social Care*. MacMillan, Basingstoke.

Mia (2011) Angermanagement.co.uk www.
hapiness-vs-depression.com

Office of Health Economics (2009) http://
www.ohe.org/page/knowledge/schools/
hc_in_uk/nhs_structure.cfm accessed
20.11.10.

Ovretveit, J., Mathais, P. and Thompson, T.
(1997) *Interprofessional Working For Health
and Social Care*. Macmillan, Hampshire.

Pearson, P. and Spencer, J. (1997) *Promoting
Teamwork in Primary Care: A Research
Based Approach*. Arnold, London

Preston-Shoot, M. (2007) *Effective
Groupwork*. Palgrave Macmillan,
Hampshire.

Quinney, A. (2006) *Collaborative Social Work
Practice*. Learning Matters Limited, Exeter.

Schiller, L. (2003) 'Women's group
development from a relational model and a
new look at facilitator influence on group
development', in *Gender and Groupwork*,
Cohen, M. and Mullender, A., Routledge,
London, Ch. 2, pp. 16–31.

Thompson, N. (2006) *People Problems*
Macmillan, Hampshire Palgrave.

Thompson, N. (2009) *People Skills* Palgrave
Macmillan, Hampshire.

Tuckman, Bruce (1965). 'Developmental
sequence in small groups'. *Psychological
Bulletin* **63** (6): 384–99. http://findarticles.
com/p/articles/mi_qa3954/is_200104/ai_
n8943663 accessed 28.11.10.

West, M. (2004) *Effective Teamwork*.
Blackwell, London.

Wheelan, S. A. (2005) *Creating Effective
Teams: A Guide for Members and Leaders*.
2nd Edition. Sage, London

University of Cambridge Counselling
Service (2010) www.counselling.cam.ac.uk/
selfhelp/leaflets/assertiveness.

10 Work-based learning

This chapter links with the Chapter 8 and should be read in conjunction, especially where reference is made to specific research methods of gathering data and data analysis.

This chapter aims to guide you through the process of conducting a work-based learning project and outlines the main areas for consideration.

Learning outcomes

By the end of the chapter you will be able to:

- Identify your own learning needs and negotiate individual learning outcomes

- Independently manage the requirements of the learning contract and respond to your own learning needs, with supervision

- Demonstrate critical awareness of a relevant health or social care issue, based on the acquisition of current, coherent and detailed knowledge

- Critically apply theories and concepts relevant to the negotiated piece of work, making use of reviews, articles and secondary data

- Devise and sustain a relevant systematic argument, using a range of established techniques of analysis and enquiry

- Present key findings of the project, adopting a critical and focused approach.

Activity 10.1

What do you know about work-based learning? List five things.

Work-based learning is a contested concept reflecting the complexity of the relationship between working and learning and the benefits of learning in the workplace.

Harvey (2007) suggests that higher education institutions (HEIs) across the UK are recognising that knowledge can be created outside of academia and that universities are no longer seen as the exclusive providers of learning. He also claims that workers and employers are being recognised more and more as relevant partners in learning programmes rather than just recipients of university designed courses.

Professor Eastwood, Chief Executive of The Higher Education Funding Council (HEFCE) supports the view that universities and colleges should tailor their offer to meet the needs of business and employees. (HEFC 2009)

> We welcome this thorough and wide-ranging report and the emphasis it places on sustaining the vision of the skills agenda. We support the view of the committee that the response from universities and colleges should be tailored and sufficiently flexible to meet the needs of businesses and employees in a time of economic upheaval.

The government sees that an increased emphasis on flexible work-based learning and other modes of flexible study are important mechanisms for meeting the country's skills agenda, and for improving economic growth (Medhat, 2008).

To meet the needs of this growing demand the universities will have to provide a different approach to learning and teaching. There needs to be a change from traditional modes of study to an increase in work-based or work-related study.

Stronger links between employers and HEIs is emerging and, Medhat (2008), argues that more intense discussions are required between the two in order fully to understand the principles of work-based learning and to transfer the language of higher education to the workplace.

O'Neill (2007) argues that British society has been preoccupied with the distinction between those who think and 'those who do' related to our education system. The very creation of knowledge is considered to be the domain of the academic whereas an increase in expertise relates to any professional or vocational education. The assessment of knowledge is through examination, which O'Neill (2007) argues creates the distinction between vocational and academic learning.

It wasn't until the late 1980s that the sharp distinction between vocational and academic learning began to weaken. The work of David Kolb (1984) introduced a partnership between education, work and personal development.

O'Neill further emphasis the work of Schon (1983) whom she believes dramatically introduced a new epistemology of practice which might be considered to be one of the most important influences in reducing the distinction between academic and vocational knowledge.

Costley (2006) argues the case for work-based learning as a new curriculum which is widening participation in higher education for those who would not normally access it. She also states that this has been made possible due to of the increased support for up-skilling the workforce and enhancing employability to become more competitive in the global markets (Costley, 2006). She suggests that there is a need for HE institutions to re-evaluate the progress they've made in the area of learning in and through work so they can embrace inclusiveness and add more value to the world of work for many people, including those who work in the independent sector, health, social care and the domestic and community spheres of work (Costly, 2006).

The work-based learning movement resonates with the government's push for economic growth and an improvement of the higher level skills of the workforce. The White Paper 'Skills for the 21st century: realising our potential' (DFES, 2003) and the more recent Leitch report (2006) call for 40 per cent of the workforce to be qualified at level 4 by 2020. This government driver has forced universities to rethink their curriculum offer and has given rise to increased activity around employer engagement (Braham and Pickering, 2007).

Nature of work-based learning

> We start with one conviction. Well-planned, on-the-job learning, with active employer involvement, leads to a better learning experience for learners and better outcomes in terms of their work-related skills and employability. (Taylor, 2001)

Work-based learning recognises that valuable learning can occur in the workplace through the investigation of work-based issues, the outcome of which is likely to be an improvement in, or change to, existing work and/or individual practice. As such it is a mechanism which promotes change and continuous improvement in the workplace, whilst also providing you with an opportunity to enhance knowledge, skills and personal development – in other words it benefits your employer as well as you.

The QAA (2004) Benchmark statement refers to:

> Authentic and innovative work-based learning is an integral part of Foundation degrees and their design. It enables learners to take on appropriate role(s) within the workplace, giving them the opportunity to learn and apply the skills and knowledge they have acquired as an integrated element of the programme. It involves the development of higher-level learning within both the institution and the workplace. It should be a two-way process, where the learning in one environment is applied in the other. (Foundation Degree Qualification Benchmark, QAA, 2004, paragraph 23)

As Tallantyre (2008: 7) summarises:

An employer is likely to benefit from encouraging employees to become serious lifelong learners, capable of identifying their own needs and interests, keen to explore how continuously to improve their performance and find new and better ways to do things, and unafraid of change. This may be more effective than to commission provision akin to mass-focused training programmes in the acquisition of functional skills, which can lead to convergent rather than to divergent thinking (the latter being critically important to creativity and innovation.

Negotiating your learning

One of the key strengths of the work-based learning module in any programme of study is that it gives the learner the opportunity to decide, often with structured support, the outcome of the learning. This is achieved through a process of negotiation, often with tutor, mentor/employer. The outcome is something which meets the needs of all those involved and more importantly it gives you the opportunity to 'own' your learning.

Negotiated learning involves a range of different approaches:

- **A problem solving and self-evaluative approach** in order to identify personally relevant learning objectives.

- **A planning and project management approach** to identify mechanisms, resources and time scales to achieve your chosen objectives.

- **An evidence-based approach** so that you can demonstrate that objectives have been achieved.

- **A reflective approach** so that you can review and evaluate your own learning processes and techniques.

The key benefit of negotiated learning is that you are able to exercise choice and control of your learning so that you can co-design a programme that best suits your needs, strengths, experience and circumstances. Being able to negotiate your learning in this way is more likely to result in a coherent programme of study, because it is has been personalised for *you*. As a result, it maximises opportunities for motivation and personal development. 'Negotiation' also means that you are not alone in working through this process. You will work with others (your tutors, employer and mentor) to identify a study programme which is tailored to suit your learning and personal development. Your tutors will not necessarily determine the content of your learning. This will be done by you, along with your mentor or employer. In some situations, the employer has an idea for a project which might bring about a change in existing practice for the benefit of the service. The outcome of your project could bring about significant change in order to improve a service or enhance the lives of a service user. The role of the tutor would be to guide you along the pathway which would enable you to achieve your academic credit. The tutor will introduce you to a body of knowledge and wider literature specifically related to your area of study which can be used to link theory and practice. The tutor will support you throughout the process of linking the theory and practice. This knowledge and experience will provide you with the evidence you require to bring about changes in the service. This is often referred to as evidence-based practice or action learning.

Work-based learning is therefore a very flexible way of negotiating study which will help to ensure that your programme of study is pertinent and manageable for both you and your employer. It also means that you will take responsibility for your own learning (with guidance from your tutors and your employer) to ensure that *your* skill and qualification needs are met, as are the business and organisational objectives of your employer, as are the needs of the service user if relevant.

In summary – the benefits of work-based learning are twofold, as shown in the next sections.

Benefits of work-based learning for you

An enhanced skillset for life. For example, you will learn to evaluate processes and situations, to identify opportunities for improvement, to receive and reap the benefits of feedback, to manage projects.

Opportunities to work with and learn from others. This not only improves your performance as a team player, working with others to exchange ideas and opinions is a rewarding and rich experience which is often far more fulfilling and productive than working or studying alone.

Improved performance at work is a typical benefit of work-based learning because of the greater understanding of your organisation and enhanced relationships with colleagues it often brings.

Opportunities to increase your professional standing and attractiveness as an employee via the acquisition of a formally recognised qualification and engagement with continuous professional development.

A study programme which suits your needs and way of life.

Opportunity for increased job satisfaction by virtue of being able to make a difference in the workplace and being supported by your employer to explore how to do so.

Integrating learning with your normal working hours. Study and working activities take place simultaneously in real time, so much of your learning takes place in time that you would have spent working anyway.

Potential for job enhancement. Work-based learning involves real projects with measurable outcomes, and can offer tangible evidence of value you are adding.

Benefits of work-based learning for the employer

Your employers will be an intrinsic and vital part of your work-based learning. As such, they will be investing time, money and other means of support. They do so because they, too, reap considerable rewards. Work-based learning drives the direct transfer and application of your knowledge and learning back to your employer, it does so in a way which is clearly visible to, and measurable by, both you and your employer at a time, cost and convenience which can be considerably more attractive than a conventionally taught programme. Quite simply you are learning to do your job better, and the university and your employer are working with you to help you do this.

Getting the most out of work-based learning

Work-based learning is a rewarding way of studying, learning, working and developing for you and adds real tangible and measurable value to your employer; but it is also a challenge for both parties. Alongside your normal professional obligations you will need to:

- Manage your time and focus.

- Be highly self-motivated and committed to the value of this style of learning, willingly participating in work-based experiences relevant to your level of knowledge and ability with the support and supervision of your employer.

- Ensure that your work-based learning respects and maintains confidentiality in relation to the individuals and circumstances you encounter.

- Be proactive in your learning, expressing your needs and adopting a questioning, reflective approach.

- Seek and negotiate guidance and support from your employer to enable you to achieve your work-based skills and knowledge.

- Utilise learning opportunities to appreciate the roles of other employees, agents and organisations that work together within your work-based setting.

- Give and act on constructive feedback.

- Reflect on your progress to increase self-awareness, confidence and competence and evaluate your achievement.

- Maintain regular contact with your tutors to access their expertise and inform them of any concerns or problems you may have either within your work-based experience, or of a personal nature, that impact on your performance.

Your employer will need to make a similar commitment and accept a responsibility to support you and optimise opportunities for you to learn from the workplace environment.

Work-based learning is therefore a tri-partite partnership between you, your employer and the university. From the start it creates a network in which all three parties are both learners and teachers and are all recognised as experts within their own domain with something of value to bring to each other:

The student enlightens the employer about different and better ways of working practice and about mentoring-style opportunities for staff development; and the university about the their personal objectives and work practices.

The employer educates the student and university about the organisation's objectives, processes and techniques and the drivers and constraints under which it functions.

The university demonstrates to the student how to identify opportunities to learn and develop; and to the employer how real work can be used to create productive learning and knowledge transfer opportunities.

The learning contract

The learning contract is an agreement between you and your tutor and it includes the methods by which you will achieve your learning objectives. There are many examples of learning contracts on the internet which could be used to do this.

A learning contract can be fairly open with no learning outcomes, which provides total flexibility.

One of the key authorities on writing learning contracts is Malcolm Knowles. His five-step model in his practice-based book, *Using Learning Contracts* (Knowles, 1986) is still relevant today. It involves:

- Diagnosing learning needs.
- Formulating learning needs.
- Identifying human material resources for learning.

- Choosing and implementing appropriate learning strategies.
- Evaluating learning outcomes.

Knowles (1986) suggests that the learning contract replaces a content plan with a process plan.

Costley, Elliott and Gibbs (2010) refer to the work of Stephenson and Laycock (1993) and suggest that learning contracts help students to reflect, collaborate and develop skills and confidence through the very process of writing the learning contract.

This activity requires a dialogue between a number of stakeholders and thus requires the student to engage at number of levels.

This is supported by Laycock and Stephenson (2000) who state that the learning contract encourages students to take responsibility for their own learning and by doing so they learn important transferrable skills. They put the emphasis on reflection action and not on action alone.

A second approach to the design of a learning contract is that of Hiemstra (2006). The use of a learning contract enables a student to learn on their own initiative, resulting in learning that will be deep and permanent. The process of developing a learning contract involves:

- Diagnosis of learning needs.
- Specification of learning objectives.
- Identifying resources and strategies.
- Stating target dates for completing activities.
- Specifying evidence of achievement.
- Articulating how evidence will be validated.
- Reviewing the contract with the work-based supervisor.
- Implementing the contract.
- Evaluating learning.

The two approaches to designing the learning contract are very similar. The most striking similarity is the notion that the student is at the centre of the process and the learning contract is an individual-centred approach to learning (Costley, Elliot and Gibbs, 2010).

The authors suggested content of a learning contract includes:

- student information section
- employer information section
- university section
- learning outcomes
- authorising signatures
- resources and methods
- documentation of methods.

It is clear from the range of approaches to the design of the learning contract that there is not one way of doing things. The learning contract should be flexible enough to meet the needs of the student, the university and the employer. The learning contract moves away from a pedagogic model of academic-led learning towards a more androgogical approach where the student is an equal partner (Laycock and Stephenson, 1993).

Lyons (2007) argues that the 'the learning contract approach has also appealed to employers who want to up-skill their employees and benefit their company. When employees get involved in commercial and strategic developments that are commercially beneficial and transfer knowledge into the workplace'.

The work-based learning module within the Foundation Degree is extremely important to you and your placement area. The module provides the opportunity to explore areas of research or practice which would benefit your placement and service users. In many ways it's a way of paying back the organisation for having you on placement. The policy environment within health and social care is forever changing. Keeping up to date with this is often very difficult. The project you choose needs very careful consideration and rarely takes place without consultation with your workplace mentor. The project could involve the design and development of a new policy or procedure. It could be more specifically related to the needs of one service user or a group of service users and involve a new or different way of working with a client.

Activity 10.2

Using the information above construct your own learning contract. You may want to do this with your workplace mentor.

Once you have an idea for your project the next step is to discuss this with your mentor. You can use this opportunity to discuss with your mentor the ideas you have for the project. The mentor will guide you through and support your ideas provided they meet with the organisational aims.

For the purpose of any Foundation Degree, work-based learning can be achieved in a variety of environments. Appropriate learning opportunities should arise within these settings where you will be able to practice, under supervision, and take advantage of these learning opportunities. This work-based experience is essential to the integration of theory and practice in your learning and development of effective care and practice.

With support, you will make sense of your practice though the application of theory, constructive feedback and reflection on your experiences. Therefore, you will have a named mentor who will facilitate and assess your learning and enable the achievement of required learning outcomes in the practice environment. It is important as a student on the Foundation Degree to work with adequate supervision and to recognise your limitations. As you progress through your programme and develop your practice skills and knowledge, you will have the opportunity to fully participate in the planning, delivery and management of care under the guidance of your mentor.

Whilst completing the work-based modules you will be supported by a named mentor. The mentor is an identified individual in the workplace who has undergone preparation for the role and can support and guide you in your achievement of the module learning outcomes, your personal objectives and key skills through work-based activities. They also act as a resource for student learning. The mentor will facilitate practice learning as well as providing an assessment of your achievement in some cases.

Responsibilities of the mentor

The mentoring function is crucial to the success of any student on a Foundation Degree programme. Without the mentor it is extremely difficult for students to continue with their studies. The mentor may guide the student through the process of learning. The mentor may assess the student through the process of learning and the mentor may provide pastoral care throughout the learning journey. Whatever role the mentor takes, it is true to say that the relationship between mentor and student is crucial to the success of the student on programme. Research into Foundation Degrees underlines the importance of mentor training and of clarity about the role of mentoring in ensuring a positive student experience.

The Open University in Partnership with Foundation Degree Forward suggest that a mentor on a FD programme should:

- Identify your particular role as a professional supervisor or mentor in the context of your own professions/ workplace.

- Understand the range of skills required for effective professional supervision or mentoring.

- Anticipate and deal with issues arising in the supervisory/mentor relationship and situation.

- Identify and develop good practice in respect of the supervisory/mentor relationship.

- Maximise the potential for effective learning in your own workplace through professional supervision/mentoring.

- Plan a supervision/mentoring framework for a specific learner.

- Understand the potential role of professional supervision/mentoring in assessment and identify good practice in practice-based assessment.

- Identify your own skill set in relation to professional supervision/mentoring and develop a personal development plan for expanding or developing additional skills.

Mckenzie (2006) acknowledges that there is little written on the role of mentorship within Foundation Degrees, possibly because the role is relatively new. However, there is a great deal of information which supports the role of mentor in a nursing and midwifery setting and a social work setting. It is important to note that there are distinctions between these roles, and the main distinction is that mentor of Foundation Degree students does not have to be on a live register of mentors whereas in nursing and social work, the mentor has a nationally recognised qualification and is recognised by their respective governing bodies the Nursing and Midwifery Council (NMC) and the General Social care Council (GSCC).

A second notable difference in the role of the work-based mentor is that nursing and social work mentors actively assess the student and in many instances 'signs off' the student as competent. The Foundation Degree mentor does not always fulfil this role.

However, there may be changes to this with the increase in the number of health related Foundation Degrees taught in partnership with the Acute and Primary Care Trusts.

Mentors have a responsibility to:

- Have knowledge and information of the student's programme of study.

- Identify specific learning opportunities that are available either within (or accessible from) their work/placement environment.

- Ensure time is identified for induction to the workplace as required by new students and conduct the initial interview with students in order to assess their learning needs.

- Identify with students the core practice outcomes and any specific personal learning objectives to be achieved by the end of each work-based learning module.

- Provide appropriate learning experiences for students to achieve the practice outcomes and facilitate students' participation in as wide a range of learning opportunities as possible.

- Be available to observe and support students practising and developing skills.

- Encourage student responsibility in active learning through the application of theory to practice.

- Encourage students to work collaboratively with clients and their families and carers, other professionals and agencies.

- Be approachable and contribute to a supportive learning environment for students.

- Provide constructive feedback and evaluation of student progress and complete mid-point review and discuss, agree and sign the learning agreement form.

- Provide constructive feedback and evaluation of student progress and complete end-point assessment, confirm completion of practice learning requirements including hours achieved in some cases.

- Communicate in good time with the Pathway Leader or equivalent any queries or concerns related to the course or the student.

Responsibilities of you the student

Learning from and for practice inevitably requires you to take responsibility for your learning, thus you are expected to:

- Read all the student handbooks relating to your programme of study.

- Keep the work-based learning record safe and secure for the duration of the course and make it available to your personal tutor, mentor, Pathway Leader or equivalent and the external examiner when required.

- Identify your specific learning needs with support from your personal tutor and mentor and work towards the achievement of knowledge and the required practice outcomes.

- Adhere to local policies and procedures.

- Act professionally with regard to punctuality, attitude and image, and dress according to requirements of the practice learning environment.

- Maintain confidentiality of service users, patients, clients and carers. Your practice record must not contain any information that could identify service users, clients, patients, families or carers, and should not include photocopies of any records.

- Be proactive in your learning, expressing your needs and adopting a questioning, reflective approach and be willing to participate in practice experiences relevant to your level of knowledge and ability with the support and supervision of your mentor.

- Use your mentor for guidance and support to enable you to achieve your learning outcomes and satisfactorily complete your practice assessments.

- Utilise learning opportunities to appreciate the roles of other professionals, carers and organisations that work together in the provision and delivery of care within your work-based setting.

- Give and act on constructive feedback.

- Reflect on your progress to increase self-awareness, confidence and competence and evaluate your achievements.

- Arrange meeting dates with your mentor to complete your learning agreement, mid-point and end-point assessment within the required deadlines if appropriate.

- Evaluate your work-based learning experience on completion of each work-based module.

The responsibilities of the higher education provider

The higher education provider has a responsibility to:

- Ensure that a current Criminal Records Bureau clearance is held by the student.

- Approve the suitability of the work-based learning environments to meet the learning needs of the student within the Foundation Degree in collaboration with service providers.

- Provide a Pathway Leader to support students and staff in work-based learning environments.

- Ensure that mechanisms are in place to enable debriefing with the Pathway Leader or equivalent in the event of a unsatisfactory assessment.

- Ensure that mentors are kept informed when changes are made in the curriculum.

- Ensure the work-based learning environments have relevant course documentation.

- Maintain good communication between higher education providers and the work-based environments through the Pathway Leaders and course leaders.

- Have in place an effective system of jointly monitoring feedback from students about their work-based learning experiences as part of the quality assurance cycle.

Activity 10.3

Identify your workplace mentor and discuss your ideas for the project.

In the event of placement/practice breakdown

It is very rare that a placement or place of work is not a suitable learning environment although this does happen occasionally.

The most important step to take is to inform your course leader immediately if you are experiencing problems. The table overleaf highlights some of the reasons why a placement might break down.

Reflective practice

As part of your work-based learning studies you may be asked to complete a reflective Learning Journal. This process of reflection is extremely important to you as a practitioner because it binds together your practice and the theory. Reflection on practice enables you to take a step back from the learning environment and assess what was good and what might you have done differently in any one situation. There are a number of very useful reflective tools such as the one developed by Gibbs (1988) discussed in Chapter 2.

Key elements of reflection

Reflection is a type of thinking associated with deep thought, aimed at achieving better understanding. It contains a mixture of elements:

Making sense of experience We don't always learn from experiences. Reflection is where we analyse experience, actively attempting to 'make sense' or find the meaning in it.

'Standing back' It can be hard to reflect when we are caught up in an activity. 'Standing back' gives a better view or perspective on an experience, issue or action.

Repetition Reflection involves 'going over' something, often several times, in order to get a broad view and check nothing is missed

Deeper honesty Reflection is associated with 'striving after truth'. Through reflection, we can acknowledge things that we find difficult to admit in the normal course of events.

'Weighing up' Reflection involves being even-handed, or balanced in judgement. This means taking everything into account, not just the most obvious.

Clarity Reflection can bring greater clarity, like seeing events reflected in a mirror.

This can help at any stage of planning, carrying out and reviewing activities.

Understanding Reflection is about learning and understanding on a deeper level. This includes gaining valuable insights that cannot be just 'taught'.

Making judgements Reflection involves an element of drawing conclusions in order to move on, change or develop an approach, strategy or activity.

This table gives an example of the course of action taken at the University of Worcester in the event of placement breakdown.

Examples of placement breakdown	Student responsibility	Mentor responsibility	Pathway Leader responsibility	Outcome
Students in employment				
Redundancy	Inform Pathway Leader and apply for mitigating circumstances for assignment if necessary evidence of redundancy will be needed	Inform Pathway Leader	Support student in finding another placement	Hours from both placements will count towards the 200 hours and need to be evidenced
Loss of job through misconduct	Inform Pathway Leader	Inform Pathway Leader	Inform Course Leader	Fail placement
Students on placement				
Unsuitable placement that is not meeting learning needs	Inform mentor and Pathway Leader	Inform Pathway Leader	Discuss possible resolution and if unsuccessful support student to find another placement	Hours from both placements will count towards the 200 hours and need to be evidenced. The new mentor will assess the practice skills
Loss of placement through misconduct	Inform Pathway Leader	Inform Pathway Leader	Inform Course Leader	Fail placement

Reflective Learning Journal

A reflective Learning Journal enables you to:

- record experiences
- facilitate learning from experience
- support understanding
- develop critical thinking and the development of a questioning attitude.

The reflective Learning Journal will form the backbone of your evidence and analysis when you come to compile your portfolio. Using this type of analytic approach early on and throughout your programme is crucial. The details you describe are important and provide the basis for subsequent analysis, synthesis and evaluation, which are the substance of effective, reflective writing.

The reflective Learning Journal is not a diary. Your reflections should be rich in insights into your own learning. The conclusions you make should be underpinned with the theories, models, views and research of others. You should draw on the information provided in your theoretical sessions and from your wider reading. Your work should be referenced where appropriate. It is most important that your reflections comply with appropriate academic conventions and avoid colloquialisms.

Activity 10.4

Using the model above, reflect on an experience you recently encountered in your workplace or placement.

Starting the reflective Learning Journal

The entries in your reflective Learning Journal will describe many aspects of your work, for example tasks, processes, how you related to and worked with others, that is inter-personal and communication skills, critical events, feelings, etc. Select significant incidents where you can extend and develop your learning rather than listing everything you have done during the day or week.

Be aware that it will take time to get into the habit of keeping a reflective Learning Journal, but it will make writing your reflections significantly easier. There is no right or wrong way to write a reflective Learning Journal, find a style that suits you.

In most cases the reflective Learning Journal is not directly assessed, but will be used to enhance your learning in other modules and in providing supporting evidence for your assignments.

Content of the reflective Learning Journal

You can keep a reflective Learning Journal in many ways but whichever way you choose, make sure it provides the information for you to address the following:

Description: Record the details of the event. For example: what happened, the sequence of events, who was involved, what you did, how you felt, how others

reacted, what the outcome was, and so on. What evidence is available that helps corroborate the description?

Descriptive reflection: Looking back, why was it a significant incident for you and what do you think were the reasons for the outcomes you described? Did it work, was it effective, or not? Are there causes and effects? Have your approaches, attitudes, behaviours changed through the experience? Ask yourself 'What have I learnt from what happened? What/how did I feel? Why? Who or what has helped me?'. What do you conclude from this in terms of what you would now do, what extra learning you need, what worked well and what you would do again or differently next time? From this you can generate action plans for further development in your knowledge, skills and attitudes, some of which will be formally assessed as 'Personal Development Plans'.

Critical reflection: Here you are establishing whether your conclusion is appropriate and/or valid by using sources of knowledge and expertise usually from

---

A student's reflective framework (Holm and Stephenson, 1994).
Ask yourself:

What was my role in this situation?
Did I feel comfortable or uncomfortable? Why?

What actions did I take?
How did I and others act?
Was it appropriate?

How could I have improved the situation for myself, the service user or patient, my mentor?

What can I change in future?

Did I expect anything different to happen?
What and why?
What knowledge from theory and research can I apply to this situation?

What broader issues, ethical, political or social arise from this situation?
What do I think about these broader issues?

Description
What happened?

Feelings
What were you
thinking and feeling?

Evaluation
What was good and
bad about the
experience?

Analysis
What sense can you
make of the situation?

Conclusion
What else could you
have done?

Action Plan
If it arose again,
what would you do?

Figure 10.1 **Gibbs' model of reflection (1988)**

outside of the situation, that is what evidence supports or contradicts your conclusion – such as theories, models, views, others' experience, or research?

A useful framework by Holm and Stephenson (1994) for this process is provided in the figure however you will have already been introduced to the reflective models developed by Gibbs (1998).

Activity 10.5

List five key benefits of keeping a reflective Learning Journal.

Work-based projects

Work-based learning projects are collaborative enterprises between you and your employer or placement provider. All projects require a research and development methodology, actual research methods may differ depending on the type of project.

Portwood (2007) argues that the interests of the learner, the university and the employer are intended to coincide through the choice of work-based learning projects used to assess learning. The projects are intended to benefit the organisation whilst meeting the formal requirements of the university to assess validity. He suggests that work-based projects stress explicit knowledge from the beginning yet require tacit knowledge to be articulated. As such, 'work-based learning projects are never a version of performity but are infused with the spirit and means contemplatively' (Portwood, 2007).

The very nature of the project will have to be considered by all the stakeholders in order to gain approval for the research to go ahead. The aim of the project is likely to be beneficial to the workplace and should add some kind of value. The aims and objectives of the project should be clearly articulated and there should be a clear understanding of the benefits and appropriateness of the project for the student, the employer or placement provider and for the university (Costley *et al.*, 2010). This tripartite arrangement should provide the support and access the student requires to continue with the research.

Ethical considerations

For some health and social care projects it may be necessary to ensure the project is ethically sound. This would require the project to be scrutinised by an Ethics Committee internal to the university or by an ethics committee external to the university.

Costly *et al.* (2010) identified three important factors for consideration when submitting a proposal for a work-based project:

1. To who is the project beneficial and is there any detriment to people (individuals, communities of practice, and members of organisations) or other living creatures?

2. Is the research feasible and will the research in some way brings about financial gain? If so, whose interests will it serve?

3. Is it likely to cause detriment to the environment?

The Department of Health Research Governance Framework for Health and Social care (2001) states that:

> The dignity rights, safety and wellbeing of participants must be the primary consideration in any research study.

Research involving patients, service users, care professionals or volunteers, or their organs, tissues or data, is reviewed independently to ensure it meets ethical standards.

Informed consent is at the heart of ethical research. Most studies involving individuals must have appropriate arrangements for obtaining consent, and the ethics review process pays particular attention to those arrangements.

Research involving human tissue must comply with the Human Tissue Act 2004.

The appropriate use and protection of patient data is paramount. Particular attention must be given to systems for ensuring confidentiality of personal information and to the security of those systems.

Relevant service users and carers and their representative groups should be involved wherever possible in the design, conduct, analysis and reporting of research.

Research and those pursuing it, should respect the dignity of human society and conditions and the multicultural nature of society.

Some research may involve an element of risk to those participating in it. If there are risks to participants, the risks must be in proportion to the potential benefit.

Methodology

Constructing a methodological framework for your project will demonstrate how you have achieved the aims and outcomes of the project. A clear methodology will clarify the validity and the reliability of the work you have undertaken. This is incredibly important if you wish to use the project as a vehicle for changing practice within your organisation.

From the beginning of the project it is important to have a broad understanding or perception about your own ideological standpoint for doing the project. This is referred to as a research paradigm. A paradigm can be described as a way of seeing the world, a frame of reference or a mental model which you as the researcher might have which drives your research.

The main components of a paradigm are: ontology, epistemology and methodologies.

Ontology is concerned with the way we might look at reality. The way you perceive the world will influence your ontological position (Costley *et al.* (2010)).

Epistemology is the component of a paradigm that is concerned with knowledge and guides you towards the development of a specific set of questions which are relevant to your study. Your view of the world and your reality will inform what knowledge is important to you.

Methodology refers to the general principles of knowledge acquisition and: 'the way you understand and select knowledge is likely to inform the methodology you construct for your project work' (Costley *et al.* (2010)).

> Ontology is the starting point of all research, after which one's epistemological and methodological positions logically follow. A dictionary definition of the term may describe it as the image of social reality upon which a theory is based. (Pramod Badadur Shrestha, 2009).

Costley *et al* (2010) provided a more detailed discussion on methodological frameworks.

> Methodologies can be described as being qualitiative or quantitative.

Research Methodology

Qualitative methodology is designed to help researchers understand people and the social and cultural contexts within which they live. The goal of understanding a phenomenon from the point of view of the participants and its particular social and institutional context is largely lost when textual data are quantified (Meyers 1997).

A qualitative approach permits the researcher to get close to the participants to obtain a great deal of in-depth information which could not be obtained by quantitative methods. It is argued that qualitative methods address research questions which require explanation and understanding (Ritchie and Lewis, 2004).

In this context, it seems natural that an approach which emphasises the use of case studies, questionnaires and focus groups is the most valid of research methodologies.

The case study is a distinct form of empirical enquiry (Yin, 2003) which allows the researcher to determine the 'what', 'how', 'why' from the study. It is a useful method for distinguishing the uniqueness of an individual and allows the researcher

to see the world in different terms (Nikolou-Walker, 2008).

The interview, both structured and unstructured, will generate rich and detailed information which will provide an insight into the lives of the individual participants. Holstein and Gubrium (2004) suggest that interviews are a special form of conversation which range from being highly structured to free-flowing informational exchanges.

The diagram below is taken from an article in the *Student British Medical Journal* archive (2007); it gives an example of how to approach the writing up stage of your project.

This section provides you with a guide to organising your project. It follows similar procedures to conventional projects.

The introduction

The introduction takes a broad look at the project, setting it against a background of previous research. The scope of the report then narrows through the methods and results sections to focus on the experiment in hand, and finally broadens out in the discussion to again relate the work to the bigger picture.

Aims and objectives

An aim is a broad statement of intent. It will say something about what it is you're trying to achieve by carrying out the project.

An objective is more specific and should be Specific, Measurable, Achievable, Realistic, and Timely (SMART).

Literature review

A literature review is a collection of information specifically related to your topic or area of interest. It can be viewed as

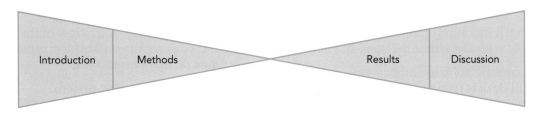

Figure 10.2 **Bow tie representation of a report's structure** (*Student BMJ*, 2007).

a critical and in-depth evaluation of previous research. A good literature review expands upon the reasons behind selecting a particular research question. The literature review may be seen as a funnel. Your search may start off rather wide, taking account of your area of interest in a wider context, and then it may become more focused as you begin to refer to sources of information which specifically relate to your area of interest.

Methods of data collection

Participant observation (overt/covert)

A method of research in which the observer joins the group being studied and participates in their activities to achieve a deep and sympathetic understanding of what motivates them to act in the way they do.

Advantages:

Participant observation generates a rich source of highly-detailed, high-quality, information about people's behaviour.

The researcher can understand the social pressures/influences/group norms etc. that may create particular forms of behaviour.

This may allow researchers to formulate hypotheses that explain such behaviour.

Disadvantages:

Restricted to small-scale studies carried out over a long period.

The group being studied is unlikely to be representative of any other social group therefore it's unlikely a researcher will be able to generalise their findings from one study to the next.

Interview

This is a conversation with a purpose – to obtain interviewees' in-depth accounts of their experiences and perceptions. The types are:

Structured (or standardised) – used in quantitative surveys.

Semi structured (or semi standardised) – qualitative.

Unstructured (or unstandardised) – qualitative.

Qualitative interviews seek to capture people's perceptions expressed *in their own words*.

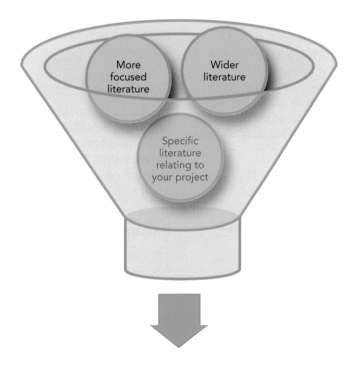

Figure 10.3

Action research

Action research is a methodology for intervention, development and change and is therefore a very useful method of inquiry for work-based learners who wish to bring about change within a placement setting. An action learning project usually involves three groups; the organisation, which in this case might be your mentor; the subject, which may be the client group or the people who are involved in the study; and finally the change agent, which could be you. These three groups of people come together to form a learning community through which the research is conducted (Nikolou-Walker, 2008).

Focus group discussion

Focus groups are a form of group interview that take advantage of communication between research participants in order to generate data. Although group interviews are often used simply as a quick and convenient way to collect data from several people simultaneously, focus groups explicitly use group interaction as part of the method. This means that instead of the researcher asking each person to respond to a question in turn, people are encouraged to talk to one another: asking questions, exchanging anecdotes and commenting on each other's experiences and points of view. The method is particularly useful for exploring people's knowledge and experiences and can be used to examine not only what people think but how they think and why they think that way (Kitzinger, 1995).

Ethnography

This method of enquiry involves the gathering of mainly unstructured data through a range of methods such as observation, discussions and interviews. This method is a useful approach particularly for those who are already playing an active role in the organisation where the research is taking place. This might be a very useful approach for those who are engaged in a project within their workplace (Costly *et al.,* 2010).

Analysis of data

The process of data analysis involves transforming raw data into something which is meaningful and representative. It involves detecting commonalities and variations amongst participant responses. It is very important to choose methods of analysis which fit the with the type of data and the intended use of the data (Costly *et al.,* 2010).

Findings or statement of results

In this section you are required to feedback your findings following data analysis. This is the very centre of the report and may be the longest. In this section you may wish to include graphs or diagrams and so on. The text that follows each diagram should highlight specific aspects of the findings and should not duplicate information (Bell, 2004).

Discussion of findings

In this section you are required to make sense of the data you have discovered. It gives you the opportunity to interpret your data and compare your results with those of others. You may also want to talk about some of the problems you encountered with your own research and what you did to put things right.

Conclusion

Your conclusion should bring all your work together. Bell (2004) warns that only justifiable conclusions can be drawn from the findings. This is not the place to give an opinion or justification. The conclusion must reflect the actual findings of project.

Recommendations

This section enables you to make key recommendations based on the findings of your project. This is likely to be a very important section for your sponsors as this will provide the catalyst for change.

And finally...

Presenting your project

At the end of the project it is likely that you'll be asked to disseminate your findings to a wider audience. This is likely to include your mentor, your employer, a service user, the beneficiaries of your project and the sponsors of your project. There are a number of ways this can be achieved. On some Foundation Degree programmes the means of dissemination is in the form of a presentation or student conference. The conference enables you to share your project with your peers and with the relevant stakeholders. In some cases the presentation forms part of a final assessment and therefore your presentation is graded by your module leader.

Giving a presentation can be a very daunting process even at the end of a two or three year programme where presentations have become the norm. However, the presentation is an excellent way of sharing your project to a wider audience.

Tips for effective presentations

- Be prepared: preparation and knowledge are vital for a successful presentation, but confidence and control are just as important.

- Good presentation is about entertaining as well as conveying information; try and find ways of making your content and delivery enjoyable by using humour and imagination.

- You have 4–7 seconds in which to make a positive impact and good opening impression, so make sure you have a good, strong, solid introduction, and rehearse it to death. Smile.

- Take a few deep breaths to begin with.

- Don't start with an apology unless you've really made a serious error, or its part of your plans and an intentional humorous device.

- Try to start on time even if some of the audience is late. Waiting too long undermines your confidence, and the audience's respect for you.

- The average attention span of an average listener is apparently between five and ten minutes for any single unbroken subject.

- Think of it like this – the audience can be stimulated via several senses – not just audio and visual (listening and watching). Consider including content and activity which addresses the other senses too – touch certainly – taste maybe, smell maybe – anything's possible if you use your imagination. The more senses you can stimulate the more your audience will remain attentive and engaged.

- Stand up.

- Vary the pitch of your voice.

- Improvise around notes rather than reading a paper out.

- Make eye contact.

- Use visual aids/pictures.

- Engage with the audience.

The following are examples of projects from Foundation Degree students at the University of Worcester.

I would like to acknowledge and thank the following Foundation Degree students for giving me permission to use extracts from their work-based learning projects:

Jenny Bolsius – Foundation Degree Learning Disabilities student University of Worcester

Neil Tonks – Foundation Degree in Health and Social Care University of Worcester

Christina Jones – Foundation Degree Health and Social Care University of Worcester

Worcester Business School for allowing me to use extracts from the Handbook for Professional Practice Awards

Foundation Degree team at University of Worcester for allowing me to use extracts from the Handbook for Foundation Degree students.

Jenny's project

Project title

An exploration of independent-living skills with a view to developing a living skills training scheme aimed at enabling adults with mild to moderate learning disabilities to make the transition from a residential supported living service into independent tenancies or home ownership.

In referring to people with learning disabilities, the terms service-user and client will be used interchangeably.

Introduction

The aim of this project was to explore the subject of independent living for adults with learning disabilities, with particular reference to the acquisition of skills required to make a successful transition. A literature review was carried out to identify the issues and ascertain the current state of research and practice in independent living and skills acquisition, which was then used to inform the project (Hart, 2001). The keywords used to focus the literature search were: independence, independent living, learning disability, intellectual disability, living skills, transition and programme. Local provision of independent living skills programmes was researched using semi-structured interviews and the findings were used to make recommendations for the development of a training programme in a specific service for learning – disabled adults.

Justification for study

It is envisaged that a comprehensive training scheme will provide a foundation of living skills that can be built upon by the clients, with appropriate support, in their new home. The service currently provides residential supported living for twelve service-users in three houses in an urban area, plus floating support for seven others in the community. The organisation was initially founded as an intentional community (Gates, 2007) for adults who had been in a Camphill college (Williams, 2002) but has since evolved into a more individualised approach to support, in line with government policy (Department of Health, 2001; Department of Health, 2009). Further to this, the funding body Supporting People (Department of Social Security, 1998) will be reducing funding for residential settings over the next few years. Following the transition by three service-users to supported independent living and the experience of supporting them during and after transition, a need has been identified for a comprehensive, living skills training programme for service-users, both current and prospective, to enable them to take on and sustain tenancies or home ownership.

Recommendations

It is not possible from this type of qualitative study to make generalisations but Bell (2005) argues that relatedness, that is how findings relate to a given problem, maybe more useful to an organisation. From this point of view my findings have something to contribute to an approach to an independent living skills programme. Skills taught need to be put into practice and clients need to be allowed to take risks and to be supported through the potential consequences. The best people to teach skills are those who have daily contact with clients and in order for this to happen a firm value base should inform the practice. Based on the literature review and my own findings, therefore, I would make the following recommendations:

- Establish a value base and common understanding among the workforce of independence and independent living.

- Build a circle of support around the individual who will be making the transition, including psychological support if necessary.

- Establish a transition timetable and keep a record of each stage with the client, from the initial search for a property to moving-in day.
- Identify skills needed through person-centred planning.
- Develop good risk-management procedures.
- Train staff in skills-teaching.
- Adopt a problem-solving approach to teaching skills.
- Establish a timetable for teaching and practising skills that fit in to the person's current life as far as possible.
- Once the client has moved, support them to establish a daily/weekly routine of work and leisure activities.

Conclusion

Although this study was made in response to the needs of a particular organisation, I envisage that this approach to a training programme could be used by any service provider. I would suggest that further research is needed into staff training and skills-teaching methods.

My research has shed some light on the effectiveness of training programmes for people with learning disabilities in transition. My findings concurred with previous research in many areas, but further identified that a firm value base and highly-skilled workforce are essential for promoting and maintaining independence for learning-disabled people.

Neil's project

The workplace project decided and agreed upon is designed to set up, deliver and evaluate Stop Smoking group sessions based on an eight week delivery program. This particular time scale framework was to incorporate both continued motivational aspects and also to cover prescribing criteria, as evidence suggest, Nicotine Replacement Therapy is usually effective between 8–12 weeks (CKS 2010). Smoking cessation has been recognised as an integral and vital resource to enable smokers to stop smoking and remain stopped through the support provided, indeed The National Service Framework (NSF) on Coronary Heart Disease stated in 2001 that all authorities and teams involved with health care should contribute to local programmes to tackle the prevalence of smoking through cessation interventions, (Health Development Agency, 2001). It was introduced due to the overwhelming evidence of nicotine dependence and the cost to health of the population. Another key factor was the financial strain that smoking related illnesses have on the department of health and the cost of drugs and hospital interventions that were needed to treat patients. Cohen (1999) reveals: 'smoking related diseases cost the British National Health service (NHS) somewhere between £1.4 billion and £1.7 billion every year'.

The work involved for the project required the setting up and delivery of fourteen groups spread strategically throughout the local area, to maximise the potential of accessing as many smokers as possible. The innovation would be extended over a period of several months, from June 2009 through to March 2010. The work is clearly linked to the student's chosen career as a Smoking Cessation Advisor, and was seen as an ideal opportunity to progress with his personal development plan. The task specified was seen as a way in which developmental progression can be made by providing responsibility through a leadership role within the framework of the project as, 'worker responsibility increases ambitions' (www.motivation-tools.com 2010). This technique can enable a natural improvement of an individual's personal development through learning how to make decisions, work as part of a team, increase ones ability to become more assertive and increase a person's confidence. Nevertheless the latter of these is dependant to a certain degree on the outcomes and evaluation on the completion of the project.

To put into place and deliver any project it is desirable and advisable to first look at existing evidence through a literature research strategy. By using already tried and tested views and outcomes and evidence based practice and data, it provides the best possible basis to engage the project, and gives a solid structure to allow the leader of the project to develop and employ the delivery plan more efficiently and effectively. The literature search can be obtained from both local and national aspects, thus comparing and contrasting the existing evidence and formulating decisions on the best and most appropriate way forward. Each new venture can use all or some of the evidence-based literature discovered to plan and deliver a robust and worthwhile project which benefits all.

The literature review used had to include the following criteria;

1. Interventions comparing groups against one-to-one therapies.

2. Research into different socioeconomic areas.

3. Documentation obtained from or supported by reputable, respected and recognised sources.

This taken into account it looked at a wide range of similar projects from a local and national level and looked at evidence from a more global perspective. By observing as much literature on the given subject as possible it is able to discard some that seem less relevant and use more pertinent material. In particular the review considered the evaluations of behavioural group work as opposed to one-to-one interventions, to assess what worked and what didn't. It used evidence from a study by the UK Centre for Tobacco Control Studies which 'found that more than a third of smokers using support groups quit smoking after four weeks; almost double the proportion of those using a pharmacy-based support scheme to help them quit' (Science Daily, 2009). However this is not to say that one-to-one interventions are not valid forms of smoking cessation work. It also realises and accepts that an innovation that may or may not work well in one chosen area may have the opposite effect in the localised area to which the project is to become applicable.

Christina's project

Introduction

The overall aim of this piece of work is to identify a gap in provision within a health and social care organisation, using current research to support the argument. The project will then apply relevant theories and concepts to establishing a solution. The Noah's Ark Trust is the particular organisation this project aims to benefit, with the intended improvement for provision being an increase in training in specific areas for volunteers, specifically working with children with Attention-Deficit Hyperactivity Disorder on weekend camps.

This will be achieved through:

▪   Identifying the reasons for this need through analysis of current volunteer training and their roles within the organisation, as well as through my own personal experience.

- Discussing the impact of ADHD on the volunteers and other children.

- Reviewing current literature related to children with ADHD.

- Exploration of training offered by other organisations.

- Identifying possible strategies that can now begin to be implemented within the organisation in order to address the issue.

Methods

In order to meet my aim of establishing a solution that will be effective, I began with a self-administered questionnaire which I emailed, along with some information about my intentions, to all Noah's Ark volunteers. I believe that this was the best way to get a higher response from my population as it is discussed by 'Creative Research Systems' (2009) that it allows the respondent to answer at a convenient time to them rather than the moment they are put on the spot. This also means that they are able to take time to think about their answers, possibly making them more valid. Other advantages are that more definable results can be produced, they can be generalised, and by using charts, percentages, and so on. may be made easier to understand by non-researchers. However, it is easy to make assumptions from answers given on a questionnaire and it may not be clear what the respondent meant by their answer. I will overcome this barrier by using open ended questions to allow for more detail.

Although I have a clear idea of how I want to conduct my research, I do expect to encounter some complications, and would like to be prepared for them. Practitioners may be reluctant to divulge information in case it gets passed onto supervisors or managers, and so on. I will ensure that this does not happen by keeping all data collected confidential, and any findings passed on or published will not include details of volunteers.

From the responses I can see that volunteers definitely feel that they would benefit from some kind of additional acknowledgement of additional needs on camp. Furthermore, the kind of support they think would be most beneficial is general information. In order to meet this need I intend to put together an information pack offering support to working with ADHD children and young people, specifically aimed at Noah's Ark volunteers on the residential camp. It will consist of an introduction to ADHD, symptoms, a section about supporting children, and a separate section about supporting teenagers. It will also contain a table displaying problems that could arise and suggestions to overcoming them during specific activities that take place over the weekend. Lastly, the pack will contain a small removable card displaying 10 quick tips which the volunteers can carry on their person for the weekend.

Summary

Work-based learning is an essential component of all Foundation Degrees and it's absolutely vital that everyone connected with the student in the workplace are well informed of the requirements and their responsibilities in order to make learning a success.

This chapter is a useful guide for students, mentors, Foundation Degree (FD) programme leads as it guides you through the important components of the work-based learning component of a FD. The chapter draws on the contributions of key work-based learning experts and includes real life examples of how students at the university of Worcester carried out their projects in the workplace.

The chapter is best read in conjunction with the Chapter on Research methodologies.

Summary assignment

Students will select and work on an individual project that explores a personal or professional interest related to a specific aspect of working in health or social care. The precise format of the project will be negotiated with an allocated supervisor via a practice learning agreement form. The report must incorporate the negotiated learning contract (500 words) and a reflective analysis (500 words) related to their personal development and relevance of the outcomes of the project to their own practice.

Summary assignment

Students will prepare an individual presentation of the key findings from the project and present these to their peer group and mentors.

References

Allin and Turnock (2007) Assessing student performance in work-based learning. Making practice based learning work. Available www.practicebasedlearning.org. (Accessed 20/11/07).

Bell, J. (2004) *Doing Your Research Project.* Open University Press, London.

Bradell, A. (2007) 'Learning through work: development on-the-job learning as a vehicle to widen participation in workplace learning.' *Learning Through Work (*Position paper for the Widening Participation Unit. Leeds).

Braham, J. and Pickering, J. (2007) 'Widening participation and improving economic competitiveness; the dual role of work-based learning within Foundation Degrees'. *Work-Based Learning Futures: Proceedings from the Work-Based Learning Futures Conference.* Buxton

Chapman, A. (1995) Presentations.http://www.businessballs.com/presentation.htm.

Costley, C. (2000) *Work-based Learning: An Accessible Curriculum. Widening Participation and Lifelong Learning. Vol.2, No 2.*

Costly, C., Elliott, G. and Gibbs, P.(2010) *Doing Work-based Research.* Sage, London.

Department of Health (2001) Governance arrangements for NHS Research Ethics Committees.

Does (2003) 21st century skills: realising our potential. London, HMSO. http://www.dh.gov.uk/en/Publicationsandstatistics/Publications/PublicationsPolicy AndGuidance.

Gibbs, G. (1988) *Learning by Doing: A Guide to Teaching and Learning Methods.* Further Education Unit, Oxford Brookes University, Oxford.

Harvey, D. (1990) *The Condition of Postmodernity.* Blackwell, Oxford.

Hiemstra, R. (2006) 'Learning contracts'. http://home.twcny.rr.com/hiemstra/contract.htm

Holm, D. and Stephenson, S. (1994) Reflection – a student's perspective. In Palmer A, Burns, S. and Bulman, C. (eds) *Reflective Practice in Nursing: The Growth of the Professional Practitioner.* Blackwell Scientific Publications, Oxford pp. 53–62

Holstein, J.A. and Gubrium, J.F. (2004) 'Context: working it up, down and across'. In C. Seale, G. Gobo, J.F. Gubrium and D. Silverman (eds) *Qualitative Research Practice.* Sage, London.

Johnson, D. (2001) The opportunities, benefits and barriers to the introduction of work-based learning in higher education. *Innovations in Education and Teaching International* **38**, 1

Kitzinger, J. (1995) 'Qualitative research: introducing focus groups'. *BMJ* 311: 299.

Knowles, M. (1986) *Using Learning Contracts.* Jossey-Bass, San Fransisco, CA.

Leitch (2006) 'Prosperity for all in the global economy – world class skills'. http://www.official-documents.gov.uk/document/other/0118404792/0118404792.pdf

Lyon, J. (2007) 'Work-based learning – a learner's perspective'. In Young, D. and Garnett, J. (eds) (2007) *Work-based Learning Futures,* Bolton, University Vocational Awards http://www.practicebasedlearning.org/resources.

McKenzie, H. (2006) Mentors for Work-based Learning and Mentor Training http://www.port.ac.uk/departments/ studentsupport/foundationdirect/research/ Literaturereviews/filetodownload,44484, en.pdf.

Medhat, S. (2008) 'The path to productivity: The progress of work-based learning strategies in higher education engineering programmes. Final report'. In partnership with the HE Academy Engineering Subject Centre and Foundation Degree Forward. Available from http://www.neweng.org.uk/ uploads/Reports/work-based learningReportFinalv4.pdf.

Meyers, M. (1997) Qualitative Research in Information Systems. http://www.qual. auckland.ac.nz/

Nikolou-Walker, E. (2008) *The Expanded University: Work-Based Learning and The Economy*. London, Pearson Education.

Pramod Bahadur, S. (2009) Research Paradigms: An Overview. http://www. scribd.com/doc/18326060/Research-Paradigms-An-Overview

Shuttleworth, Martyn (2009). 'What is a literature review?' Retrieved [9 March 2011] from Experiment Resources: http://www. experiment-resources.com/what-is-a-literature-review.html.

Stevenson,J. and Laycock, M. (eds) *Using Learning Contracts in Higher Education*. Kogan Page, London.

Tallantyre, F. (2008) 'Workforce development: Connections, frameworks and processes'. http://www.heacademy.ac. uk/assets/York/documents/workforce.

Taylor, S. (2001) *Getting Employers Involved – Improving Work-based Learning Through Employer Links* Learning and Skills Dev. Agency, Tamworth.

Udani, R. (2007) 'Writing up your research'. *Student BMJ* **15**:383–426 November. ISSN 0966-6494 http://archive.student.bmj.com/ issues/07/11/careers/406.php.

Glossary

Absolute poverty – the lack of minimum resources for survival

Action research – research which is active in nature and grounded in practice. A form of self-reflective enquiry, encouraging participants in a setting to improve practice by addressing understanding and making changes

Advocacy – speaking on behalf of someone to enable them to meet needs

Analytical psychology – Jung's description of his own approach as a way to healing and personality development

Andragogical – The art and science of helping adults to learn

ANOVA – analysis of variance

Anti-discriminatory – the prohibition of treating people in an oppressive or unfavourable manner

Attitudes – a like or dislike or a favourable or unfavourable response to a person, object or idea

BASW – The British Association of Social Workers

Behaviourist perspective – a psychological approach that tries to explain behaviour in terms of its interaction with the environment and the events observed.

Beliefs – opinions we hold about the nature of the world in which we live.

Bibliography – a list of everything read for an assignment or written piece of work

Biomedical – a mechanistic view of health based upon the belief that health was to be free of disease.

Body kinesthetic – the movement and action of the body through dance, athletics and other such medium

Body language – the non-verbal cues that the body communicates; gestures, eye contact and body position

Care value base –the major values in care work which are based upon the rights to which we are all entitled

CBT – cognitive behavioural therapy concerned with thinking, feeling and the impact on behaviour

CCDC – consultant in communicable disease control

CCETSW – Central Council for Education and Training in Social Work

Classical conditioning – a behavioural theory put forward by Pavlov; we learn to respond to a separate stimulus which is paired with a natural stimulus

C. Diff – *Clostridium difficile*

Cognitive perspective – a psychological perspective concerned with explaining behaviour in terms of an individual's thoughts, beliefs and interpretations and the meanings they ascribe to their actions.

Confidentiality – a health and social care worker must not discuss client related information to unrelated staff

Congruence – Gerard Egan; the helper is genuine, honest and true

Core conditions – According to Gerard Egan; empathy, unconditional positive regard and congruence

COSHH – The Control of Substances Hazardous to Health Regulations(2002)

CPR – Cardio-pulmonary resuscitation

Critical analysis – analysing an event or literature by looking at the strengths and weaknesses

CSCI – Commission for Social Care Inspection

Cultural sensitivity – being aware and sensitive to people's different cultural beliefs and practices

Discrimination – the treatment of a person less favourably than another based on: age, class, colour, religion, gender and sexuality

Dysfunctional – functioning outside the realms of what is generally considered to be normal behaviour or performance

Diversity – difference

EBP – evidence-based practice

E. Coli – *Escherichia Coli*

Egan's Three Stage Model – a counselling model developed by Gerard Egan, describing stages in the counselling relationship

Empathy – the ability to understand the client's internal frame of reference; to be able to 'put yourself in their shoes'

Empowerment – to enable the client to solve a problem

ESBL – extended-spectrum β lactamases

Ethnography – a particular type of research methodology often used when investigating people and their behaviour

Evaluation – to assess or appraise, or find the value of something

Experimental hypothesis – a proposition in scientific research made as a basis for reasoning.

Functionalist – a sociological perspective developed by Auguste Comte (1798)

Generalisation – the degree to which the work can be applied to the whole population and not just the sample used

Gibbs reflective cycle – stages of reflection Gibbs (1988) including; Description, Feelings, Evaluation, Analysis and Conclusion

Action plan – identifying the stages involved in making a change or solving a problem

GORs – Government Office Regions

Grounded theory – research methodology coined by Glaser and Strauss (1967)

Grow Model – framework for coaching developed by Whitmore (2002)

GSCC – General Social Care Council

Harvard System – a referencing system

HCAIs – Health Care Associated Infections

HEIs – Higher Education Institutions

HPA – Health Protection Agency

HPP – healthy public policy

Holistic – an approach to health care placing emphasis on the whole person

HSE – Health and Safety Executive

Humanistic theory – a study that focuses on human values pioneered by Carl Rogers and Abraham Maslow

IAPT – Improving Access to Psychological Therapies

Immediacy – responding straight away

Inequality – lack of equality particularly with reference to resources and access to health care

interpersonal skills – the skills we use in order to get on and communicate with each other

Intrapersonal – the communication that occurs within ourselves or 'self talk'

Institutional Politics – the interaction between different parliament, local government, pressure groups and the media

learning journal – a written record which describes a learning journey

Linguistic – referring to language

LSE – London School of Economics

Marginalised – the social process of becoming or being made marginal and confined to a lower social standing or outer circle

Maslow's Hierarchy of Needs – a triangle which is separated into stages representing a hierarchy of needs humans strive towards achieving

MDT – multidisciplinary team

Mind map – a process of putting ideas to paper

MMR – measles, mumps and rubella (vaccine)

MRSA – Methicillin resistant *Staphylococcus Aureus*

NEETS – not in education, employment or training. A term coined to describe young people who leave school at 16 who do not find work or stay on in education

NICE – The National Institute for Clinical Excellence

NMC – Nursing and Midwifery Council

Non-judgemental – adopting a stance which does not judge an individual which might lead to their disadvantage

Non-verbal communication – communicating using signs, symbols or other means which is not spoken

Norms – the socially acceptable ways to behave which are linked to values

OFSTED – The Office for Standards in Education

Operant conditioning – a behavioural concept which shows how our behaviours are changed in response to positive and negative reinforcement

Paralinguistic aspects – the different ways which we moderate our speech, for example pitch, volume, rhythm, tone of voice and timing alongside grunts, ums and ahs.

Paraphrasing – the skill of rephrasing what you understood to be the core message of the client's communication

Person-centred counseling – a counselling technique devised by Carl Rogers

PDP – personal development planning

Personality structure – a transactional analysis term used to explain patterns of behaviour

Phenomenology – a psychological perspective

Political ideology – a package of ideas and values that affect how people define social welfare issues and formulate social policy

PPE – Personal Protective Equipment

Prejudices – an adverse judgement or opinion formed beforehand or without knowledge or examination of the facts

Primary research – original research

Psychodynamic perspective – a psychological theory put forward by Sigmunfd Freud and his followers

QAA – Quality Assurance Authority

Qualitative – a method of inquiry used to gather information about people in their natural setting

Quantitative – a formal, objective, systematic process in which numerical data are utilised to obtain information

Receptive reading – reading actively and selectively to gain a better understanding of the material

Reference list – a list of the sources or ideas cited and used in a piece of work

Reflective learner – a person who considers the what, why and how in relation to a previous activity in order to improve on their future performance

Relative poverty – individuals with a standard of living which is below that which is generally acceptable in the society in which they area living

Reliability – is the extent to which the findings of research may be replicated with the same or similar results

Restating – a counselling term which involves the process of repeating back to a client what they have just told you but using different words

RIDDOR – Reporting on Injuries, Diseases, and Dangerous occurrences Regulations 1995

Sample – a group of people under study from a larger population all sharing similar characteristics.

SATS – colloquial term commonly believed to mean Statutory Assessment Tests or Standard Attainment Tests

Sick role – a term coined by Talcott Parsons to describe a person who identifies with the role of the sick person and disengages from social duties

Skimming – browsing a text quickly to get the gist of the work therein

Scanning – rapid reading of a text to find specific material quickly

Secondary research – the presentation of other writers 'primary' research

Self-awareness – a process of having insight into our own behavior and its impact on others

Social exclusion – the process by which some groups in society, due to deprivation and poverty, are excluded from mainstream activity

Social learning – learn other attitudes and values through association, reinforcement and modelling

Socialisation – the process by which we learn our values, beliefs, norms and attitudes

Social policy – academic study and the activity of policy making to enhance the well being of groups in society

Sociology – the study of society and the people in it

SOLER – an acronym suggested by Gerard Egan (1990) used the acronym SOLER in order to help us remember the importance of body language and how to our non-verbal communication to create a therapeutic relationship

Spatial – to do with space

Stereotyping – ascribing characteristics, usually negative towards members of groups

Strokes – a transactional analysis term which describes verbal and non-verbal communication

Summarising – gathering together client's statements to identify their specific thoughts and feelings

SWOB analysis – a reflective model used to analyse strengths, weaknesses, opportunities and barriers

Symbolic interactionism – a major sociological perspective that emphasises social interaction

Therapeutic relationship – one in which the client is helped in some way

Transactional analysis (TA) – was created and developed by Eric Berne; it is a theory of how personality is structured in the ego state model, and helps us understand and analyse communication and interactions between people

Transactions – communication between one person and another

Transference and counter transference – an idea developed by Freud to explain the unconscious mind's ability to project and transfer phenomena onto other people in order to deal with memories and emotions

Triangulation – the use of several methods to test the results in a data set

Unconditional positive regard – the ideal attitude for counsellors which indicates respect of the highest order for their clients

Validity – refers to 'trueness' in research. The extent to which the researcher has measured what they have said they were going to measure

Values – the worth, desirability or utility of a thing, or the qualities on which these depend

VRE – Vancomycin resistant *enterococci*

WHO – The World Health Organization

Index